ICONIC

HOW ORGANIZATIONS AND LEADERS ATTAIN, SUSTAIN, AND REGAIN THE ULTIMATE LEVEL OF DISTINCTION

SCOTT McKAIN

AUTHOR OF *CREATE DISTINCTION*

Original edition named one of the
"Ten Best Business Books of the Year"

by *Miami Herald* and other major newspapers

Published by Forefront Books.

ISBN: 978-1-948-67706-6 (Paperback)
ISBN: 978-1-948-67707-3 (eBook)

To Gerard Mauvis in thanks
for his integrity and his inspiration

CONTENTS

Part 3
Bringing It All Together

INTRODUCTION

With tears forming in his eyes, the CEO of the once-distinctive and revered company slowly took the stage for the press conference. The organization he served was founded the same year President Lincoln was assassinated. Yet, in its long and storied history, there had never been a moment like this one.

As he sat on the dais, he must have noticed many of his colleagues scattered around the room. Several were already sobbing in anticipation of the announcement that they knew was forthcoming.

Their company—named for a local river—began when a mining engineer established a small ground wood pulp mill. Over the years, the company received countless accolades for anticipating—and regularly driving—marketplace change. It frequently had been named as a global leader. Those descriptors were a thing of the past.

From that initial pulp mill, the company added electricity generation to its portfolio, then expanded to become a major manufacturer of galoshes—those weatherproof rubber boots that slip over your shoes to protect them from water. The company had long been a model of both innovation and adaptation. In the 1930s, they merged with a Finnish rubber company. As regional, then global demand for infrastructure grew, the company became a leader in the cable and wiring industry—essential for transmitting not only electricity but also telephone and telegraph communications.

The company diversified its pulp production and soon became a key producer of various paper products. The rubber business continued to grow as they made everything from bicycle tires to footwear. The cable division expanded as well, and they began manufacturing television sets.

The company had once flirted with bankruptcy, due to the political and economic devastation in the aftermath of World War I. After the Second World War, however, business rebounded—partly by providing the then Soviet Union with the cables required to rebuild their country. This effort also provided a cornerstone for the organization's future growth.

The company's visionary leaders recognized the potential of telecommunications—even though that division operated at a loss for many years. They poured resources into a digital switching product that became an industry standard for telephone equipment in early network architecture. Their engineers even developed a mobile telephone network that provided 100 percent coverage to their home nation—in 1978.

For a long time, many people marveled at how adept and adroit the organization and its leaders were. The company created a new tool for mobile networking—cellular handsets—that were used by everyone from global trendsetters to average workers. They expanded into products such as computers and high-quality displays. After divesting itself of its formative businesses—paper, tires, footwear, and various consumer electronics—the company's decision makers chose to concentrate exclusively on one industry: telecommunications.

This company that started from humble origins became a global icon.

That day at the press conference, however, none of those achievements were being celebrated. Instead, the CEO was about to address the more recent failures. Relative startups were running rings around the company's operating software. The CEO had recently sent a memo to employees describing the team as being on a "burning platform" in a "war." The mobile devices the company released—once viewed as the vanguard of technology and scooped up by the tens of millions—languished on the shelves as customers bolted for easier-to-use alternatives.

In 2013, after a long downward spiral, the company that enjoyed a rich tradition and iconic standing for almost 150 years was being acquired—bailed out, in actuality—

by a business that had about one-fourth of the longevity and history. At this press conference, Nokia CEO Stephen Elop announced that Microsoft was purchasing his company.

As he looked over the assembled crowd of reporters and his colleagues, Elop attempted to address the spectacular failure of the global icon he led. He gave his take on what had decimated the formerly successful conglomerate, as well as the events that presaged the termination of about half of the company's employees.

"We didn't do anything wrong," he tearfully and defiantly claimed. "But somehow we lost."

Maybe Mr. Elop's inflated compensation clouded his judgment. It is hard to imagine that such a highly remunerated global executive would think that he didn't do *anything* wrong while at the helm as a distinctive company lost its iconic status.

Maybe Mr. Elop totally missed the mark. Perhaps Nokia lost its iconic status because of mismanagement, because of poor organizational focus.

There is no doubt that *attaining* success is critical. However, knowing the steps to *sustain* and *regain* it are vital as well. Could it be that Nokia's leadership knew how to create their lofty status in the marketplace—

but not how to preserve their position, or reclaim it once it was lost?

That question is the one I've been pondering for the past several years. When I wrote a book on how to create distinction, I did not focus on how a leader or an organization maintained or enhanced the marketplace advantages they generated. A few years after teaching people how to make their company stand out, I had a blinding flash of the obvious. I realized that I now needed to focus on how to sustain, or possibly regain, the distinction they had created.

As I spoke at corporate events on the elements of setting yourself apart from the competition in the marketplace, it became clear that there was another level beyond distinction—beyond setting your company apart—that extraordinary leaders and organizations could attain as well. The companies that are widely recognized and frequently used as illustrations of "best practices" (some to the point their example has become clichéd) are not merely distinctive. They are much more than that!

For instance, Samsung has created distinction—and left many other mobile device manufacturers, such as LG, HTC, and Motorola, eating their dust. Apple, however, is on a higher level. It isn't merely distinctive. It has become iconic.

Your local neighborhood probably has a coffee shop that stands above the rest because of its customer experience or a special blend that attracts java enthusiasts. That little local store has found a way to create distinction. Starbucks, however, is iconic.

Apple and Starbucks are global companies, yet worldwide recognition is not a requirement for iconic status. For example, there is a plethora of steakhouses. Some national chains—Del Frisco's, Morton's, Fleming's—have risen to the point of distinction. St. Elmo's, however, is iconic. You may not have heard of St. Elmo's if you have never been to Indianapolis. It is the place where almost every visitor to the city wants to go. In downtown Indy, none of the distinctive national brands are even in the same ballpark in terms of recognition—or revenue. It has become a model for all types of businesses in the region—not just restaurants. (You'll learn much more about St. Elmo's in the concluding chapter of this book.)

As the Nokia example powerfully illustrates, attaining iconic status does not ensure that lofty perch will be maintained.

Think of Sears, Arthur Andersen, MCI, Lehman Brothers, Wachovia, Saab, Compaq Computers, JC Penney, and Abercrombie & Fitch. This is just a short list of companies that have disappeared or are in significant difficulty, even though they had been well known and highly respected. Certainly, we could debate if a company like Wachovia was iconic or simply distinctive. Nonetheless, every one of these organizations—and their respective leaders—were perceived to be powerhouses at one period or another (and some for a very long time.)

So how does a local steakhouse like St. Elmo's maintain and even enhance their iconic status since 1902 while these formidable global organizations fail? Or as an executive in the hospitality industry at one of the most incredible resort properties in the United States asked me, "How can we move from great to distinctive to a truly iconic hotel?" Perhaps you want to learn how to stand out from your competition and enhance marketplace advantages. It could be that you've enjoyed a degree of success in setting yourself apart and now you want to move to the highest level.

Or maybe you have already achieved iconic status and you're ruminating on how you can keep your standing from slipping through your corporate or professional fingers.

Great is not good enough in today's hypercompetitive marketplace. With all the technological advances in the past decade, starting a business has never been easier. That means being distinctive has never been more difficult. And, unfortunately, distinction may not provide all of the extraordinary advantages it formerly did for you and your company.

I researched my first book on distinction because I could not find any significant advice on how to make my own business stand out. I used what I learned to grow my own small enterprise and help others create their own distinction. Now, there are so many authors and speakers helping businesses and individuals stand out from the competition that it's hard for even the so-called thought leaders to stand out from *their* competition.

Since then I've come to the realization that standing out isn't good enough anymore. How can you possibly succeed if nothing that you offer engages your customers or prospects—or inspires your employees to deliver the results they desire?

Let's face it, you do not want to be the CEO speaking at a press conference, or the entrepreneur standing in front of your employees, or the sales manager addressing your team, naively and defiantly insisting that despite the fact that your people are losing their jobs and your company is now toast—you did *nothing* wrong.

That is why it's time for you to become *iconic*!

How to Get the Most Out of This Book

This book has three goals. To help you...

1) **Attain iconic status.**

   What does it take to be perceived not merely as *distinctive* within your specific field or industry—but also recognized as a significant organization or professional across a wide spectrum?

2) **Maintain and enhance that status once you've achieved it.**

   You've often heard that once you're out front, you also have a target on your back. After you've made it to iconic status, what do you do to maintain and enhance your position so you don't get disrupted in a hypercompetitive environment?

3) **Regain that status should you find it has eroded in the marketplace.**

   Perhaps through no fault of your own, you are in a position where your status—and the perception about your relevance in the marketplace—has slipped. Can you regain your previous level of prestige? And, if so, how is that accomplished?

There may be some aspects of this book that challenge your thinking. (I certainly hope so!) Some things you may not have heard at your last business meeting:

- **Go negative for greater success.**
- **"Underpromise/overdeliver" is a horrible way to deal with customers.**
- **There are only two factors by which customers will judge your organization.**
- **There is a single aspect that your organization must cultivate—for if it doesn't, you can't compete.**
- **You need to stop selling your products and services.**
- **If you aren't distinctive locally (meaning in your geographic area or in your specific industry), you can't become iconic.**

You'll also learn some aspects about becoming iconic you may not have previously considered. For example:

- **Iconic companies know there is great room for improvement on the things they already know how to do.**
- **Iconic organizations and leaders have captivated our attention and attained a level that transcends their individual and specific field of endeavor.**

- **Iconic businesses have resolved they will not be reactive to external events outside their control.**
- **Iconic institutions understand that sales metrics can be misleading in terms of organizational growth and achieving their potential.**

To get the most out of this book and attain your target of becoming iconic, you should read this book at least two times.

The first time, read this book straight through and absorb the content and ideas. The second time, review this book with a journal or notebook by your side. Make notes and plans about how you'll implement the concepts I've outlined. For example: the first time through, consider the concepts in the context of how Nokia was fundamentally destroyed as an iconic leader in mobile telephones.

The second time through, ask yourself questions specific to your own situation, such as:

- What am I not seeing in my business?
- Am I obsessing about our own products and services and missing key market indicators?
- What or who could disrupt us the way that Apple and Samsung disrupted Nokia?

Reading Groups

If you are reading this book, you are likely a leader of a company or organization looking to take your business to the highest level. Even if you are an individual—perhaps an entrepreneur, sales professional, or sole proprietor—wanting to do more than just stand out from the crowd, it is important to note that you should not try to analyze your business and market by yourself. Just as the software sharing company Github utilizes the collective brainpower of hundreds of engineers to accomplish complex tasks in record time, the power of collaboration can have a profoundly significant impact on your business as you analyze your distinction and how to achieve the highest level.

One organization I worked with developed a path to iconic status by forming reading groups. They challenged every person in the company to read a chapter a week. Next, they split into departments and had detailed conversations every Wednesday about how that week's chapter impacted their individual department or team. Finally, they executed tactics every week on one specific change they made based upon the points of a chapter. This was part of their recipe to move from being considered as one of many strong players in their field to becoming an iconic business, respected throughout the world. No matter the size of your business or division, you can do the same.

At the end of each chapter, you'll find a set of questions that will both stimulate your personal thinking and provide discussion starters. I highly recommend you form reading groups in your company or organization and discuss these questions. If you are an individual professional striving for higher achievement, do it with your team, mentors, or friends. This type of collective thinking will have a significant impact on the way you do business. For you to advance your organization (and yourself) through the process, answering these questions precisely—and specifically to your situation—is critical.

If you're familiar with my previous work, the initial part of this new book will be an updated review and expansion on the content you've already consumed. You will likely note a couple of significant changes as well. It's important to reintroduce this information before we move to a higher level.

If you haven't read any of the information and stories that I've provided earlier on creating distinction, don't worry. The next couple of chapters will get you up to speed.

While you may have previously been exposed to some of the information in this book, it is my fervent hope that you won't toss it aside and say, "Ah, I've heard this before." What if Billy Graham would have said, "You've heard this material from the Bible before, so there's no need for me to preach about it again"? What if Steven

Spielberg had said, "There have been movies about aliens out before, so there's no need for me to make *E.T.*"?

Please don't misunderstand me. I am certainly not comparing this book to the Bible or *E.T.* The point I'm attempting to make is that it's not about whether you're familiar with the concepts or not. It's about whether the material that you're absorbing is presented in a manner that compels you to think and act. In other words, even if you've heard it before, I promise you that the themes discussed here are critical to your success—and we all have room for improvement. In fact, every iconic leader and organization knows there is room for improvement on the things they already know how to do.

If you've heard it before but aren't doing anything about it—perhaps, just *perhaps* you need to consider the material once again.

This book presents the best that I can contribute on the topic. I'd love to hear what you think—and how it has been of value to you. Send me a note at: iconic@scott-mckain.com. I promise to personally read every message—and use your input to improve and enhance the content. I would be grateful if you'd take a moment to share.

That is how you will get the most out of this book. *Let's get started!*

PART ONE

WHAT IT MEANS TO BE ICONIC

CHAPTER ONE

WHAT IS AN "ICONIC" ORGANIZATION?

For every Amazon, there is a Sears. For every Apple, there is a Nokia. For every Starbucks, there is a HoJo's. When we mention an iconic company of today, we often forget there was one in the past that was equally dominant.

Remember the goals of this book are to help you or your organization achieve iconic status, maintain that status, and if your reputation has slipped, how you can regain that level of distinction. In this chapter we will examine the Four Levels of Business Distinction and what is so special about those businesses that have attained iconic status.

THE FOUR LEVELS OF BUSINESS DISTINCTION

You may not be as different as you think.

On a recent flight I enjoyed a brief conversation with the person sitting next to me. As we landed at our destination, my seatmate turned to me and presented her

business card. Coincidentally, I discovered that she was involved in a similar business to the one my late wife, Sheri, worked in for many years. Naturally, I was interested in knowing more about her organization, so when I got home I looked up her company's website. The headline I saw there—What Makes Us Different—really struck me. As I'm fascinated by elements that make any organization stand out from their competition, I read the four bullet points listing the aspects that her company believed were the ones separating them from the others in their industry.

- experience
- depth of knowledge
- founded by innovative entrepreneurs
- depth in multiple market segments

I thought about each point on this list. *Experience* is just longevity. It's as if they're suggesting their competitors are staffed with rookies who have no background. Using the same logic, when they say *depth of knowledge* makes them unique, it seems they're asserting the competition is dumber than they are. The fact that they are *founded by innovative entrepreneurs* doesn't strike me as an extraordinary trait since, by definition, every business had to be founded by an entrepreneur. I guess their competition was started by unimaginative entrepreneurs. Finally, the company claimed to have *depth in multiple market segments.* My wife said the same thing about the company where she worked in the late nineties. I promise you this is nothing new or unique.

None of these points make the company *different*. There is absolutely zero here that would truly qualify to be listed under the heading What Makes Us *Different!* These points merely make that company moderately *relevant* in the hypercompetitive industry in which they play.

Could you be making
the same mistake?

If you and your rival are both claiming
that your great service is what makes
you different, then from the customer's
perspective you *aren't*.

This company has inadvertently displayed that they don't get it. They don't understand what would make their customers perceive them as superior to the competition.

If your prospects think that you don't understand your own uniqueness, wouldn't they also surmise that you might not grasp other salient aspects of doing business together? And just because you say it is so doesn't make it so.

ICONIC

You cannot attain differentiated, distinctive, or iconic status by demand.

In other words, no individual or organization can stand up and announce, "We are iconic, dammit!" Well, I guess they could—but based solely upon their declaration, no one else would recognize them as such.

Obtaining iconic status happens only through hard and smart work that leads to overwhelmingly enthusiastic evaluations from your customers in a competitive marketplace. Attaining the highest level of distinction is something that you attain because you have *attracted* it—not because you have demanded it.

There are too many companies and a multitude of professionals proclaiming they stand out from the competition. What they evidently fail to recognize is that the *marketplace* decides their status—not them.

I'm acquainted with—and a big fan of—the iconic Fox Sports personality Colin Cowherd. One of the segments on Colin's show that I love is, "Where Colin was right, where Colin was wrong." He presents a few of the predictions and opinions that he's previously expressed, then he reviews where he was on target and analyzes where he missed the mark.

Well, in reviewing my previous book, *Create Distinction*, I confess that there was a point where I missed the mark. I wrote about the three levels of business distinction. However, after sharing the concept with thousands of leaders, I realize now that I failed to recognize a fourth level. Ironically, it is the most significant level of all.

Let's first examine the Four Levels of Business Distinction. Then, I'll help you evaluate where you fall on that spectrum, so you can design your plan to elevate your standing.

LEVEL 1: SAMENESS

Do customers perceive a compelling difference between you and your competition on something other than price? Do they see you as something more than a commodity? If not, you fall into the first level of business distinction: sameness. This, I believe, is the worst spot in which any organization or professional can reside.

Years ago, I had a manager tell me that customers were loyal to his company's product because, "We are the cheapest in the market and that's what customers are looking for—the lowest price." I explained that his customers weren't attached to his product; they were just committed to being cheap. All his competitors had to do was start selling a similar product at a lower price and his customers would run for the door.

The problem for this manager—and many like him—is that it seems to be easier to keep cranking out what we've been doing for years than to try to move up into a higher station. Many people think that continuing to do what's worked in the past will continue to be safe. This approach isn't safe at all. In fact, it's the most unsound and unhealthy place to be. At this level—where margins are small and competition is intense—the failure to provide an aspect that sets you apart from your competition can be deadly.

LEVEL 2: DIFFERENTIATION

When customers perceive there is something about your product or service that is unique from the competition, you have differentiated yourself in the marketplace. It simply draws more attention to you and your efforts. In addition, customers are willing to pay more for products or services that have some aspect that sets them apart from the swarm of the similar.

This approach works for individuals as they seek to grow their career as well. The professional who has something special about her background, knowledge, or approach will naturally find her talents more highly valued than one who has taken the same path as the horde of others seeking advancement.

The challenge here, however, is that it is easy to presume that mere differentiation translates into superiority. It doesn't.

Different is not better.
Different is just different.

As I've noted many times, if I slap every customer in the face, I am different. That does *not* mean I am better.

DOES "WHY" MAKE YOU DIFFERENTIATED?

There is a lot of discussion these days about a little word *Why*. In 2009, business consultant Simon Sinek wrote a megabestselling book *Start with Why* in which he espouses that we start by asking why questions:

- Why are we in business?
- Why do we get out of bed in the morning?
- Why does our company exist?

Many entrepreneurs, business leaders, and professionals began asking themselves about the *why* of their business or their careers. Sinek instructed his readers to use their *why* as the foundation upon which they will differentiate themselves in the marketplace. He suggests when we do this, we begin the process of becoming more valuable.

I agree that *why* is a great question to ask yourself. It is one that can lead to higher levels of understanding and insight that can be important to your personal and professional journeys. It requires deeper thinking about your purpose and priorities.

Sinek takes it a bit further, though. He advocates that people don't buy *what* you do; they buy *why* you do it.

On this point, I respectfully but fervently disagree.

For instance, the burgers at Shake Shack are unbelievably good. They are so tasty, I believe that is what differentiates Shake Shack from the standard burger competition. As their customer, I don't give a damn *why* they make them so delicious—I just care that they *do*.

Author, speaker, and close friend Joe Calloway has brilliantly observed that even at a company like Apple (one that Sinek cites as a primary example of starting with the *why*), this approach does not work. "Go into any Apple store," Calloway says, "and ask an employee at the Genius Bar why he is there. He likely won't cite any Apple corporate mantra. Instead, he'll probably say it's to pay off his student loans."

"In any business—large or small—there are many varied 'whys,'" Calloway continues. "People buy what you *do*—and, more importantly, *how well you do it*. The key is not the 'why,' it's to be the best at what matters most to customers."

> *Problems in differentiation are usually not about your* why, *it's that you need to deliver a better* how.

In many of the organizations I've observed, three of the most frequently asked *how* questions are:

- How do we sell more?
- How do we cut overhead?
- How do we enhance our profits?

Notice what all these statements have in common? *They're all inwardly focused.*

What if, instead, we asked questions like:

- How can we be of greater service to our customers?
- How can we make the experience of doing business with us more compelling?
- How will the steps we are taking impact the prospects we want to convert to clients?

While Sinek states the *how* is important in everyday decision making—and that your *how* should align with your *why*—there's a critical difference that I've noted among iconic companies and leaders.

Disney is unquestionably an iconic company. Through the leadership of CEO and Chairman Bob Iger, it continues to navigate the difficult waters of the changing media and entertainment environment. So what is the *why* of Disney?

Perhaps in an earlier time, one could say Disney was in business to create, promote, and distribute family entertainment. But now they own or have a controlling interest in, among other ventures, ESPN, A&E Network, Hyperion Books, Reedy Creek Energy Services, ABC Television Network. So how do they define their *why* in today's world? None of those subsidiaries is devoted exclusively to family entertainment.

"If you want to thrive in a disrupted world, you have to be incredibly adept at not standing still," Iger told *Vogue* magazine.[1] It would be very difficult to pivot as quickly and move as rapidly as Iger suggests if you're dogmatically focused on an esoteric *why* as opposed to the more practical *how*.

If a customer decides to do more business with you, which of these two comments do you suppose is most likely to express the reason for their choice:

- "I like *why* they are in business."
- "I like *how* they do what they do better."

Moving from level one to level two does not commence with asking *why*. Instead, it begins with creating and executing a better *how*.

Differentiation based upon the quality of how you do what you do lifts you above the level of sameness.

LEVEL 3: DISTINCTION

Once you have differentiated yourself or your company from the competition, it is time to become distinct. There are some organizations that have attained a higher level of differentiation from those with which they compete. They have created an advantage of such an extraordinary level of significance that customers are attracted to them. This is the essence of distinction.

PURSUIT VERSUS ATTRACTION

Companies and individuals that have not created distinction in their marketplace have to pursue their customers. Unfortunately, the problem they encounter is that there is a fundamental difference between pursuit and attraction. Please don't misunderstand—I'm not talking about some New Age "law of attraction." Instead, I'm referring to the viewpoint of late business philosopher Jim Rohn, mentor of famed motivational speaker, Tony Robbins.

Rohn said that "success is something you attract, not something you pursue."[2] If you choose the path of pursuit, you might constantly be chasing after an elusive objective. Rohn espoused growing your value as a person and a professional to such a significant level that you would attract more opportunities and, therefore, have a greater chance of becoming more successful.

Yet, many organizations and leaders simply set the bar too low. They exhort their teams to close the next deal or build a better product or deliver a better service without ever contemplating what it would mean if they would truly become distinctive.

Ask Phil Mickelson what his goal might be for any tournament in which he is entered. Do you think he would *ever* say, "Gee, I hope to make the cut"?

Ask LeBron James what his goal is for an approaching NBA season. Do you think he would ever say, "I think that maybe we can make the playoffs"?

Yet, sales professionals seek to grow their performance by 2 percent. Customer service leaders hope to enhance their Net Promoter Scores by a few points. C-suite executives set a target to improve EBITDA by a modest amount.

Are you so busy pursuing
customers that you haven't considered
what might *attract* them?

Customers and employees that you attract
typically become much more valuable than
those you've had to pursue.

Incremental improvements add up over time. And you must realistically assess your current situation to set targets that are meaningful for the immediate future. However, here's another point we must understand: champions think like champions. They invest whatever is required to get there.

That's part of the challenge for many professionals and organizations. It's much easier to say, "We're going to grow our Net Promoter Score by 2 percent," than it is to commit to delivering an Ultimate Customer Experience (more on this later) so we become the standard by which others are judged. It's more common to say you're going to grow sales by a certain percentage than it is to do what it takes to create distinction.

Never forget the high price champions pay to become the distinctive best.

Have you set the bar too low? It's a critical question we must all ask ourselves—and be honest in our response. You cannot play small and simultaneously attain the level of distinction.

In the next chapter, we'll review the four cornerstones of distinction. You cannot reach iconic status without first becoming distinct. For now, it's time to look at the highest level of business distinction.

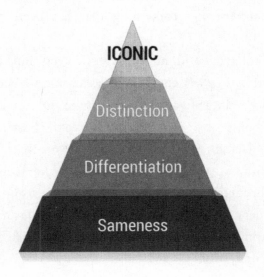

LEVEL 4: ICONIC

The ultimate level of distinction for any organization or leader to attain is to become iconic.

Today, we may think of icons as the small symbols on our phone or desktop that denotes an application or document. The word was first used in that sense in 1982. The root of the word *icon,* however, is much older. *Icon* originally came from the Greek *eikon* meaning "likeness, image, or portrait." In the sixteenth century, the Latin word *ikon* was used by the churches—particularly the Eastern Orthodox Church—as the word for depictions of Jesus or other important Christian figures in oil paintings or wooden panels.

Whether you think of the ancient *eikon* or the religious ikons or today's digital icons, they are all symbols that represent something that has been deemed important.

In today's world, an icon can be everything from a movie star to a leader of the latest fashion trends. For example, every generation has its iconic entertainers who are symbols of their times: from Elvis to the Beatles, from Michael Jackson to Jay-Z, from John Wayne to Al Pacino, from Tom Cruise to Dwayne "The Rock" Johnson. Likewise, throughout the years there are iconic companies and leaders: from GE and Jack Welch to Apple and Steve Jobs, from Berkshire Hathaway and Warren Buffett to Microsoft and Bill Gates.

Performers, organizations, and leaders became iconic when they move from being distinctive in their respective marketplaces to becoming broadly recognized as captivating.

If you're into rap music, you probably know Dolla $ign, XXXTentacion, and Migos—all of whom have top ten songs on the charts at the writing of this chapter. If that style of music doesn't suit your tastes, you probably have never heard of them. However, if you know nothing about rap—even if you abhor it—you likely have heard of Jay-Z. While the first three rappers I mentioned can fill clubs with fans, Jay-Z can sell out arenas and stadiums—in part, because he has transcended his specific genre of music. He is iconic.

I'm a big fan of Ray Dalio, the billionaire investor and hedge fund manager who recently authored a terrific bestselling book, *Principles: Life and Work.*

Despite Dalio's incredible financial track record and a *Forbes* estimated net worth of $17.4 billion dollars, I will bet the farm that he's nowhere nearly as well known as the Oracle of Omaha, Warren Buffett. It's not just Buffett's greater wealth—estimated at $84.7 billion—that makes him iconic. His status is not exclusively because he owns companies that the masses do business with daily— Geico, Duracell, and Dairy Queen. While Dalio is distinctive in the world of finance, Buffett is iconic because his seeming accessibility to the public and down-home attributes have transcended his specific field.

Therefore, the fundamental
difference is this:

Iconic organizations and leaders have captivated our attention and attained a level that transcends their specific field of endeavor.

Iconic organizations and leaders have become such universal symbols of distinction they are not only irresistible to customers in their marketplace, they compel interest and admiration across a wide spectrum.

At the risk of sounding like the professor whom I had for a class on logic in college, you can become distinctive and not attain the level of iconic. However, you cannot become iconic without first reaching the level of distinction.

The next chapter will get you up to—and through—the first step: creating distinction.

Questions for Chapter 1

Take some time to go through these questions with your team, study group, or mentor. Share ideas and insights that will help you drill deeper into the strategies and tactics that can apply to your specific organization.

- At which level of distinction would I currently place my organization or department (or myself)? Why?
- What level do I reasonably believe that my organization or department (or that I personally) could attain? Why?
- What are the specific points of differentiation that customers or others would recognize about us?
- Are we distinctive within our industry or field? Why or why not?
- If we are distinctive, what do we need to do to become iconic? If we aren't distinctive, what could we do to attain that level?

CHAPTER TWO

THE FOUR CORNERSTONES OF DISTINCTION

THE ORIGINS OF DISTINCTION

After my first wife, Sheri, passed away from ovarian cancer in 2005, I had to hitch up my pants and get to work. Left with an enormous amount of debt from medical bills and more, I found myself in a floundering financial status. At the same time, I was emotionally devastated and adrift. As her sole caregiver, I had cut back on my speaking to stay home with her. Now, I had to jump back into a hypercompetitive market and try to reestablish my professional speaking career.

At that point, if someone asked, "What do you talk about?" my answer was usually, "Oh, about an hour." In other words, I had made my reputation as a proficient speaker on any number of generic topics. You name it, I probably had a speech for it: sales, leadership, customer service, motivation, team building, time management—just to name a few.

The first step to rebuilding my career was to contact the speakers bureaus that had previously been a primary source of my bookings. I wanted to let them know I was back in gear and ready to work with them again. During the conversation with the first bureau I contacted, I asked a simple question: "When you recommend me to your clients, what do you say about me?"

The immediate response was, "We say that you are a great speaker and a really nice guy!"

While the person on the other end of the line thought they were giving me a great compliment, I was nothing short of *horrified*! I've worked at my craft, and I aspire to be considered a great professional speaker. And don't get me wrong: there's nothing bad about being nice. However, all I could think of was a ridiculous scenario: the vice president of marketing for some major corporation turns to a staff member and says, "You know what we really need for this year's meeting? We need a speaker who is a *really nice guy*!" That would *never* happen! Instead, the staffer would be instructed to find the best speaker on marketing or sales or life balance.

"Great speaker and good gal or guy" was about as generic and unremarkable of a description as I could imagine. What could possibly blend into the background more than that?

Sadly, this conversation played itself out repeatedly with numerous speakers bureaus. My branding—or lack thereof—was "the good speaker who is a really nice guy."

Naturally, I decided that I had to reposition my business. It's hard enough to *position* yourself in a marketplace. That requires a message compelling enough to move people to think about a product or service in a positive manner—and remember that concept. To *reposition* requires a new message so compelling that it makes you forget what you already know—then moves you to consider and remember the new concept in its place.

Initially, I started looking for books that would teach how to stand out and move up in a hypercompetitive marketplace. Jack Trout's book *Differentiate or Die* was excellent, but I wanted something to help me become distinctive—not just different.

That's when it hit me. "If I am having so much difficulty finding this," I asked myself, "what's the likelihood that others are as well?" If I was having trouble making my business stand out from the competition, the odds were good that there had to be more professionals dealing with the same problem. I had found my niche.

My personal pursuit to learn about distinction for my own little company had turned into a quest to research, study, write, and teach organizations and leaders around the world how to become distinct.

The irony doesn't escape me that I've just told you my *why*.

Sales of our company's books on distinction, speeches, virtual training programs, and more have totaled in the millions of dollars. Yet, not one client has ever asked me to explain *why* that's my topic.

Clients have something more important in mind:

How does what you do help them to become better at what they do?

I hope you have a compelling *why*. Certainly, I hope you do not have a *why* that is grounded in tragedy as I do. But always remember—it's the *how* that will make you stand out from the competition.

Let's examine the steps to create distinction in your marketplace—and the *hows* that will ensure your customers perceive that you are on a higher echelon. These *hows* I discovered are the elements that make up the four cornerstones of distinction.

1) CLARITY

Several years ago, I read in the *Wall Street Journal* that Procter & Gamble announced they were getting rid of more than half of their brands. "CEO A.G. Lafley said that P&G will focus on seventy to eighty consumer brands, including Tide and Pampers, which together account for some 90 percent of the company's sales and 95 percent of profits, and either divest or find ways to exit between 90 to 100 smaller brands."[3]

This reminded me of Dr. Sheena Iyengar and her research. Dr. Iyengar, famed Columbia University professor and author of *The Art of Choosing*, is perhaps the world's leading expert on why people select one option over another. (She was featured in Malcolm Gladwell's 2005 book, *Blink*. I'm honored that she has been one of my coaching clients.)

The more options you provide customers, Dr. Iyengar discovered, the more difficult you make it for them to choose any particular one.

The same phenomenon happens internally in organizations. The more brands, options, projects, initiatives, and KPIs you have, the more difficult it becomes to focus with clarity on what really matters for the company.

The first cornerstone of distinction is clarity. Obviously, if you aren't focused, you cannot exemplify the clarity required to stand out from your competition.

Well-known public speaker, leadership consultant, and author Greg McKeown wrote in his book *Essentialism: The Disciplined Pursuit of Less* that "the word *priority* came into the English language in the 1400s. It was singular. It meant the very first or prior thing. It stayed singular for the next 500 years. Only in the 1900s did we pluralize the term and start talking about priorities."[4]

P&G took a step toward clarity—focusing on their brands that are most critical and establishing performance as *the* priority not *a* priority.

If your product line is diffused, it's difficult to gain clarity. And if you're constantly analyzing your *priorities*, consider if you've been specific enough to be perceived as unique in the marketplace.

As you look at your priority and seek to gain clarity, think about your *high concept* statement. The high concept model is one I've been a fan of for a long time, devoting significant space to it in previous books. A basic premise is that if it takes you longer than six seconds to express a thought, idea, or attribute of your product or service, you aren't clear enough on it. A high concept statement is a brutally brief, powerful phrase that will interest and engage the listener.

Going back to P&G, their high concept statement is "We provide branded products and services of superior quality and value that improve the lives of the world's consumers." When they became so diversified, they began providing inferior products under the P&G name. This meant their performance wasn't congruent with their high concept. CEO Lafley realized that had to change.

The idea of a "high concept pitch" originated in Hollywood. Producers have to sell their ideas to studio executives in order to get the funding required to create their television or movie projects. Studio executives hear requests for funding for projects all day, every day. In order to pique their interest, producers had to learn to convey their concepts in six seconds or less. If they could do that, the executives knew the film could be marketed to moviegoers—who don't want to listen to a long explanation of the plot of a movie, either. That's how films like *Snakes on a Plane*—where the high concept line became the actual title—are sold.

Consider the more recent comedic movie, *Blockers*. Imagine the pitch: the producer simply says to a studio executive: "Envision every outrageous teen comedy you've seen—*American Pie, Superbad, Fast Times at Ridgemont High*—only this time we will tell it from the *parent's* point of view."

That high concept statement is brutally brief—it takes six seconds to say, yet is compelling. Every parent has worried or wondered about their teen and all the potential trouble that awaits them in the world. Most of the previous comedies focused on the perspective of teens seeking their independence. This high concept grabs our attention because it moves us to consider a different point of view from what we would expect from a raunchy comedy.

(Perhaps that's why one reviewer wrote, "Beneath the whacking, smutty, in-your-face teen sex farce, *Blockers* is a mature, thoughtful exploration of parental responsibility and the capacity of burgeoning adults to navigate life's difficult choices."[5])

During a break at a conference where I was giving a speech to financial advisors, one professional approached me to ask my opinion about his high concept statement.

"I'll build your financial future!" he exclaimed. I acted as though I were dozing off.

"The problem with that statement," I said, "is that everyone in the room could claim exactly the same thing. It does nothing to make you distinctive. Tell me a little bit about you and your background." It turned out he was a retired Air Force fighter pilot.

Together we came up with his new high concept statement: *I fly people through financial turbulence.* Significantly more interesting, right?

Don't miss the importance of what this statement did for his practice. It's not just catchphrase or tagline. His high concept statement focused his business and made him distinctive. This financial advisor now is clear about his special place in the market. He focuses on risk-averse investors, those who aren't interested in aggressive growth but want safer investments. He's focused. In other words, he's taken the first step in creating a unique practice in financial services—the first step for anyone who wants to be distinctive.

Achieving Clarity is not easy. And it's not exclusively for owners, managers, and leaders. Your entire team must be focused too.

At a consulting day I spent with an IT firm, the owner told me I could move directly to the second of the four cornerstones, as he was certain they required no help with Clarity. I challenged him to tolerate a little exercise with his executive team. I gave each of the six department heads a blank three-by-five-inch notecard. I asked those leaders to write a brief statement on the card that would clearly describe their company and what made it distinctive in their competitive market. When the executives read their statements to the rest of the room, the owner was stunned. Five of the six statements varied widely. The owner simply assumed that because he had Clarity, it was shared by his team. The exercise proved he was wrong.

It doesn't matter if we're talking about a small business or an international conglomerate. If your company's leaders aren't clear about what advantages you have in the marketplace, how in the world do you expect your employees to grasp it? If your employees aren't clear about why someone should buy from you instead of the competition, how can you assume customers get it? Make Clarity a key goal across the company and in the marketplace.

In our next section, we'll expand on this. For now, your goal is to develop a high concept statement for your business, your product or service, your department—and yourself.

Have a high concept statement ready.

Your goal is to be extraordinarily precise
about what makes you stand out to
customers. Create a compelling statement
that requires six seconds or less to convey.

2) CREATIVITY

From the last section, it's easy to understand the clarity
of the high-concept pitch for *Blockers*. However, did you
also notice the creativity? It is, to my knowledge, the
first comedy to approach the coming-of-age theme from
the parents' perspective. (And, as of this writing, it has
earned $90 million at the box office against a production
budget of $21 million.)

Enterprise Rent-A-Car is another excellent example
of creativity. The Ford you rent from Hertz is the same as
the one you drive from Avis. There is zero product variation in the rental car business. Enterprise, however, was
innovative on how they could serve their customer. They
asked, in essence, "What is one thing we can do that is
unique in the rental car experience?" Enterprise decided
to bring the car to the customer rather than make the customer come to them. Since they couldn't rent a different
or better automobile than the competition, they got cre-

ative in how they could connect with their customer. That one point of creativity is essential to why Enterprise has become the biggest player in their industry.

There are two challenges that I consistently encounter when discussing innovation with leaders. They often perceive that

1) Creativity equals chaos, and
2) Being creative is only for startups in the hi-tech industry

First, note that both Enterprise and *Blockers* didn't blow up the model—they just changed a single aspect about it. There was no chaotic disruption, just a mere adjustment. Enterprise brought the car to the customer; *Blockers* looked at the same situation from a different point of view.

In business, any innovation in how you reach or serve your customer can make an enormous difference. And it doesn't even have to be product related—you can be creative in a single aspect of service.

At Moe's Southwest Grill, employees shout, "Welcome to Moe's!" with enthusiasm every time a customer enters the restaurant. As they say on their website, "We're not trying to scare you or anything. Our signature 'Welcome to Moe's' greeting represents our passionate promise to always welcome everyone with open arms and a smile. It's safe to say this rally cry is infectious, especially among the little ones." It's true—we have toddlers in our extended family who shout, "Welcome to Moe's!" every time we pass a Moe's.

If you've dined at Chick-fil-A, you know that—even when you're at the drive-thru—you'll be met with, "Good afternoon! Welcome to Chick-fil-A! How may I serve you?" That approach stands out from the mumbled greeting that we frequently hear at the typical burger joint. And instead of saying, "You're welcome," employees of Chick-fil-A will always tell you, "My pleasure!"

You might be saying, "Wait a minute, Scott—isn't this just a customer service issue?"

Yes and no. This is initially about a commitment to creativity. It's about being innovative. It's asking, "What can we do in our approach that will be imaginative, unique, and memorable?" Perhaps you come up with a slight alteration in your approach to communicating with the customer. It could be a tweak in the method of delivery of your product or service. It may be in the app your company makes available to clients.

If you really think about it, the suggestion box on the floor at a factory is just an invitation to creativity. It's asking for ideas or innovation that could improve the productivity and workflow of the plant.

Yet, I've witnessed a disdain for these kinds of efforts. In many organizations, the perception that leaders create is apparent: the managers think they know everything about plant operations—why would they ask the frontline workers for input? The home office has all the answers—why take the time to ask the cashiers in the stores for ideas?

Then, we wonder why our customers—and employees—are leaving us for the competition!

It matters less *where* you deliver a creative approach than whether or not you *do*.

Examine every point of contact you have with your customers. Where is *one* point where you can "flip the script" and deliver creatively? It only takes one.

---

3) COMMUNICATION

Never in history have we had so many tools of communication at our disposal. Change happens so fast that some people long for the "good old days" when mail (or snail mail as it's now called) and the telephone were our primary tools of communication. While every organization has some degree of proficiency when it comes to communication, those that quickly adapt to the newest forms of communication are more competitive. However, distinctive organizations and professionals take communication to a higher level in two critical aspects:

1) They communicate with their customers in the manner of the customer's choosing.
2) They use narrative as their foundation of communication.

Following the Customers' Lead

Given all the varied forms of social media—texting, FaceTime or Skype, What'sApp, Snapchat, Instagram, Facebook, email—not only do we have more ways than ever to connect, we have more opportunity to be communicating with customers in a manner they *do not* desire.

Distinctive companies will ask their customers how they wish to be contacted. If you want a text, that's what you'll get! Want a phone call? No problem. In other words, these distinctive companies aren't focused on a set policy or what's more convenient for them or the way they've always done it. They deliver their messages in the format the customer has chosen.

Use Narrative in Communication

According to a study from the National Academy of Sciences, "People can remember more than 2,000 pictures with at least 90% accuracy in recognition tests over a period of several days, even with short presentation times during learning. This excellent memory for pictures consistently exceeds our ability to remember words."[6]

How do you transmit information to customers when they don't remember words?

You tell a story. Stories are, in essence, word pictures. They paint memorable mental images of events and create an impact in the imaginations of the listeners.

Distinctive companies are masters at narrative. They tell effective stories in which customers see themselves in a particular situation and the business as providing the solution to their problem.

To make the film *Titanic*, it cost a staggering $200 million (in 1997 dollars!). However, not many stepped out of the theater marveling over the fact that a special Russian submarine was used or that every detail on the ship matched the original Titanic down to the doorknobs. The audience walked away swooning over Jack and Rose's romance, saddened by the massive loss of life—or enraged that Jack's death could have been prevented had Rose just shared the door she was floating on!

The fact is people rarely remember the details—but they will remember how something made them feel. The power of a great story is the power to create emotional connectivity with customers and employees.

For example, I could simply say, "Your employees should make your customers happy."

Or I can tell you about the time that Jia Jiang decided to work on his fear of rejection by making at least one outrageous request a day. His plan was to go to a different business every day to ask for things he was certain would be refused. Then his plan was to post stories of each of these denials of service on his blog, "100 Days of Rejection Therapy."

However, on only his third day on the project, Jiang entered a Krispy Kreme in Austin, Texas, where he encountered shift leader Jackie Braun. Without her knowledge of his effort or his blog, Jiang asked Braun if Krispy Kreme would create a special order for him. His "sure to be rejected request" was that he wanted five doughnuts linked together like the Olympic rings, with each of the pastries matching the specific color and position on the logo.

And he told her he needed it in just fifteen minutes.

"I was honestly just hoping for a no and to go home," Jiang said later.

After exactly fifteen minutes, Braun emerged from the back with five interlocked doughnuts, looking much like the famed Olympic rings.

However, she wouldn't charge Jiang for his order! "It wasn't exactly what he wanted," Braun said. "To my eyes it wasn't perfect, so I didn't think I should charge him for it. It was the best I could do in the time allotted."

Why did Jackie Braun go to such extraordinary lengths? Her answer was simple: "We're here to make people happy."

Do you want your employees to become as committed to customer happiness? Do you wish your local Krispy Kreme had an employee like Jackie Braun? What do you suppose Braun's manager said about her efforts—especially since she did not charge the customer for all her work? I'll wager that you asked yourself at least one of those questions as you were reading the story or just after you completed it. Telling you that "employees should make customers happy" did not have a fraction of the impact that a narrative about one customer and one clerk in one donut shop delivered.

One of the stories I often tell during my speeches is of an extraordinary cab driver—Taxi Terry—from Jacksonville, Florida. (This story formed the basis of my book, *7 Tenets of Taxi Terry*.) When I tell the example of this taxi driver from the stage, practically no member of the audience is visualizing *me* in the back of the cab. Each person is seeing *herself* sitting there. When customers personalize the visualization, it has become memorable.

Many leaders have no problem retelling well-known stories about Steve Jobs, Southwest Airlines, or some other anecdote their customers or employees have read or heard. However, they frequently won't tell the stories of their own organizations. Why?

We run from our own uniqueness.

For some strange reason, we love to hear and tell the stories of others—but many have significant challenge in being able to recognize and relate their own. It's as if we have a huge blind spot regarding our own distinction.

And, by the way, if your first reaction to that statement was, "The difference is that we don't have a good story to tell," you've just confirmed your blind spot. There is a compelling story within each person and every organization.

If you find yourself with that dilemma, reach out for coaching—and there are many such consultants available. For example, Doug Stevenson (storytelling-in-business.com) teaches salespeople how to tell better stories via a method he calls Aikido Selling. According to his website, "In the ancient martial art called Aikido, you use your opponent's energy and momentum to defeat them without doing harm. In Doug's unique sales approach, the salesperson welcomes resistance, questions, and objections because they know they are prepared to embrace the objection and answer it with the appropriate story."

Larry Winget (LarryWinget.com) is a close friend I mention several times in this book. In addition to his highly successful career as a speaker and author, he consults with a limited number of executives and entrepreneurs to improve and enhance their storytelling abilities.

And this is an area in which I've helped executives with coaching and consulting. My experience has been that most of us have been well trained in data and analytics—and poorly educated in creating compelling narrative that advances our causes and careers.

Just as an editor can notice mistakes in a manuscript that have eluded the author—just as the manager can improve the swing of the famous hitter in baseball—having a professional assist you in crafting and delivering your narrative can help you see the proverbial forest amid all the trees.

By the way, that is not a solution exclusively available for corporations with big budgets for public relations. I promise there is a community college literature professor—or even a local high school English teacher—who would love to help you craft your compelling narrative. You're not asking for expertise in creating marketing copy—that's not in their wheelhouse. You are requesting their insights on your narrative, just as they would grade and improve a student's essay.

Create a compelling narrative—then start sharing it with customers and employees. The story you keep to yourself has the same value in the market as not having a story at all.

4) CUSTOMER EXPERIENCE

Distinctive organizations and leaders have an obsession for sensation. They are consumed with the question "What does it *feel like* to do business with us?"

Leaders who believe they can cut their way to success are fascinating to me. You've seen this play out repeatedly when an organization finds itself in difficulty. The immediate response from the leader may be to terminate senior staffers—meaning customers now can't find anyone who knows what they're doing to serve them. Maybe they scrimp a bit on maintenance—so now customers face dirty stores that are poorly stocked.

When I was growing up, my dad owned a small grocery store. He faced some tough competition when a new, larger store opened in town with greater selection and longer hours of operation. In response, my father didn't cut our staff or their pay. He did the opposite. He reduced the number of hours our store was open, increased the number of people working at the times you could shop with us, and intensified the customer experience. We would offer to carry your purchase to your car—even if you only bought a pack of gum!

While the competition was a supermarket, our store became known as the "super service market." Although I am certainly not an objective observer, the experience of shopping at that little store was beyond compare. It's why our grocery survived the impact of "big box" competition—the supermarket eventually closed its doors and left town. And it's why, with the new owners who followed when my dad retired, that little store in Crothersville, Indiana, still thrives today.

Take a moment to think about your own business. Would *you* do business with you?

Ask yourself if the experience you offer is so compelling that you would become a loyal customer. Obviously, customers want to repeat and refer extraordinary experiences.

> *It's important to note that these Cornerstones—even this final one—are for every business of every type.*

For many, it's easier to think about customer service in a retail setting. However, even companies that support other businesses—freight companies, ad agencies, accounting service providers, data repositories, law firms, and the like need to focus on their delivery of the customer experience as well. Unfortunately, some of these business-to-business (B2B) organizations assume that an intensive approach to customer relationships is only for companies selling directly to consumers. Nothing could be further from the truth!

"Today's B2B buyers bring their B2C [business to consumer] digital commerce expectations for functionality, personalization, and service to B2B eCommerce," says a recent study from Forrester Research conducted for Accenture Interactive and SAP Hybris. "Buyers want more personalization across all stages of the customer journey," the study continues, "and they're willing to reward the businesses that offer it to them. *If you don't deliver that B2C-like personalized experience, someone else will.*"[7]

For many years, I've discussed the Ultimate Customer Experience (so much so that I trademarked the term). Here is a list of steps to help you create an Ultimate Customer Experience—regardless of whether you're B2B or B2C:

1. What if *everything* went *exactly* right? Write a list of what would occur if everything—from the first point of contact to the close of the transaction—went perfectly from the customer's point of view.

2. What does it take to make it work out this way? Next, determine what you need to do—the specific action steps required—to enable the result as outlined in Step 1.

3. What are the roadblocks preventing execution? Consider any old policies or procedures that are getting in the way of delivering the Ultimate Customer Experience. Could the way it's always been done be preventing outstanding service? Whatever is delaying the delivery of the Ultimate Customer Experience—*fix it!*

4. Are we providing the tools required to deliver an Ultimate Customer Experience? Make sure your frontline people have been educated and

trained sufficiently. Do they have the tools—physical and technological—to deliver an ultimate experience?

Your goal should be to create the Ultimate Customer Experience for every customer—every time!

From Distinction to Iconic!

As mentioned previously, you cannot rise to the level of iconic status without first creating distinction. Developing an extraordinarily high level of Clarity, Creativity, Communication, and Customer Experience can take you to the top of the particular market that you serve. Some organizations and leaders, however, have transcended their specific industry to become recognized as iconic.

What did they do above and beyond the four cornerstones to advance beyond distinction?

That is the question that we will explore in the next chapters of this book.

QUESTIONS FOR CHAPTER 2

- What is your organization's high-concept statement? What's your personal high-concept statement?
- Select a specific point of contact you have with a customer. What's one aspect you could approach in a more innovative manner?
- Craft a story about how doing business with you has impacted a customer—whether another business or an individual. Tell the story from the customer's point of view. (To make the story memorable to other customers and prospects, it must be about the customer—not you!)
- How would you assess the experience that customers currently receive from you? Is it systemic to your organizational culture, or is it random and dependent upon which employee they encounter? (It cannot be "ultimate" if it is random!)

PART TWO

FIVE FACTORS OF
ICONIC
PERFORMANCE

CHAPTER THREE

#1 PLAY OFFENSE

When I hear the expression "Take it to the limit," I immediately hear the Eagles' hit song featuring Randy Meisner's soaring vocals playing in my head. It may be a cliché, but iconic companies and leaders do take it to the limit. They attain the highest level of distinction.

In my research, interviews, and observations, I've learned that there are five factors of iconic performance—those aspects that take an organization or leader to a level beyond distinction:

1. Play Offense
2. Get Promise and Performance Right
3. Stop Selling
4. Go Negative
5. Reciprocal Respect

We don't imagine that Amazon is inhibited about their plans for the future and their speed of execution. It's difficult to envision Elon Musk instructing colleagues to "take it easy"—to use another Eagles analogy—as they're executing a project. Iconic companies and leaders are widely recognized for being the ones who are constantly on the offensive.

Iconic performers concentrate
on playing offense.

In today's business, you may hear phrases such as "We are knocking it out of the park" or "Today's performance was a grand slam." While sports metaphors potentially can cause confusion with certain clients, it does help to illustrate the point that iconic leaders are aggressive in their thinking—they want to win. In my study of organizations, the phrase "We stay on offense"—or the variation "We don't focus on defense"—is repeated with great frequency. For that reason, it's what we'll use here.

In September 2015, I gave a talk on distinction in Cancun, Mexico, to all the general managers of Fairmont Hotels & Resorts. A short time after that conference, I was booked at the Fairmont Scottsdale Princess in Scottsdale, Arizona, at an unrelated event for a different company. When the team at the Princess learned I was coming as a guest, they decided to prove to me they took my material on distinction very seriously—and delivered an Ultimate Customer Experience. The director of operations, Gerard Mauvis, arranged an incredible welcome. He placed me in a magnificent suite and arranged for my rental car to be a Ferrari. (Yes, he was making a *phenomenal* impression—one that reminded me I was a long way from that small grocery in Crothersville, Indiana.)

Gerard told me he planned to develop reading groups throughout the Princess to discuss my book *What Customers REALLY Want*. Each department would read a chapter a week, then discuss how the content could be applied to housekeeping, valet parking, and every other position. He wanted to then repeat the process with *Create Distinction* to discover distinctive ways for every professional there to do their jobs. (I *loved* that idea—distinctive housekeeping, distinctive bartenders, distinctive valets.)

When I returned to visit the Fairmont Scottsdale Princess several months later, Mauvis asked a question that stopped me in my tracks.

"What's *next*, Scott?" he inquired. "What comes *after* you achieve distinction?"

Gerard Mauvis's question got me thinking—what *does* come next? I had focused on how to create distinction—but not how to maintain it, grow it, and expand beyond it. "Next you will become iconic!" I blurted out.

He smiled a broad smile. "*Yes!*" he responded. "We will become *iconic!*"

Gerard introduced me to Jack Miller, the general manager of the Scottsdale Princess—now also regional vice president of Fairmont Hotels & Resorts. Miller is a legend in the hospitality industry. In 2016, he was

ICONIC

named the Outstanding General Manager of Large Properties in the nation by the American Hotel & Lodging Association.

Over breakfast one morning, Miller and Mauvis told me they were frustrated that a local competitor was imitating the innovations that made the Princess distinctive.

"It almost makes you want to stop innovating," Miller said. "We work so hard to create something special and unique—and they step in and rip us off."

As the discussion continued, we concluded that if the Princess ceased to innovate, it was certain the competition would catch up with them. Miller knew he had to continue innovating, he had to stay on the offensive if he was going to establish the Princess as an iconic hotel.

"I see now that every moment I spent being upset at the imitation we were seeing from the competition was a moment wasted that could have been invested in innovating to take our business to the iconic level," Miller told me later.

Every moment you are playing defense
against the competition wastes a moment
you could be innovating to make them
irrelevant.

Choosing to be on the offense—rather than defense—means you have decided to be the initiator of action. You have resolved that you will not be as reactive to events outside your control. Primarily, it means you are exercising your power of choice regardless what others may be doing.

Besides, as Comcast CEO Neil Smit says, "It's a lot more fun than defense. It's a way of life. You get more externally focused when you play offense."[8]

When you focus on offense, you choose to spend the vast majority of your time and effort—probably at least 75 percent—planning and progressing down your desired path without any regard for what others in your industry are doing.

When the executives at ABC determine their programming schedule for the next season, they probably make their decisions based on what the other major networks—NBC, CBS, and FOX—are planning. Netflix, on the other hand, likely considers only what their customers are watching. They refuse to be bound by the traditional seasonal scheduling format and make their determinations based on customer preference instead of the competition.

Think Netflix is worried about the networks? I don't. I don't even believe they're too concerned with Hulu, Amazon, or Apple. They have taken the offensive and are charting their own course. Netflix is iconic.

While Netflix doesn't focus on Amazon, the reverse is equally true. Amazon founder Jeff Bezos has often said, "Our number one conviction and idea and philosophy and principle . . . is *customer* obsession, as opposed to *competitor* obsession."[9]

Notice a pattern here?

SIX STEPS TO AN OFFENSIVE MINDSET

It is important to note that iconic businesses or leaders understand that playing offense is a strategy of growth and innovation. Unfortunately, some marketing consultants have an alternative approach to this point. We are all aware of marketing organizations—particularly those focused on politics—that view offensive marketing strategies as "full frontal attacks." They even engage in character assassinations and assail their competition's strengths in an attempt to twist them as weaknesses. Some of the specific strategies include:

- *flank attacks*—named for attacking weak spots of competitors
- *guerilla attacks*—subversive "hit and run" attacks to undermine your competitor
- *bypass attacks*—leapfrogging the competition through introduction of new products or services

These tactics may work, but the strategy behind it is too small. To be an iconic business, you must think much bigger—long-term. Instead of this combative type of marketing approach, your innovative thinking needs to be what Smit called "a way of life." It's both an organizational commitment and a total mindset makeover by the leadership.

Many years ago, entrepreneur and former congressman Ed Foreman related the story of the time he turned the financial results of his several companies over to his accountant. Noting the strong expansion in each sector of Foreman's diverse organization, the CPA shook his head and said, "Ed, this growth is amazing. Haven't you heard about the recession?"

Foreman responded, "Yes, but we decided not to participate."

Foreman set his own rules. Choosing how you will play the game is essential to delivering the results and building an iconic organization. It creates the kind of business that Jack Miller has generated at the Fairmont Princess and builds the type of organization that Neil Smit has at Comcast Cable. You do not have to participate in the games that competitors are playing.

Let's look at the six steps to taking the Iconic offensive mindset.

1) CHOOSE THE GAME YOU WILL PLAY

One of the most profound statements I heard about becoming an iconic company was from Gerard Mauvis during our initial discussions. He said: "We realized we couldn't become globally iconic until we were locally distinctive."

Remember, you must create distinction before you can achieve the iconic level. The Fairmont Scottsdale Princess exemplifies that approach. They chose the game they would play, created amazing distinction at the local level, then rode their success to iconic recognition.

Imagine you are managing a hotel in Scottsdale, Arizona. What do you think the slowest times of the year might be? You'd naturally think of the summer months—it's probably difficult to fill your resort when the temperature is 120 degrees. Another time that might be tough for you is around the Christmas holiday. There are no conventions held then and business travel drops to zero. Few families view that time of year as one to spend in a resort hotel. In addition, Arizona is home to many transplants who want to return to the East Coast or Midwest to spend Christmas with their families back home. (There's a reason Bing Crosby never sang about dreaming of a cactus and sand-filled Christmas "like the ones I used to know.")

How do you pack your hotel with guests during the time of year that the fewest number of people want to travel to your location?

Combining the ideas of the offensive mindset—choosing the game you will play and becoming locally distinctive—Jack Miller and team made a critical decision. "We decided," Miller said, "that we were going to *own* Christmas in Scottsdale."

That meant at least three things to Miller and his colleagues:

1. We will create a local tradition for the entire community.
2. What we do will be so spectacular that it will inspire repeat and referral visits.
3. It will grow our local reputation to the point that we are considered *the* distinctive property in our community.

No one else in the community was playing that game. In fact, some properties were reducing their number of employees working over the holiday and providing a lower level of service because of the sparse business. Miller, Mauvis, and their team committed to playing the game that they had chosen in a very unique manner. They created a winter wonderland with a desert ice skating rink, a build-a-toy workshop, millions of lights and light shows, a s'mores land complete with a campfire, carousel, and Ferris wheel, and much more.

The Fairmont Princess did not submit to certain "rules of engagement" and pack up for the winter because it is just the way "it's always been done." That's the essence of not selecting the game you're playing.

Don't get me wrong. I realize that for many of us, we're not going to have total control over the rules of the game. If you're a financial advisor, you must adhere to governmental and industry regulations. If you're an architect, there are certain rules of physics that will always take precedence. Even if you're the general manager of the Scottsdale Princess, you will still have to rent rooms to guests. I'm certain you already know in today's fast-changing environment that doing business as it's always been done is not going to cut it. The question is what will you *do* about it?

Tesla didn't say, "Automobiles are only sold through independent dealerships." Instead, Elon Musk and team took the offensive and decided how they would play the game. You can only buy a Tesla through Tesla showrooms—which are usually in shopping malls, not in suburban "auto malls"—or online. Tesla followed the Apple model of selling products direct to consumers. In the early days, Apple didn't say, "Most computers are sold to companies through highly organized corporate sales teams." Instead, Steve Jobs and associates decided on a different field of play. Both of these companies are examples that you can make how your product is sold as distinctive as the product that you sell.

You can choose—and change—the game in every organization and at every level. A payroll department in a large organization decided to do exactly that. Instead of just "cutting payroll checks," they decided to reframe the game. They changed their motto to "We deposit the money that funds the dreams of 5,000 families—including our own."

The department leaders then started sharing the stories of the fulfilled dreams. They told their colleagues of employees who had saved to buy a boat or pay for a college education from the money the payroll team had deposited in their accounts. The results were higher productivity, lower turnover, and significantly greater job satisfaction in that department. This department is now both distinctive within the organization and iconic as a payroll team across many industries.

They decided to play a different game.

What game are you choosing? Or are you even choosing? Are you just going along for the ride—just mindlessly playing the same old game—and wondering why you aren't standing out from the competition and winning the contest?

2) DEVELOP AN INNOVATIVE GAME PLAN

At the core, our game plan is both the overall strategy for success and the specific tactics we will execute to win.

Remember the Fairmont Scottsdale Princess. The manager decided the game was to be locally distinctive and that would start with "owning" Christmas in their hometown. The next step was to deliver the tactics to accomplish that strategy.

Similar to the strategy of McDonald's with its Happy Meals and playgrounds, the team at the Princess realized that if they would appeal to kids, the parents would naturally come along. Hotels tend to market to business travelers—resorts often focus upon meetings, couples, and families. The Princess developed an aspect of their unique Christmas program that would focus on kids. (After all, parents love to give their kids memorable experiences.) If the Princess could wow the family, they would get the repeat and referral business they desired.

How would you develop such a plan? For Jack Miller and his team, it started with outlining the traditions that make Christmas special. Some were obvious—Santa Claus and Christmas lights—others took a bit more creativity given their Southwestern setting—ice skating in the desert and roasting marshmallows around a campfire. The Princess team set up a "Santa's Secret Headquarters" where kids could write a letter to Santa. Next, youngsters walk through a hallway of snow-covered trees to place their message to St. Nick in an oversized mailbox.

The Princess didn't slow down for the winter like the competition. Instead, it decided the game it wanted to play and developed strategy to play that game—and become the best at it. At no point in the process did the Princess team ask what any other resort in the area was doing. They didn't wonder, "What does the Phoenician serve for Christmas brunch?" Or "How many lights does the Four Seasons string up?"

You cannot create an innovative game plan if all you do is focus on what everyone else is delivering in your marketplace. Naturally, you have awareness of your competition. However, when you choose to play the game your way, what the opponent is doing is never a primary aspect in your game plan.

The week before Super Bowl LII, a story in *Sports Illustrated* featured the planning process that Philadelphia Eagles coach Doug Pederson employed in the attempt to win against an iconic competitor. "In the pre-game mayhem this week," famed reporter Peter King wrote, "there is sure to be this story line: *Belichick vs. Pederson: Mismatch of Super Bowl 52*. Pederson gets it. He was a Louisiana high school coach ten years ago when Belichick already had three Super Bowl rings."

(The Patriots are the NFL's reigning dynasty and Patriots coach Bill Belichick is recognized by most football experts as one of the—if not *the*—greatest coach in the history of the NFL.) Coach Pederson was asked how many times he had mentioned the Patriots or Belichick to his team of coaches or the players.

"Zero," Pederson said. "I have not."

Pederson called his strategy the "faceless opponent."

"I just think you can't get caught up with who's on the other side," he said. "Everybody in the NFL is good. Every team is good. I've always believed you just go about <u>your</u> business. You prepare. You get your team ready to go every week, and you treat it that way. It's about doing *your* job. That fits with the faceless opponent. Do what you've been coached to do this week...win your matchup, the one-on-ones, and let's see what happens. *Nothing else matters, so why introduce anything else?*"[10]

When you decide to approach the marketplace with an offensive mindset, it strengthens the likelihood that you can create an innovative game plan.

3) PLAY TO YOUR STRENGTHS

A team of researchers wrote a great piece published in the *Harvard Business Review* on managers playing to their strengths. It is the best way to reach your highest potential. "After all, it's a rare baseball player who is equally good at every position. Why should a natural third baseman labor to develop his skills as a right fielder?"[11]

A fundamental element of playing offense is to play to the strengths of your organization and the people on your team.

You likely know the result of the Super Bowl LII. The underdog Eagles "beat the (New England Patriots) Belichick-Brady conglomerate—the greatest coach/quarterback duo in the game's history—and he did it with a backup quarterback [Nick Foles] who nearly retired in 2015 because he questioned whether he had enough enthusiasm left to continue playing."[12]

"'We just wanted to stay aggressive,' Pederson said afterward. 'My mentality coming into the game was to stay aggressive until the end and let playmakers make plays,' Pederson said."[13]

The Fairmont Scottsdale Princess believed they had advantages in the areas of both property and people. The goal became to play to their strengths.

The physical facility was a critical aspect that would permit them to create a memorable experience. The resort is on sixty-five acres in the heart of the Sonoran Desert next to the McDowell Mountains. The sheer size of the property was a strength that allowed the team to create special areas within the resort for the Christmas project—such as a six-thousand-square-foot ice skating rink (with real ice in the middle of the desert) and a giant four-story Christmas tree with seventy thousand LED lights and a five-foot snowflake tree topper.

Yet, Miller and Mauvis constantly reminded me that it was the team of professionals at the Princess who made it all happen. They believed in their staff that included industry "playmakers"—and they were called on to make some big plays.

"Our people are our greatest asset" is a phrase we've heard leaders exclaim time and time again. However, many recite this line while simultaneously treating their employees as nothing more than an expense. So what's your initial, gut-level reaction to this question: are your employees *primarily* an asset or an expense to your business?

Many leaders claim their people are their greatest asset but then go on to treat them as nothing more than an expense. Consider this report from CityLab in 2013:

> The average American cashier makes $20,230 a year, which in a single-earner household would leave a family of four living under the poverty line. But if he works the cash registers at QuikTrip, it's an entirely different story. The convenience store and gas station chain offers entry-level employees an annual salary of around $40,000, plus benefits. Those high wages didn't stop QuikTrip from prospering in a hostile economic climate. While other low-cost retailers spent the recession laying off staff and shuttering stores, QuikTrip expanded to its current 645 locations across 11 states.[14]

If you see your people primarily as an expense, you naturally will seek to minimize them.

If you see your people primarily as an expense, that expenditure becomes an aspect of your business that you typically seek to minimize. In other words, we're taught in business that profit is enhanced—at least in part—by reducing expenses. The more we keep our expenses in check, this basic theory of business goes, the greater the likelihood we will become more profitable.

That's not the *total* picture, though. Assets are vital points in our business that we seek to amplify. When we go on the offensive, we seek to make our assets more valuable. When you see your employees as assets to be cultivated and enhanced—as opposed to expenses to reduce and minimize—those assets become more productive—and, therefore, more profitable—for your business.

CityLab found that "entry-level hires at QuikTrip are trained for two full weeks before they start work, and they learn everything from how to order merchandise to how to clean the bathroom."

Why is that important? "As global competition increases and cheap, convenient commerce finds a natural home online, the most successful companies may be those that *focus on delivering a better customer experience*."[15]

That experience is delivered by your "playmakers."

> *To attain iconic status, you must seek to enhance and play to the strengths of your team.*

The *Harvard Business Review* report states, "It is a paradox of human psychology that while people remember criticism, they respond to praise. The former makes them defensive and therefore unlikely to change, while the latter produces confidence and the desire to perform better."[16] When it comes to praise and playing to the strengths of the team, I don't know that I have met any leader who is as relentlessly positive as Jack Miller at the Scottsdale Princess.

- Imagine working for someone who sees you as an asset, has confidence in you, and gives you the tools to succeed.
- Visualize a coach who tries to take pressure off you by not harping on the competition.
- Consider what it would be like to be an employee under a leader whose core principle is to play to the strengths of her team members.

Do you suppose that type of commitment and trust would inspire greater performance, engagement, and loyalty with your team?

It's not a coincidence that QuikTrip paid its cashiers almost *double* the industry standard and simultaneously grew the business. It's not merely by chance that the *Forbes*, Glassdoor, and LinkedIn lists of Best Places to Work constantly feature iconic companies like Salesforce, Wegman's, In-N-Out Burger, Google, Lululemon, and SAP. We'll explore the iconic corporate culture later, in chapter seven of this book.

> When you play to your strengths—
> recognizing your strength is in your
> people and how you help them develop—
> you can take an offensive position in the
> marketplace.

4) CAPTURE ATTENTION

Ben Parr is a journalist, author, and venture capitalist. When we were both speaking at the Brand Manage Camp in 2017, he talked about capturing people's attention.

> Your long-term success depends on winning the attention of others. If your boss doesn't notice your work, how will you get a promotion? If your team doesn't listen to you, how can you lead effectively? And if you can't capture the attention of clients, how does your business or career survive? . . .

The most effective employees, managers, and executives are the ones who shine a spotlight on their ideas, projects, and teams. Understanding the science of attention is a prerequisite to success in the information age.[17]

In the case of the Scottsdale Princess, three million dazzling LED lights, an animated holiday light show, a large Ferris wheel, a Christmas carousel, and an ice slide are among the innovative elements that capture the attention of the entire Phoenix metropolitan area and beyond.

In the age of the Internet and social media and blogging, attention spans are shorter than ever. You must ask the question: what are we doing to capture the interest of our audience?

To take the offensive, you cannot major in minor projects.

---

5) HOLD THE PLAYERS ACCOUNTABLE

The late Pat Summitt, legendary Tennessee women's basketball coach, said, "Responsibility equals accountability equals ownership. And a sense of ownership is the most powerful weapon a team or organization can have."

Coaches of top athletes and management experts agree that an essential component to staying on the offensive is to hold the players on your team accountable for their actions and results. According to Gordon Tredgold, business coach and consultant, there are three purposes for this:

1. It lets them know that they will be held accountable for the activities.
2. It gives you an opportunity to provide support in case things start to go awry.

3. It offers you the opportunity to offer praise and encouragement to move people further if things are going well.[18]

Could you imagine the coach allowing a player who was performing badly—or not caring about the outcome of the game—to continue to play in the game? While that's unheard of in athletics, it is often the case in business. For some reason, there are many who seldom choose to call out a colleague when their attitude is below par. It seems in today's sensitive and litigious world, managers are afraid to upset or offend. The problem is that by failing to hold their team members accountable, they frequently upset and offend those who *are* performing at the levels we expect and desire.

Peter Bregman is renowned author and leadership coach. Bregman began his career teaching leadership on wilderness and mountaineering expeditions, then moved into the consulting field. Since 1989, he has trained and coached all levels of management. He teaches that there are five clear ways to hold people accountable:

1. **Clear expectations**: be precise about what you expect in terms of performance and outcomes.
2. **Clear capabilities**: be exact about what's needed to get the job done—and whether that individual team member has the capacity to achieve it.

3. **Clear measurement**: be open about how the performance will be evaluated—and what constitutes success or failure.

4. **Clear feedback**: open, honest, and transparent reviews throughout the process are required to keep everyone on track.

5. **Clear consequences**: be certain there's no ambiguity on what will happen when performance is delivered—or the team member fails to achieve success. [19]

French philosopher and playwright Moliere once wrote, "It is not only what we do, but also what we do *not* do, for which we are accountable."

You cannot develop iconic performance
without accountability.

You'll never stimulate a culture that's
constantly on the offense if you fail to hold
your players to a high standard.

---

6) CELEBRATE THE VICTORIES

When I entered my room during a recent visit to the Fairmont Scottsdale Princess, a video was playing on the flat-screen television. At first glance, it appeared to be the performance of a circus. On closer examination, I noticed that the ringmaster was none other than Jack Miller and many of those in the audience were members of the Princess team I had grown to know over the past few years.

To celebrate their becoming an iconic hotel and resort, the leadership team had thrown a private circus performance for the entire resort staff and their families. It was the leadership's way of congratulating the employees on a job well done—and served as another reminder of the family-oriented culture that Miller and his colleagues work to ingrain throughout the organization.

When you decide to celebrate a success:

1. Don't wait
2. Make it special
3. Deliver a tangible

DON'T WAIT

Picture an NFL game where the official says to the players, "You have to wait until halftime to dance in the end zone for the scores you have accumulated over the previous two quarters of football." Are you kidding?

Could you even imagine an announcer prior to a basketball game warning the fans, "To enhance the concentration of our players, do not cheer after each basket—please wait until the designated breaks to display enthusiasm for your team." Obviously not!

Players dance and fans cheer *immediately* when their player scores or makes a big play. It's a visceral reaction. We have to cheer.

So why do we frequently take a different approach in business? Why do we wait to schedule a meeting to read a list of accomplishments from the past several weeks—or even months? That's a poor approach to recognition.

When someone has done something deserving of recognition, don't wait. You may debate the appropriateness of instant expressions of commendation. However, in this day and age, it is a proven and effective leadership tool.

Make it special

I have been at conferences where awards for exceptional performance were being presented and the chief executive officer has commented, "This is the most important—and enjoyable—part of my position as CEO of this company." I *love* hearing that!

One idea is to reconsider the names that you assign to the awards and recognition.

For example, being named a customer service *superstar* is infinitely more special than receiving an award for fewest customer complaints. (I've actually seen both of those awards presented to exceptional employees!) I swooned when a CEO presented a receptionist with an award titled Hero of First Impressions—instead of handing a gift and unemotionally thanking her for her service to the company. Review how you recognize achievement and find ways to enhance the level of excitement it creates for your team. Be creative and distinctive even in this area.

DELIVER A TANGIBLE

Jack Miller not only is ringmaster of a circus to reward his team, he is a master at handwritten notes of appreciation. Miller understands that customer and employee experience is critical. He makes sure to "leave behind a trail of tangibles," as my close friend and president of High Point University Dr. Nido Qubein suggests.

In other words:

- Don't just send an email to give a high performer a day off. Hand-deliver a printed "day-off pass" to them and personally thank them.
- Do not simply buy a meal at a nice restaurant. Arrange to have the menu signed by the chef and framed as a keepsake of a special occasion.

The point is to go above and beyond not just in the way you reach customers but the way you treat employees too. They "respond to appreciation expressed through recognition of their good work because it confirms their work is valued by others," writes consultant Kim Harrison.[20]

Our job is to deliver tangible recognition in a manner that keeps our teammates delivering and on the offensive.

THE IMPORTANCE OF PLAYING OFFENSE

"Defense wins championships," goes the old saying.

Except it isn't true. The better defense does not win even half of the time.

Consider this: thirty-eight Super Bowl winners had a top-ten *offense*.

According to an analysis on Freakonomics.com, "There have been 427 NFL playoff games over the last 45 seasons. The better defensive teams have won 58 percent of them. The better offensive teams have won 62 percent of the time."[21] (The winning team sometimes is better on both sides of the ball, explaining why the total exceeds 100 percent.)

Maybe I'm a bit prejudiced when it comes to this statistic because my favorite NFL team, the Indianapolis Colts, won Super Bowl XLI with a team rated nineteenth in the league on defense—but *third on offense*.

It's interesting to me that when the NFL, NHL, NBA, or MLB presents their respective Most Valuable Player awards, it is almost always for the player who has had the best season in terms of offensive statistics. Many of those leagues even have a best defensive player award to recognize a player's excellence on that side of the ball or puck. Yet, "most valuable" is, in many cases, the best *offensive* player.

In other words, the best *offensive* efforts are the ones considered as the most valuable to the team and the sport.

To emphasize my point: "Which of the following set of names is more recognizable? The top five touchdown leaders in NFL history: Jerry Rice, Emmitt Smith, LaDainian Tomlinson, Randy Moss, and Terrell Owens? Or the top five interception leaders: Paul Krause, Emlen Tunnell, Rod Woodson, Dick Lane, and Ken Riley?"[22]

Those of you who follow football likely remember more offensive players than defensive ones.

The same is true for iconic companies or individuals. We remember the ones who take charge and lead the offense. Remember, every moment you are playing defense against the competition wastes a moment you could be innovating to make them irrelevant.

Stop playing defense. Start now to create and deliver an innovative and dynamic offensive approach to your customers and employees.

You cannot make your competition irrelevant while worrying about them all the time. Play offense!

QUESTIONS FOR CHAPTER 3

- Do you feel your organization is primarily playing offense or defense? Why? If playing defense, what could you be doing to strengthen your offense?

- Are you choosing the game you play—and the way you play it—or is that dictated by external forces like the economy and the competition? If you are controlled by external forces, what can you do to be more independent of them?

- Is your game plan innovative—or do you feel as though you're just repeating traditional approaches?

- What are the strengths of your organization? What are your personal strengths? How could you play to them more of the time?

- Do you have the attention of those you need—customers, prospects, and employees?

- What do you need to do to enhance the attention you receive?

- Are people held accountable in your organization? Are you holding the people who report to you accountable for their performance? How do you enhance the level of accountability in your organization?

- Do you celebrate—quickly, publicly, and tangibly—the successes of your team members? How could you improve?

CHAPTER FOUR

#2 GET THE PROMISE AND PERFORMANCE RIGHT

You might take your car to a shop for a regularly scheduled service. Maybe you hire an IT company to manage your company's systems. Perhaps you select an advertising agency to create a campaign to tell the world about your products. It might be that you decide on a financial advisor to administer your family's resources and plan for your retirement. In every case—personal or professional—you need to ask:

- How will you evaluate the results?
- How will you determine if the decision you made was good or bad?
- How will you decide to continue the relationship—or search for another provider?

Iconic companies and leaders don't make it right—they get it right.

The research is clear: iconic companies and leaders don't *make* it right—they *get* it right. They are precise about the two primary factors that determine how we consciously—and subconsciously—evaluate them: promise and performance. These two factors are fundamental in our decisions whether we will repeat our business with them—and whether or not we will refer friends and colleagues.

> *The two primary factors of customer*
> *evaluation are promise and*
> *performance.*

"Gallup research has shown that if customers don't have a firm foundation of confidence and trust in a brand, customer loyalty erodes," wrote William J. McEwen, author of *Married to the Brand.* "In fact," he continued, "across an array of brands in six different product categories, Gallup found that customer loyalty plummets an average of 29% if customers do not have a strong belief in the company's ability and commitment to keep its promises."[23]

Customers judge companies primarily upon how they perform relative to their promise.

Customers judge companies not only upon what they promise to do but also on how they deliver on that promise. Iconic companies are superior in the alignment of a compelling promise with consistent performance. That may sound basic and simplistic, but the more you drill down into this principle, the more complex it becomes.

> *Iconic companies are superior in the alignment of a compelling promise with consistent performance.*

A few years back, a principal business catchphrase was, "Your brand is a promise." In other words, the promise and commitment that your organization makes to customers—and employees—determines the primacy of your brand in the competitive marketplace. Often-cited examples were Safety = Volvo or Joy = Disney.

Yet, you might be asking, if your brand was simply your promise, does that mean all you have to do is make a bigger, better promise than your competitor to gain an advantage? Not exactly. An organization or leader must deliver on the promises made. Your brand is not your promise, for the promise may not be the most critical aspect in the brand equation.

As you know, Jeff Bezos is many things: founder of Amazon, owner of the *Washington Post*, and currently the world's richest person, to name a few. He also has delivered my favorite definition of what a brand *really* is: it is what people say about you when you're not in the room.

> *"Your brand is what people say about*
> *you when you're not in the room."*
> *—Jeff Bezos*

That's perfect! Your brand is not what you promise your customers. It's what customers say about how you have performed—based on the promise to others.

- The brand of the Scottsdale Princess is what I—and other guests—tell my friends about my experience when I return home from a trip.
- The brand of my financial advisor is what I say over a cup of coffee to my wife about our advisor's performance and the experience she's created.
- Amazon's brand is, in part, how you feel about getting a delivery from them on time, even when you don't expect it—and telling all your friends. (More on that later.)

Your brand isn't just your promise.

Your brand is how customers evaluate
the performance you have delivered
based on the promise they perceive you
have made.

This means that we must examine both:

1. The promise we are making—and how it is perceived.
2. How our performance is stacking up against the standard that our promise implies.

PROMISE

What are you promising your customers? What should they expect when they do business with you? How about your employees—what are you promising them?

A promise, in the sense we are considering it here, is interpersonal. In other words, it is a commitment between two or more companies or two or more people. At its core, a promise is simply a commitment for action. Promises can be

- between individuals in their personal lives ("I promise to remain faithful.")
- between professionals ("I promise I'll have the report completed today.")
- between organizations ("We promise to complete the building on time and under budget.")

For over fifteen years, I've written and spoken about the importance of perception and understanding the elements of a transaction that a customer has a right to expect. Note that if I "expect you to deliver," it presumes that I perceive that a promise of some kind has been made. Why would I hold the expectation that you'll deliver something you haven't promised?

Frequently, I will ask the leadership team of an organization to list the basic elements of their product or service that any and every customer has a right to expect they deliver based on their sales pitch or promise.

The results of this exercise never cease to amaze me. In all my years of facilitating this exercise, I don't think I've ever had but a few companies—or leaders—tell me they have such a list. They usually have a list of things they don't do because of liability issues—hardly any have lists of what they always deliver for the customer. Only a small fraction has developed the list of *nonnegotiables* that a customer will always receive.

Let me explain what I mean.

I'm a Global Services-level flyer on United Airlines. Would I fly United if their motto (or stated promise) was, "We don't crash—often!" Absolutely not! Safety is a nonnegotiable; it's a given. United—and every other airline—*must* get safety right every time. If they don't, nothing else matters to their customers. Some other promises I expect from airlines include:

- The flight should be on time (if weather and other safety-related circumstances permit).
- Service should be friendly and efficient.

- The airline should deliver the promised frequent flyer rewards.
- Baggage should reach the same destination that I do—at the same time I do.
- Planes will be clean and well maintained.

You get the idea. This list should be easy to develop; however, few leaders take the time or make the effort to do it. Stop right now and create the list for your organization. In addition, make a list of what employees (your "internal customers") have a right to expect from you and your engagement with them. After you've developed your list, the next step is to ask an important question: what is the primary promise that customers believe we have made to them? You might need to:

- take a look at what your marketing efforts are suggesting;
- inquire from your sales professionals what they find most persuasive to prospective buyers;
- seek insight from your call center on what issues customers are talking about the most; and
- examine every other segment in your organization where a promise has been made or implied to customers or employees.

It's critical that you become totally clear and precise about the promise you are making. If you fail to perform, customers *will* hold you accountable. And—as many businesses, entrepreneurs, and frontline professionals already know—through social media channels, such as Yelp, Trip Advisor, Twitter, and Facebook, customers now have a bigger megaphone than ever to voice any dissatisfaction.

What happens when you feel you have delivered on the promise you have made—and customers still aren't happy? The obvious answer is that the level of "performance" you are delivering may be different from the customer's standard of expectations. We will examine that point later in this chapter. The answer that I believe is more prevalent—and much less obvious—is that you and your customer are *perceiving* the promise differently.

> *The challenge is that customers will always evaluate your performance based on the promise from their point-of-view . . . not yours.*

This is an issue that every organization and leader must confront. There is a fundamental problem with perception: customer and employee perceptions are subjective and influenced by past or comparable performances. Even iconic companies are not immune to this challenge.

We know that our promise to customers is an interpersonal commitment. But the perception of what is being promised is *intrapersonal*.

In other words, an individual will perceive a promise based on their own experiences and beliefs. Their perception is very personal and unique. If you fail to deliver based on the customer's perception, the result will be disconnection, distrust, dissatisfaction— or in the case of employees, significantly higher levels of turnover.

For example, it is my contention that the iconic company Apple is experiencing a growing gulf with their customers because of the perception problem. Apple is known for making intuitive and simple-to-use products. My first computer was the Apple IIe. Because of my lack of computer acumen, it was really nothing more than a glorified word processor for my new small business. My one significant accomplishment on it was figuring out mail merge—so I could easily address multiple envelopes and send letters that appeared to be personalized to a database of prospective clients.

When I got my new Macintosh Plus, I became a devoted fan. Every program had a similar interface and was easy to use—everything just *worked*. When Apple released the Mac SE, I was at the front of the line. It had an 8 MHz processor (my Mac Pro now has a 1600 MHz processor). I hardly knew what to do with all the computational power. It also came with 2 GB of memory, a floppy disk drive, and a hard drive with 40 MB of space for documents—less than some of my individual files today. Although it had amazing power for its time, the reason I was thrilled with it was because it was the "computer for the rest of us"—and it really was. Frankly, I don't recall ever cracking open a manual, because the Mac was so intuitive.

Fast forward to today—as I type this chapter on my MacBook Pro and I look at my iPhone X on the table beside me and the Apple Watch on my left wrist—I'm still a devoted customer of the company and am honored to have it as a client of mine. But quite frankly, my passion for them has eroded just a bit. The products aren't as simple as they once were—or as I once perceived them to be.

Now, it seems as though there is something different and unique about each program or product for the Mac that has a bit of a learning curve for the user. Certainly, Final Cut Pro is infinitely more complex than a program like Adobe PageMaker that I purchased many years ago. However, the promise of uniformity—while not absent—certainly has been ablated a bit.

The same is true with my iPhone. I became accustomed to having just one button—a tradition at Apple starting with the first iPod. Now I must learn gestures on how to swipe the screen or push the proper button in the correct sequence to get the device to do what I want it to do. With the iPhone X, I have to learn at least a dozen "intuitive" gestures that seem about as easy and natural to me as understanding the hand signals of a third-base coach. Then there are ten gestures to learn to get the basic services of the Apple Watch. That's twenty-two gestures to memorize. On the other hand, there's still just one button for my iPad.

Certainly, I realize that I'm getting very close to older generational "get off my lawn" bitching here. Yet, it's not that I'm upset about a relatively high number of gestures or methods of use of their products—it's that I feel that Apple hasn't delivered on what I perceived to be their fundamental promise: *ease of use*.

Perhaps part of this phenomenon is because our perceptions *change* based upon our performance. According to research by University of Virginia Professor Dennis Proffitt and his then-graduate student Jessica Witt, now a professor at Purdue University:

> "In their (Profit and Witt's) experiment, 23 volunteers had to kick an American football through the field goal from the 10-yard line. After a warm-up, participants were asked to judge the height and width of the goal by adjusting a handheld, scaled-down model of the goal made out of PVC pipes. They then each performed 10 kicks. Immediately after the final kick, participants repeated the perceptual measurement.
>
> The result was striking. Before kicking, both groups had the same perception of the size of the goal (incidentally, an inaccurate one: everybody underestimated its actual width-to-height ratio). But after 10 kicks, the poor performers (those who scored two or fewer successful kicks)

saw the goal as about 10 percent narrower than they had before, whereas the good kickers (those who scored three or more) perceived the goal to be about 10 percent wider.

How well you have performed over the past few minutes influences the way you see the world! Not just metaphorically, but on a physiological level—it changes your actual perceptions."[24]

Perhaps part of the problem is that your customer's perception changes as their performance with your product changes.

My perception of Apple's promise has always been "insanely great products that are easy to use." Therefore, it's likely that as Apple products have become more complex and I find them more difficult to use, my perception about the organization and how it delivers has been altered. In other words, as I'm swiping the wrong way (missing kicks, so to speak), I'm also perceiving the company is not delivering what I desire (they're making the goal posts narrower).

The more I've considered it, however, I suggest that there has been a shift at Apple's headquarters as well. CEO Tim Cook states that the "North Star" of Apple is "making insanely great products that really change the world in some way—enrich people's lives."[25]

Is it possible, though, they have come to believe that the only way they can do this is through the most advanced—and thus complex—technology achievable?

(Perhaps, too, they have their eye a bit more on the competition than they should. We all know that a new feature on the next Samsung device has a good chance of being included on a future iPhone—and vice versa.)

Please don't misunderstand me. I'm one of the 97 percent of satisfied Apple Watch customers. [26] It's just that I've moved from being "over the moon" and "thrilled" to being just "satisfied." And, while certainly not scientific, I cannot help but notice that every time I use this illustration in a speech, many members of the audience enthusiastically nod their heads in agreement.

The significant point here isn't even about Apple. It's about the fundamental importance of having a deep understanding of what your customers perceive your promise to be—because that is their benchmark for evaluation.

Apple is probably doing it exactly right, based upon what Tim Cook perceives is the proper execution of their "North Star." But what if your customers are using a sextant with a different alignment?

Here are three significant steps for achieving iconic status as it pertains to perception:

1. Clearly and precisely craft your promise to your customers.
2. Adjust and tweak your promise so it aligns with the perception of the majority of your customer base.
3. Ensure congruency between the internal and external perceptions of your promise. If your team holds one perception and your customers have a different version, it is a breeding ground for disconnection.

PERFORMANCE

How effective you are at delivering exactly what you've promised to your customers is the essence of performance. As my pal Larry Winget says, "Do what you say you will do, when you said you will do it."

"Do what you say you will do, when you said you will do it."

Many companies and professionals have difficulty executing at even this basic level. They concoct reasons—what customers call "excuses"—for why they didn't deliver as promised. However, when we do what we say we will do, customers are not only appreciative—in many cases, they want to tell the world.

A longtime friend and former coworker of mine, John T. Howard, recently posted a powerful message for his thousands of followers to read on Facebook. It was about an experience he had with an iconic company:

> "Here is a precise reason why Amazon is killing traditional retail as we know it. . . .
>
> On Friday I needed a specific lawn treatment application and went to Menards to buy it. Menards was out of stock.
>
> I also needed a specific health supplement recommended by my cardiologist that turned out to be unavailable from local retailers. In other words, I was looking two places for two separate, completely different items. When I got home from the futile 'snipe hunt' on Friday, I found both items on Amazon for less money.
>
> Because I am an Amazon Prime member, two-day delivery is guaranteed—including Sundays.
>
> I forgot when I ordered that Sunday (today) is Brickyard 400 day. (*Author's note: The Brickyard 400 in Indianapolis is one of the major races on the NASCAR circuit. Even though attendance has declined in recent years, there were still about 50,000 fans crowding into the few blocks surrounding John Howard's home on this day.*)

Our usually quiet neighborhood is now crawling with cars, cops, helicopters, and people on foot—some of whom are already inebriated—who are walking in the street oblivious to traffic.

Thirty minutes ago, my 8-pound Amazon box arrived—*just as they had guaranteed!* It was delivered by a guy ON A BICYCLE with a basket.

When I asked about the bicycle, the delivery guy stated that—given the race—the packages he was delivering in the neighborhood today required something more agile than a truck.

The truck with the goodies ordered by Amazon customers in my neighborhood is parked next to Kohl's near Crawfordsville Road. Two guys with bikes are shuttling packages on race day throughout the neighborhood—so that Amazon can *keep its promise* of delivery.

I find this amazing. Amazon's success in this case seems well-deserved."[27]

It shouldn't escape us that John Howard is thrilled with Amazon not because they gave him a discount, offered an upgrade, or any of the other "underpromise, overdeliver" gimmicks that we've assumed are business gospel. Instead, he was amazed because they *did what they promised they would do.*

THE PROMISE-PERFORMANCE MATRIX

The promise-performance matrix is comprised of four possible combinations that can occur in any business transaction:

1. Low promise, low performance
2. High promise, low performance
3. High promise, high performance
4. Low promise, high performance

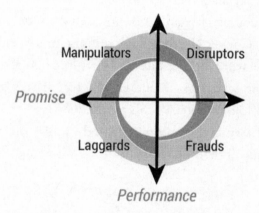

First, let's define the four styles on the matrix. Then we'll discover the "sweet spot" where iconic companies place and maintain their organizations.

LAGGARDS (LOW PROMISE, LOW PERFORMANCE)

In 1962, eminent sociologist Dr. Everett Rogers proposed the "diffusions of innovations theory" in which he developed five categories of businesses or people: innovators, early adopters, early majority, late majority, and—at the trailing end—a group consisting of approximately 16 percent of the market that Rogers designated as the laggards.

One positive comment you can make about laggards is this: they keep their word!

Certainly, laggards do not deliver much to customers. Conversely, they don't promise much, either.

The word *laggard* dates to 1757. Its original meaning was "one who lags, a shirker, loiterer." That's precisely how customers perceive this group: they lag behind their competition in their promises and they shirk the industry standards in their performance.

> *Laggards are low on promise*
> *and low on performance.*

While Rogers first described laggards over fifty years ago as bound by tradition and conservative in approach, today's laggard is more difficult to pigeonhole. Yet we could analyze some famed national companies and categorize them as fitting into this segment.

Sears is a good example of a laggard. They offer discounts on about everything. Low prices and wide selection seems to be their promise. Yet we know that there are other retailers—Walmart comes to mind—stocking a range of anything from lawn mowers to leisure wear at lower prices. One problem is that Sears is trying to compete from higher priced real estate. When I visited a Sears store recently, I had trouble getting anyone to help me, and when I finally did get help, they weren't knowledgeable about the product.

Sears' promise is dated and old, and their performance is poor.

Frauds (High Promise, Low Performance)

There's no kind way to put this.

If you intentionally promise what you cannot deliver, you're a fraud. Or as they say in Texas, "You're all hat and no cattle."

It has been easy to find stories in the news about companies that were fraudulent—leaders and organizations who promised customers and investors the stars but delivered nothing. I wrote specifically about one that had deceived me in a previous book.

You may be familiar with the story of Elizabeth Holmes. She was CEO of a biotech startup called Theranos that has been charged with fraud by the Securities and Exchange Commission. Holmes "once promised to revolutionize the multibillion-dollar blood testing industry with innovative finger-prick tests she said would deliver results quickly, painlessly, and cheaply."[28]

The company could verify none of those results. Their web of deceit was vast and their false promises were stunning. Holmes claimed, "The US Department of Defense was using Theranos's products on the battlefield in Afghanistan and on medevac helicopters, bringing in more than $100 million in revenue in 2014." The SEC said otherwise. Apparently Theranos' technology was never deployed by the DoD, and it generated only a little more than $100,000 in revenue in 2014. Holmes "promoted a key blood-testing product using unfounded claims." [29]

While high-profiles stories like this leave us aghast, you and I encounter smaller but similar promise-performance fraud on a regular basis:

- The waiter who promises the specials are "fantastic"—not because they are but because he's been told to push them.
- The salesperson who assures you that customers "love our product"— not because they really do but to make the sale.
- The business owner who tells the creative professional how much he "values her work"—then rips off her ideas so he doesn't have to pay for her concepts.

There was a service provider I did business with regularly because I liked the charismatic owner a lot. I considered the owner to be a personal friend and a good guy. When we were having difficulty with their product, though, his response was always, "Just wait until you see our next version—it will knock you out!" I'm not proud to admit how long I continued to do business with them, but he finally crossed the line. Make no mistake, there is always a line in the sand for every customer.

Because of the shortsighted approach of the frauds, they seldom recognize that those customers who finally see through their con game will not only stop doing business with them—some will make it their mission to do what it takes to help drive other customers away.

- If you are dealing with a fraudulent business, stop immediately. It will only get worse.
- If you read this and feel a little pang of guilt for some fraudulent claim you made, stop immediately. Make a list of the promises you've made to your customers and employees. Attempt to repair the damage of your falsehoods before you make any additional promises.

ICONIC

Disruptors (High Promise, High Performance)

Disruptors begin at a point of pain and dissatisfaction with the options currently available and work tirelessly to make high promises and overdeliver.

The genesis of all disruption is dissatisfaction.

No one truly liked standing on a street corner in the rain, waving frantically at passing yellow vehicles, desperately hoping that one would decide to favor you with a pickup. Entering the cab, you might be met by a surly driver you could barely understand and with an odor you could barely endure. You wondered throughout your experience if he was taking the most direct path to your destination or taking advantage of you. By the time you exited, you may have been happy to simply depart with your luggage and your health.

Uber and Lyft changed all of that. From your smartphone, you merely indicate where you want to be driven. Almost instantly, you receive information about your ride—complete with a picture of the driver, the type of car she is driving, and her license plate number. You can track the ride on your device—both to view the arrival of your car and to ensure you're taking the right route during your trip—and it's totally cashless. The ride is instantly billed to your credit card, and you tip the driver on the app.

Uber and Lyft made their promises big—they were highly innovative and disruptive. Yet it goes beyond that. They *performed* on their promises. It just works. That is what has enabled Uber and Lyft to become disruptors and iconic companies.

Certainly, there have been challenges that Uber has faced as an organization—many because of the boorish behavior of founder and former CEO, Travis Kalanick.

Kalanick's conduct reportedly included rude comments to employees, leadership that was certainly sophomoric for a CEO and perhaps misogynistic, and a displayed disregard for the rules ranging from violation of app guidelines and restrictions by Apple to accusations by Google of stealing trade secrets. [30]

Yet most of us kept on using the Uber app. The reason is promise/performance. Their big promise was still compelling, and the performance we personally received as a customer was delivered in a manner that was congruent. While the CEO was saying and doing reprehensible things, the organization was doing what they said they would do for customers—at the Disruptor level.

This is not to suggest that I believe we should ignore reprehensible behavior from corporate executives. We *shouldn't*. The reason to mention this situation is that simple observation confirms the average customer was able to put aside the lack of congruency from one executive so as not punish many hardworking drivers for a single individual's behavior—an issue over which the drivers had no control. The Uber Board of Directors did what was required to get bad behavior out of the corporate suite, just as we appreciated the promise/performance execution of the larger team of about 12,000 employees and 160,000 independent contractor drivers.

Disruptors understand that the customer's perception of their promise is high—in part because it goes against the bland, standard approach that consumers have grown to find dissatisfactory. Therefore, when an organization can deliver on a new kind of promise, customers naturally assume that your high benchmark of performance will make a powerful impact on the marketplace.

When Professor Jeff Wilson said he wanted to change housing, he proved that he meant it. Wilson wanted to learn more about the limits of how much space we need as human beings. So he decided to put himself to the test.

Wilson made a thirty-three-square-foot dumpster his home for a year. "While the experiment was extreme, the experience he gained by living small and simple made a big impression," his company's website states. "At the end of the year, he left the dumpster with the concept for a new category of housing — a beautiful, small footprint home designed as a solution for the growing housing crisis."[31]

Wilson formed Kasita in 2015, which now manufacturers 374-square-foot micro-homes that can be anything from a guesthouse, cabin in the country, unit for a rental home on your existing property, or just about anything else you could imagine. Features on these micro-homes can be upgraded to include exclusive Bosch appliances, Casper mattresses, and Sonos sound throughout.

The units are even stackable—meaning they could become apartment communities, condo groups, or home/office units.

Wilson and his team in Austin, Texas, have made an interesting and aggressive promise. The marketplace will determine if their performance throughout the range of services they need to provide—including quality manufacturing, safe delivery, financing, assistance with zoning regulations, and more—will move Kasita to the level of an iconic disruptor. (The future looks good for them. *Inc.* named Kasita as one of the 25 Most Disruptive Companies of the Year in 2017.)[32]

Why does the type of disruption we've talked about here—from Uber to Kasita—seem to happen through start-ups instead of established companies?

It's partly because of the phenomenon Dr. Clayton Christenson describes in his 2013 book *The Innovator's Dilemma*. Companies tend to seek to improve existing products incrementally to protect their franchise. Start-ups aren't burdened with economic and emotional loyalty to past products or way of doing things. They are free to raise the standard.

Another facet is that start-ups are nimbler. After a while, the high promises that have been made by disruptors lose their luster and are no longer valued to such a significant degree by customers. We become accustomed to the new higher standard.

For example, I landed at Chicago's O'Hare with no ride planned. That would not have been the case a relatively short time ago. Not wanting to deal with long cab lines—particularly in bad weather—whenever I had business in Chicago, I always made a reservation for a ride to downtown well before my arrival. This time, while walking through the airport and dragging my carry-on, I whipped out my iPhone and connected with Uber. I instantly ordered my ride. What was amazing in the not too distant past is now standard operating procedure.

What does this mean for a disruptor?

For disruptors to become iconic companies, they will have to find a way to continue to advance and enhance both their promises and their performance—or they will fall into another category.

After a long road trip, the last thing I want to do when I finally return home is to go out to a restaurant. However, there's no way that my wife wants to cook another meal for herself after being home alone for several days. What do we do? Well, sometimes—if we're both feeling brave—I do the cooking. However, more often than not, I don't want to cook because I'm tired from my travel. In those cases, we use Uber Eats. She doesn't have to cook, and I don't have to leave the house.

The disruptor Uber raised the bar with its instant car service and then expanded their promise from "taking you where you want to go" into "*and* we can bring your favorite food to your door, so you don't have to go anywhere." By enhancing and expanding their promise—and performing at a high level by executing on those promises—they continue to disrupt.

Uber has also recently announced Uber Health. Uber recognizes that transportation is one of the challenges for some patients in receiving proper care. Caregivers, patients, and staff may find easier access to their doctors and clinics by utilizing the Uber system of drivers and technology. They've even made it possible to access Uber Health without a smartphone to be of greater service to senior citizens, who may not possess the latest in technology. It's another way that Uber continues to expand both the promise and performance of the company.[33]

I realize that it's possible that you—and probably others that you know—have had an inferior personal experience with Uber, Amazon, or any of the companies that I'm writing about. The important point is that while no organization is perfect, Uber usually works as it promises and Amazon usually delivers to your door on time. Performance—like beauty—is in the eye of the beholder.

Most of us behold that they're doing it right, but I recognize that "your mileage may vary" in your personal experience.

What happens when you can't keep up?

When *Sports Illustrated* was founded, a weekly magazine devoted exclusively to sports was highly disruptive in the publishing marketplace. The problem was that *SI* believed their promise was to "publish a magazine on sports." What the customer wanted was "sports information." Enter ESPN. The cable sports network filled the gap and raised the bar. *Sports Illustrated* was woefully unprepared to expand and enhance their promise. Despite forays into television with CNN and other very modest efforts at innovation, they were late to the game. Sadly, *SI* is swiftly falling into irrelevancy. Concurrently, other new entries like Barstool Sports are growing a raving fan base—ironically consisting of the very engaged sports enthusiasts who would make up the natural market that *Sports Illustrated* previously attracted.

In the case of *SI*, the disruptor eventually became a laggard. *How do you keep this from happening to* you?

> *It's not enough to evaluate if your promise is* relevant *in today's marketplace. Rather, evaluate whether your promise is* compelling *in today's marketplace.*

In chapter 8, we'll look at the steps that organizations and leaders can take to regain iconic status if they discover their position has slipped in the market.

MANIPULATORS (LOW PROMISE, HIGH PERFORMANCE)

You read that correctly. If you consistently underpromise and overdeliver, you aren't *serving* today's customer—you're attempting to *manipulate* them.

Don't misunderstand me—I am *not* suggesting that you stop making strides to create Ultimate Customer Experiences by doing the extra steps that create high levels of customer engagement.

If you're a service department at an auto dealership, this does not mean you stop vacuuming the floorboards or putting a rose on the seat. If you're a B2B company, it doesn't mean that you halt the practice of taking your best client to a sporting event or nice dinner. Whatever you're doing to ensure an experience that thrills and amazes your customers or clients, *keep it up!*

The point here is that I've learned that many organizations skew their promises so the company is set up to exceed their performance for the customer.

Many organizations skew their promises so the company is set up to exceed their performance for the customer.

It's an insincere attempt to become a hero.

Let's say Ms. Smith takes her car to the auto dealership for an oil change. She's told that her car will be ready at 5:00 p.m. Later that afternoon, the service advisor calls his customer. "Ms. Smith, great news! It's only 3:00 p.m. and your car is ready. Because you're such a valued customer, we wanted to exceed your expectations here at Jones Auto!"

The problem is that Ms. Smith has made plans to pick up her kids at the sitter at six, because she was told her car would be ready at five. The extra two-hour window means nothing to her in terms of convenience. If she would have known that her car could have been completed by three, she would have made arrangements at work and skipped paying for a couple of extra hours for her kids to be with the sitter. This "overdeliver" from the dealership has cost her both time and money.

Ms. Smith also notices that the dealership seems to do this every time she takes her car in for service. It seems that getting the car done ahead of time is just a gimmick that she's getting tired of. In other words, the precise activity that the dealership presumes is positive is, in fact, reducing the level of trust that the customer has in them.

Hmm, she might be thinking. *If they're that phony when it comes to service, could they also be playing games with me when I buy my car there?*

A hotel chain where I often stay never has an upgrade available when I make a reservation online. They can almost never let me check in early and cannot promise they will ever allow me to check out late . . . until I arrive onsite. Once I get there, they always are able to do all the above. Don't get me wrong—I appreciate being able to get into my room early and have access to the room a little bit after posted checkout time to change after a speech into something more casual for the trip home. It's just that I know they can easily let me check in a little early and check out a little late. It's not really "overdelivery," but they want me to *feel* like it is. They're trying to manipulate me.

"Oh, no, sir. We could not possibly accept reservations at this late juncture for a table on a Saturday night!" you are told. "We are a very popular restaurant. You are free, however, to stop by and see if there is a cancellation or if we could squeeze you in."

The first couple of times you show up and attempt to dine there, the restaurant discovers to great astonishment that they can "squeeze you in." Naturally, you have a positive feeling about the establishment. However, when they to do it every time and you repeatedly notice empty tables after being informed they have no availability, you realize it's just a ploy.

I'll say it again: it's important to deliver the Ultimate Customer Experience, but don't repeatedly underpromise and overdeliver. Your efforts become undervalued by the customers you want to impress and in doing so you take your focus off what really matters: *doing what you said you would do when you said you would do it.*

In a study conducted by behavior scientists at University of California San Diego, they found that

- keeping a promise increases its *perceived value*;
- exceeding a promise is less important than keeping one; and
- keeping a promise has a more positive outcome than exceeding one.[34]

When your performance is congruent with your promise, it delivers the outcomes you desire. When you exceed the promise with your performance, your efforts are undervalued by the customers you seek to impress.

The study found that people place a high value on people (or companies) who keep their promises—and that there is no added value for exceeding the promise.

It might be hard to keep your promise, but it's definitely worth it.

The results go on to show that "it is wise to invest effort in keeping a promise because breaking it can be costly, but it may be unwise to invest additional effort to exceed one's promises. When companies, friends, or coworkers put forth the effort to keep a promise, their effort is likely to be rewarded. But when they expend extra effort in order to exceed those promises, their effort appears likely to be overlooked."[35]

If we are overdelivering when it comes to enhancing the service experience, customers tend to appreciate it as long as it does not become the standard operating procedure. If it does, customers recognize the game and share their experiences with one another on social media.

The fundamental question is: are you promising and performing or manipulating?

Pros and Cons of Each Group

Obviously, each group can have positives—and, they all have negatives as well.

Group	Pros	Cons
Laggards	deliver what they promise	fail to promise or deliver anything significant

Group	Pros	Cons
Frauds	excite us with the promise	deceive us regarding ability to deliver
Disruptors	change the game with promises	must continue to advance the promise and performance
Manipulators	engage us with higher performance than promised	eventually creates distrust because of consistent discrepancies

If each of these groups have their faults, where do iconic companies fall on the scale? What do they do to maintain their status?

Most iconic companies would fall in a sweet spot somewhere in the bottom left quarter of the disruptor quadrant. Their promises are slightly more aggressive and advanced from the pack. And they perform at a higher level than others, not only in their specific industry but in the entire marketplace.

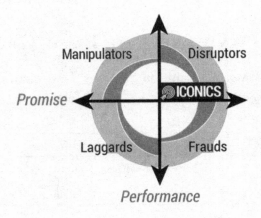

The Sweet Spot

As with any matrix, there are variations within any specific group. For example, some manipulators may wildly overdeliver and underpromise more than others. Nonetheless, both would fit into the category.

Iconic companies typically are going to be found in the disruptor quadrant. However, in most cases, they are going to be neither radically promising nor outrageously delivering. They constantly are looking to improve and expand upon their promises.

An example would be Uber's efforts to add restaurant delivery and helping you make it to health care appointments. And they don't skimp on performance either, like Amazon making sure my friend received his package on race day in Indiana. This runs true with the Scottsdale Princess too. After establishing their resort as *the* place for Christmas, they are now striving to become the go-to destination for other holidays.

Iconic companies find a way to accelerate their promises while improving their performance to a public that has already become predisposed to expect their excellence.

WHAT DO *YOU* DO NEXT?

Briefly, here are the five steps you need to be taking to move your organization—and yourself—closer towards iconic status:

1. Examine your promises
2. Evaluate your performance
3. Create strategies and tactics for alignment
4. Advance your promises
5. Accelerate your performance

1) EXAMINE YOUR PROMISES

Take a close look at what you are promising your customers and employees. As we discussed earlier in this chapter, examine what is the most prevalent customer perception regarding those promises. Is the promise you are making compelling to customers and/or employees? Is the promise one that you will be able to fulfill?

You should be coordinating throughout the organization—or your department or team—to ensure that everyone is on board and committed to your promise.

2) EVALUATE YOUR PERFORMANCE

Assess your performance based on your customers' perception of your promise. Is it possible that customers think you are good at your performance—just not in a manner that is congruent with your promise?

A fast food franchise may measure success based on the speed at which the customer proceeds through the drive-thru line and reward the performance accordingly. Customers, however, believe the promise includes receiving the right order in the bag. If Apple evaluates itself based on the technological quality of its devices, they will naturally believe that they are delivering extraordinarily well for me. The problem is, as I mentioned earlier, I thought the promise was "ease of use."

The old saw is that "you can only manage what you can measure." The challenge is that you need to be measuring the right elements to create customer loyalty and engagement.

Don't just evaluate how your team is performing; evaluate how they are performing based on the customer's perception of your promise.

3) Create strategies and tactics that align

In a previous book, I wrote about organizations that have had a less-than-successful quarter or year and decide the problem is that they aren't as productive as they should be. With that in mind, they double down: salespeople are required to make more contacts with clients, call centers must handle more in-bound conversations, and marketing is pressured to come up with more creative advertisements.

For many, the problem is that they are
working harder on the wrong plan.

Instead of pushing more intensely to achieve what has already left your customers and prospects indifferent, why not use this as the time to ensure your strategies and tactics are in alignment?

Every customer can probably tell you a story about seeing an advertisement about "great customer service" but are placed on "hold" for twenty minutes every time they call for assistance. Don't permit your team or company to be perceived as a fraud! Make sure your performance matches your promises before you do anything else.

4) ADVANCE YOUR PROMISES

Now that you've taken the first three steps, you can examine how to advance your promises. Just as Uber did with health care and food delivery, just as the Fairmont Scottsdale Princess is doing with other holidays, you can do with your team or organization.

It's not about being revolutionary or chaotic at this juncture. It's about taking a step to set yourself apart.

For example: in my company, my team schedules a conference call with every new client. This helps me learn more about their organization and ascertain their goals for my presentation so I can customize my talk to their specific event. As you might imagine, this is standard procedure for every speaker. We decided to see how we could advance our promises. We started promising that my programs would be not only highly customized—we would also offer something to every audience member before and after each event.

Our clients loved this. It meant their investment in a keynote speaker would have greater impact than just the hour I was typically on stage. They knew I wasn't just delivering a "canned" speech and the impact of the meeting would extend beyond just the conference.

Advancing our promise gained attention in the marketplace, served as a terrific sales tool, and demonstrated our understanding of the challenges our clients were facing.

5) Accelerate your performance

It's not enough to advance your promises. You must accelerate your performance to match. Remember, you must do what you said you will do.

This can be done by departments, teams, leaders, and organizations—no matter their size or industry.

So what did we do to deliver on our advanced promise? We now provide our clients with a survey for everyone to complete before the event. This short (usually four-question) survey not only helps me learn what my audience is concerned about before the speech, it also gives me the ability to say to them at the beginning of my talk, "Here's what *you* indicated were important issues, and I constructed this program to what *you* identified as critical." Following each presentation, I shoot a short video recapping my talk. Our client then sends that video to each audience member.

The results have been fantastic: more repeat and referral business, deeper engagement with clients, the privilege of being of greater assistance to our customers, and more profitability for our company.

It's not remaking the business; it's simply finding and delivering advanced promises and accelerated performance for your customers in ways that make a difference for them. You can do the same!

WHAT'S NEXT?

Getting your promise and performance aligned is critical—and one step where you need to spend resources that are more important than money. Your investment of *time* and *commitment* is essential. However, if you execute on this step, you may create iconic results!

Now that I have my promise and performance congruent, you might be thinking, *I'm ready to start pushing my products and services, right?*

Wrong. And that leads us to the next step.

Questions for Chapter 4

- What is the promise that you are making to your customers? Is this what they perceive it to be?
- How do you believe that your customers view your performance? Is it congruent with your promise?
- What group do you believe you fit into? In which group would you choose to be placed?

  o Laggard?
  o Fraud?
  o Disruptor?
  o Manipulator?

- How can you accelerate your promise?
- What does it take to advance your performance?
- What can we do starting today to move closer to iconic status?

CHAPTER FIVE

#3 STOP SELLING

Let me start by freely admitting that of course you cannot cease selling and survive, much less become an iconic organization or leader.

The problem is that too many people emphasize the old-school, hard-sell approach to selling. They fail to recognize that times have changed dramatically. Arm-twisting, "always be closing," and "getting the prospect to surrender" tactics will cost you and your company more sales than you gain through your aggression.

Stop it.

SELLING IS NOT ABOUT SELLING

My friend, Ian Altman, has a great idea: sell like an expert, not like a salesperson. "Effective sales," according to Altman, "is not about persuasion or coercion, it's about getting to the truth as quickly as possible."[36]

Notice how his philosophy tracks so well with the "attraction" aspect we discussed in chapter 1? We are attracted to take the advice of experts; we are repelled at being pushed into a purchase.

Leigh Ashton is a top sales consultant and speaker who works for Sasudi, a sales training organization. She wrote, "Selling is *not about selling*. It means simply the art of selling has moved on from the 'always be closing,' 'sell anything to anyone and to hell with the consequences' era."[37]

> *Iconic organizations and professionals*
> *have grown beyond the need to hawk*
> *their products and services.*

Iconic organizations and professionals have grown beyond the need to hawk their products and services. In fact, many would be embarrassed if customers perceived that was their customary practice. Again, this does *not* mean that they don't make an effort to sell their products or services. It's that they realize making the sale isn't the end game. Building a relationship is.

Porsches, for example, are purchased through dealerships and from the sales professionals who work there. Successfully concluding transactions and turning prospects into customers in no way diminishes Porsche's iconic status. In fact, they'd be bankrupt without it. However, the Porsche salesperson is taught to be committed to providing the best service he or she can because the reputation of the almost ninety-year-old automaker depends upon it.

When executed properly, I truly believe that there is no professional more admirable and beneficial to a customer than a salesperson. If the salesperson is assisting the customer correctly and the product or service delivers as promised, then he or she is improving the customer's life in some manner and stands a good chance of establishing a long-term relationship.

To stop selling is to understand growth
comes from building the relationship
and enhancing the experience—not
overwhelming the customer with aggressive
prospecting or closing techniques.

THE IMPORTANCE OF THE EXPERIENCE

More times than I care to remember, I've had sales professionals or managers challenge me on this. They suggest the old saw that service is the first step of the next sale—as if the *experience* did not contribute to making the initial sale possible. That's asinine!

While you may have seen these (or similar) statistics quoted previously, now is a good time to review the importance of the customer experience in generating sales for your organization:

- According to the [customer experience research firm] Temkin Group, 86 percent of those who received an excellent customer experience were likely to repurchase from that company, compared to only 13 percent of those who had a very poor customer experience (*more than 6 times more likely*).
- The Temkin Group also found that those who received excellent customer experiences were *11 times more likely to recommend the company* than those who had a very poor customer experience (77 percent vs. 7 percent, respectively).
- Forrester Research found that customer experience leaders grow revenue faster than laggards, with leaders seeing a *17 percent compound average revenue growth rate*, compared to only 3 percent for their customer experience laggard counterparts.
- When it comes to down competing on price or the experience, Gartner found that 64 percent of people found customer experience to be *more important than price* when it comes to purchasing something.[38]

The critical aspect is that iconic businesses
know that enhancing the experience
increases sales.

Can you imagine Apple having a "get out there and crush it" sales campaign? Imagine a semicrazed, half-balding salesman in front of boxes upon boxes of Macintosh computers, shouting, "We've stacked them deep and we're selling them cheap!"? Not in this lifetime, I'll wager.

Yet many companies would rather take that approach than do what it takes to create iconic status for their organization. Their leaders prefer hammering their sales force to push harder to sell than to encourage their teams to build a greater experience. Don't think that's the case? Then ask yourself these two questions:

1. When was our last sales rally or meeting?
2. When was our last customer experience meeting?

I know a plethora of companies with annual sales meetings that have *never* had a customer experience conference. Then they wonder why neither sales nor customer loyalty are growing. "Customers' expectations have fundamentally changed," said Lynn Vojvodich, board member for Ford Motor Company and Priceline Group and former CMO of Salesforce.com. "They want you to know who they are, what they've bought, and what they like. So, if you cold call them and don't have any information about their company and their industry—if you don't know what they've purchased, what they called for service help on—they're going to hang up on you."[39]

Why, then, don't all companies focus on the experience?

> *It's easier to berate sales teams to work harder and to cut your prices than it is to stop selling and build iconic experiences through customer relationships.*

Many organizations—and their leaders—typically prefer to take what they see as the path of least resistance. This is especially true in smaller businesses where an entrepreneurial founder may have vast experience in his respective industry—but little training in creating the Ultimate Customer Experience.

THE "EASY" PATH IS COSTLY

This ridiculous practice is seen every day on social media—and, perhaps, especially on LinkedIn. Consider this example from a spam message I recently received—along with my comments.

Message	Comments
Hi Scott,	1) I find a comma in the salutation on the initial message you send me to be a bit informal and perhaps unprofessional. Not a good start.
This is Anne of XYX Central. I was wondering if you're available for a chat.	2) You've told me nothing about why I would be interested. Why would you ask me to invest my time as the very first point in your message?
I'm reaching out to see if your company would be interested in finding new clients.	3) Ugh! What a trite, manipulative line. "I'm wondering if you'd like to improve your profitability?" is another. Do you really believe your prospect is *that* stupid? If you do, you're too dumb to be selling to them.
Our services can reach out to your target audience not only by calling but also email and LinkedIn messaging.	4) So you're offering to spam my prospects the way you are spamming me? Anne, you have given me zero indication that you have any idea what I do. So how do you know anything about my "target audience" or what I need to do to "reach out" to them? And nothing you have told me assures me you have the experience and depth to be able to do so.
Allow us to do the complex and tedious legwork of sales and marketing for you so you can focus on what you do best—improving your products and services and closing deals.	5) Anne, you have no idea what my products and services are. How can you possibly know that improving them or closing the sale is what I do best?)

Message	Comments
It will only take a brief phone call with us to discuss the details of this opportunity. Is your calendar open on Tuesday at 1:30 PM for a quick call? Please let me know what's the best number to reach you.	6) Why should I block my calendar to educate you? This is your opportunity for you to sell me—it's not an "opportunity" for me at this point. I know nothing about you

*This is beyond cold calling—
it's more like frigid pleading.*

Observe the aspects of her message that are so off-putting to a prospect. For example, in point 6 above, notice how she wants to set up a call with me to pick my brain and prequalify my prospective clients. She should have done that homework before spamming me! In other words, it appears she knows just one aspect about me: I have an account on LinkedIn. There's nothing in her message that indicates she knows anything about my potential problems or needs. She wants me to commit to investing my time to help her do what she should have done before initial contact. This is incredibly distasteful to a prospect. Don't ever do it.

Remember the earlier line quoted from Lynn Vojvodich? "If you cold call them and don't have any information about their company and their industry, they're going to hang up on you."[40]

Which is what I did to Anne. I asked to be removed from her mailing list. However, it's worse for Anne's company than that. I've *blocked* her. I don't have time for spam. It means that because of this effort on her part to "sell" me, she doesn't get a second opportunity to try to serve me.

While we have never met personally, I am connected through social media and mutual friends to a *New York Times* bestselling author who also owns a company that helps aspiring authors get published. He was contacted on LinkedIn by a publishing company that asked him, "Have you ever considered publishing a book?"

The author posted the ridiculous message and called out the spammer online. He received a plethora of venomous responses telling him, in essence, "Sales is a numbers game" or "If you don't like it, too bad. This is the future." My take is that if you send a stupid spam message to someone, you should be prepared for any consequences. And the consequence of the easy path can be a lost relationship—or even worse, a bad reputation.

THE PROBLEM WITH THE NUMBERS GAME

Is there is a relationship between number of outbound calls or emails and sales?

When you're sending out thousands of messages, you get the metric on how many opens, clicks, and responses that your missives have received. You may naturally assume that if you send out thousands more, you'll hit on more companies or people who need what you're selling.

Unfortunately, you're only seeing one side of the equation.

Imagine for a moment that you have created the first antiviral drug that cures the flu. You inject people who have come down with the flu. To your amazement and gratification, for every one thousand people to whom you give the shot, four hundred are completely cured of the flu. You're really on to something, aren't you?

Perhaps. However, first you need to know if the drug is causing any unintended side effects. What if four hundred are cured from the flu, but the medication is simultaneously killing five hundred from heart attacks? Would you still administer it?

Professional spammers know the metrics on clicks and responses. What they often *don't* know is how many prospects are so turned off that the seller will never get another chance. Do you really want that many upset prospects?

Sure, it's easy to hit send and fog your sales pitch to tens of thousands and then see who clicks. Unfortunately, it is just as easy to ignore the collateral damage you're causing because it's usually less obvious and often not immediately painful.

In situations like this, prospects go so far as to become a "reverse referral." These are people who go out of their way—in person and on social media—to strongly recommend that people *not* do business with you. How many sales will the path of least resistance cost you over the long haul?

The first time I posted my disapproval of these types of inane messages on LinkedIn, I received a response berating me for my attitude. "If you're so smart," the responder's message implied, "how would you do it?" Well, the message just so happened to be from a sales professional in a city where I had lived years ago. He worked at a car dealership where I had purchased multiple automobiles when I lived there. It turns out I also knew a relative of his. The salesman had no idea he just alienated a person who had spent tens of thousands of dollars with his employer—and he was probably going to hear about it from his family too! (You can almost hear the song, "It's a Small World After All" playing in the background, can't you?)

All it would have taken was just a couple of moments to enter my name into the dealership database just to be certain he wasn't about to offend a customer. It seems as though when it comes to hitting the send button on posts and tweets, we have a new mantra: "Fire...Ready...Aim." Some want to immediately put in their two cents to get their point across—and perhaps even troll the person whose views are in opposition—without considering the bigger picture of how this makes one appear.

It's not just those idiots with "keyboard courage" who cowardly hide behind anonymous avatars and rip everything to shreds. It's also marketers who spam without thinking of the consequences—and then are somehow offended when someone calls them out over their errors. Others can make these mistakes—don't be that guy or gal . . . or organization.

You're aiming for iconic.

How Do You Stop Selling?

Iconic organizations take a more difficult path.

For example, I also receive a lot of sales messages from Amazon. Yet each one says something like, "Here are some recommendations based on your past purchases." Or "If you liked that . . . you'll love this!" The subtle message is, "We *know* you—that's why we are advocating these options."

As my great friends Scott and Alison Stratten—authors of several books, including *UnSelling: The New Customer Experience*—say, "Stop selling; start engaging." It cannot be expressed better than that!

When we engage, we attract. When we attract, as mentioned previously, the results are relationships with high lifetime value in terms of both repeat and referral business. Yet in my experience many people would rather rush into getting business without investing the time and effort required to build the relationship. It's like asking someone to marry you on the first date! There must be engagement and relationship-building first. Pushing hard and fast too early can propel your prospect away. It's akin to saying "Trust me" in the first moments in the initial conversation with someone. If you feel compelled to beg for their trust so quickly, you've raised the issue that maybe there's a reason that they shouldn't.

So how do you slow down and build a relationship instead? Here are three steps to stop selling and approach prospects the way iconic leaders and companies do:

1. Appeal to their aspirations—then invite them to savor the experience
2. Provide value before an ask
3. Stop thinking like a professional

APPEAL TO THEIR ASPIRATIONS—THEN INVITE THEM TO SAVOR THE EXPERIENCE

The Fairmont Scottsdale Princess almost never discusses specific room rates in their marketing materials. Instead, they appeal to what you would like to do for a fun break at a wonderful resort—or a productive meeting at a prominent conference center—and then invite you to partake in that experience. They present pictures of their Trailblazer's Kids Club and show young people— maybe children just like yours—having a great time. They share shots of gorgeous weddings held on the property—maybe just like the one you and your fiancé desire.

How does that differ from a sales pitch?

First, unlike the spam email, it requires zero commitment from me.

Second, in almost a subliminal manner, it appeals to something I may desire and *attracts* me, rather than tries to push me into staying there. Their visuals assure me they will successfully accomplish my goals for my stay, that if I go there with my meeting or my family, I'm going to savor a superior experience.

How can you appeal to your prospects' wants, needs, desires, and aspirations—and invite them to partake in your experience?

Consider the Volkswagen Group Australia and the amazing way it drives (pardon the pun) this type of customer experience—in an industry primarily known for anything but. The Volkswagen dealers in Australia promise to provide "Premium for the People." Who doesn't want a premium level of automobile service, and dealership experience? And "for the people" suggests that it's accessible to everyone, so VW invites you to join them and experience what they have to offer.

If you run a transmission repair shop, don't talk about fixing the car. Appeal to the aspiration of safe transportation and a car that doesn't break down on the side of the road in a bad part of town. If you own a dry cleaner, don't get caught up in a race to the bottom on the price of laundering a shirt. Appeal to the aspiration of looking great at work, school, or a party. In every case, clearly demonstrate how you will provide a superior experience that the customer will want to encounter for herself.

Appeal to the aspirations of your customers and prospects. Then invite them to savor the experience that they desire through your product or service.

PROVIDE VALUE *BEFORE* AN ASK

Legendary motivational speaker and broadcaster Earl Nightingale, known as the dean of personal development, used to say many people sell like someone sitting before a woodstove. "If you give me some heat," they say, "then I'll put in some wood."

That's the case with many marketers. It's like they are saying to their cars, "If you will drive me to where I want to go, then I'll fill you up with gasoline." How many sales pitches do you receive that ask you to do something before the organization or sales professional will make a commitment?

"Is your calendar open on Tuesday at 1:30 p.m. for a quick call? Please let me know what's the best number to reach you." That's what was requested in the LinkedIn sales pitch from someone I've never been contacted by before. Why should I invest my time in something that may have zero return?

The prospect who talks to you has made an investment whether she buys or not. She has invested something more precious and valuable than money—her time and attention. Yet that investment seems so lightly valued by so many who just keep on selling (or attempting to sell, anyway.)

Iconic companies get the order right.
They provide value first and then ask
for your time.

While author, speaker, and internet personality Gary Vaynerchuk may be perceived as the aggressive, pushy type when you watch his style on social media, there's no doubt he has it exactly right when it comes to the "value first, ask next" philosophy.

"My entire business philosophy pretty much revolves around the 'jab jab jab right hook' method," Vaynerchuk writes. "Jabs are the value you provide your customers with: the content you put out, the good things you do to convey your appreciation. And the right hook is the ask: it's when you go in for the sale, ask for a subscribe, ask for a donation. You've got to throw several jabs before you throw your hook. [And], just because you jab and jab and jab doesn't mean you automatically get to land the right hook. It just allows you to have the audacity to ask. You have to earn the right to ask people for a sale. In fact, you have to earn the right to ask people for anything. That's just life."[41]

Vaynerchuk cites iconic contemporary performer Taylor Swift as an example of someone who provided value to fans first. Among the many things Swift has done for fans, she

- got tickets for a fan who missed her flight tickets to another sold-out show,
- made a playlist for a fan who was sad over a breakup,
- donated to a family's Kickstarter campaign after a horrific car accident, and
- tracked down a fan who waited in the cold for 20 hours for tickets and took a selfie with her.[42]

Scott Swift, Taylor's father, was in the audience for one of my speeches years ago prior to his daughter's becoming a pop icon. He related to me many instances where Taylor had reached out to her then small group of fans before she achieved global recognition. I've thought of our conversation often in the years that have followed. Even as a teenager, Taylor Swift intuitively knew that if you want more fans, start by treating the ones you already have amazingly well. By offering all those jabs, as Gary Vaynerchuk calls them, because she first provided such terrific value and experiences for her fans, guess what they did when she later gave them a right hook, or asked them to buy her next release of new music?

What is the specific value that should you provide? Obviously that depends on your product or service. This method works, however, regardless of what business you are in.

The Ultimate Business Summit is a program for entrepreneurs that two of my friends—bestselling authors and Hall of Fame professional speakers Larry Winget and Randy Pennington—and I host annually in Las Vegas. We help small businesses create this values-based, results-oriented, distinctive approach. We have landscapers in our seminars who are now doing videos on YouTube on how you should plant your spring flowers, chimney sweeps posting blogs about fire dangers in your home, and specialty food companies doing podcasts on simple changes in diet that can help you feel better. In every case, both sales and profitability are growing for these small businesses because of the value they are providing to prospective customers before they ask them for anything.

You do not have to be an international behemoth like Amazon—or a company with a gorgeous setting like the Fairmont Scottsdale Princess—to make this work. All you have to do is plan, create, and deliver something of value before you invite prospects to do business with you.

STOP THINKING LIKE A PROFESSIONAL

Every business wants to sell and grow more than the competition; few actually do. Every sales professional desires to become highly successful; only a fraction really do.

What's the problem? What is stopping us from coming up with the innovative approaches required to sell more and grow our market share over the competition?

Interestingly, in 2012 some neuroscientists at the National Institute on Deafness and Other Communication Disorders in Bethesda, Maryland, conducted a study to "identify the neural correlates of spontaneous lyrical improvisation."

Twelve rappers "freestyled"—strung together unrehearsed lyrics, a difficult and highly valued skill in the world of rap music—while connected to an MRI machine. Next, Doctors Siyuan Liu and Allen Braun and their colleagues had the rappers recite memorized lyrics. Finally, the researchers compared the two sets of brain scans.

"We think what we see is a relaxation of 'executive functions' to allow more natural defocused attention and uncensored processes to occur that might be the hallmark of creativity," said Dr. Braun.

The results of the study were in line with the discoveries from previous research that Dr. Braun conducted with Charles Limb, a doctor and musician at Johns Hopkins University that looked at MRIs of jazz musicians.

This isn't about being a rapper or jazz artist. It's about how all of us think innovatively—which, of course, can have significant impact on your approach to business.

Michael Eagle, a study coauthor who raps under the name Open Mike Eagle, agrees: "That's kind of the nature of . . . improvisation. Even as people who do it, we're not 100% sure of where we're getting improvisation from."[43]

In other words, rappers and jazz musicians cannot simultaneously freestyle and analyze their performance. Without "breathing space" between innovation and evaluation, we shut down the flow of our creativity.

The article states that the study suggests there are two phases to creativity:

- Phase One is spontaneous and based upon improvisation to create unique ideas and approaches.
- Phase Two is where we process, revise, and improve our original thoughts.

What does this mean regarding your sales methods and connecting with customers?

The study illuminates the problem that when we want to become more innovative, typically our "executive function" or "sales professional" thinking quickly kicks

in. In other words, we attempt to be creative and evaluate
at the same time.

This frequently results in the "we've never done it
that way before" or "do you know how much it would
take to do that?" syndrome. We don't stretch ourselves to
become spontaneous and "off the cuff." Unfortunately,
we usually attempt to innovate as we simultaneously
appraise and process. This kills the very type of innovation that is required to stand out in today's marketplace.
Don't shut down your opportunity to be innovative in
your approach by overanalyzing new methods.

Perhaps this explains why many companies typically fall back into the old methods of hardcore selling.
That style may have worked thirty years ago when customers didn't have as many alternatives to that aggressive
approach as they do today. However, there's little doubt
that old, hardcore techniques fall woefully short of establishing the relationships that customers crave today.

Strange as it may sound, if you want to follow the
lead of iconic companies and stop selling, maybe you
need to think less like a business professional and, if only
for a little while, think more like a rapper—let it flow.

Michelle Stacy, former president of Keurig—the
famed maker of K-cups and coffee brewers—and a
coaching client of mine, used this innovative strategy
to make a profound impact on the company she led. If
you're a coffee company and you want customers to drink

your product, who would you consider as your primary competition? There's no doubt—the iconic Starbucks.

The typical, traditional "executive thinking" would ask

- How can we sell more and grow our market share in an industry dominated by such an iconic presence?
- What do we need to do to gain a foothold against Starbucks?

Stacy stopped thinking like an executive and instead decided to think first like an innovator. "What if," she asked herself, "we were *collaborators* instead of competitors?"

Consider how revolutionary that approach would be considered in her industry. It's the CEO of Ford asking how they could do more business with GM. It's the CEO of McDonald's asking how they could partner with KFC. It's Steve Jobs asking how he could collaborate with Bill Gates. (Oh, wait! That one really *happened*. Just another example of "rapper think.")

Michelle Stacy decided that instead of fighting the traditional industry battles, she could innovate. She would get Starbucks into Keurig's K-cups. The results were astounding. K-cups and brewer sales grew, making Keurig happy. Starbucks had an additional revenue stream, making them thrilled. The innovative collaboration increased sales for both companies.

In other words, Michelle Stacy sold more when she stopped selling.

It's Not All a Happy Place

It's not easy to stop selling and start focusing on the experience. As my friend Jason Bradshaw, chief customer officer and director at Volkswagen Group Australia, says, "It takes a lot of energy and focus to move from a very product-centered industry to one that matches its product experience with a seller/customer experience as well."

While most would look for a positive approach to this challenge, the next chapter may provide you with a controversial alternative. In fact, I'm positive that you should go negative.

Questions for Chapter 5

- How do you sell your products and services? Would you describe your efforts as primarily pushing—or engaging?
- On a scale of 1 to 10 (10 being the best), how would you rate your customer retention? How could you enhance the experience of doing business with you to the iconic level so you could retain more customers?
- On a scale of 1 to 10 (10 being the best), how would you rate the amount of referral business you are receiving from current customers? How could you enhance the experience and inspire more customers to refer you to their friends and colleagues?
- How do you appeal to the aspirations of your customers and prospects? What could you do to improve?
- What are you currently doing to provide information, insight, and value to the marketplace—even to prospects who are not yet customers? How could you provide more value to your customers—*before asking for a sale?*
- Develop three innovative ideas about your business. They do not have to be practical or something you could start doing today. Explain how these ideas would attract more customers to you (or better employees to work with you).

CHAPTER SIX

#4 GO NEGATIVE

Now is the time in many business books where—after you've navel gazed at your "why" and read all of the wonderous stories about how Disney, Starbucks, Amazon, and Apple make their customers and employees so "happy"—the author suggests that this positive approach is the key to your future success.

Surprisingly, that's not what iconic companies do. Instead, they go negative.

Leaders who are constantly putting on a happy face and organizations always seeking a sunny outlook may be taking the wrong approach. Consider these shocking facts:

- "A study of data from British households found that across two decades, especially optimistic self-employed people earned about 25 percent less than their pessimistic peers."

- "National Cancer Institute researchers found that people who lowballed their risk of heart disease were more likely to show early signs of it."
- "Married couples who were extremely optimistic about their relationship's future were more likely to experience relationship deterioration."
- "Homeowners who underestimated their chances of radon exposure were less likely to buy radon test kits than were those with a more realistic sense of risk—their optimism left them vulnerable."[44]

It seems natural to want to overlook or gloss over our own faults. We frequently work exceedingly hard at developing our strengths, making it difficult to then examine where we are falling short. In fact, managers in many organizations view merely discussing areas in need of improvement as a sign of weakness in the employee.

Ironically, not drilling deeply enough on our weaknesses is a limitation that holds back companies. In the 1960s, consultant Albert Humphrey at the Stanford Research Institute came up with the SWOT analysis. As you probably know, SWOT stands for: Strengths, Weaknesses, Opportunities, Threats. The typical approach of this method is to discuss and dissect where our team, department, or organization stands in each of the four categories.

SCOTT McKAIN

The challenge is that frequently, we don't focus enough on our specific weaknesses.

A friend of mine who manages a sales team wanted to poll her department to determine their strengths, weaknesses, opportunities, and threats. They are in the tech industry, so they constantly face a lot of threats and disruption. Here is an example of the results of their brainstorming:

Strengths	Weaknesses
Well-recognized brand in marketplace	Brand not as innovative as competition
Young team of energetic sales professionals	Sales team lacks depth of experience
Opportunities	**Threats**
Expanding market means more sales	40% of revenue from 8% of clients
Many clients with old equipment to replace	Competition investing more in R&D

We know that most professionals are reluctant to admit shortcomings. However, it is even harder during a SWOT analysis because we are called upon to identify our weaknesses and threats immediately after the excitement of noting our most important strengths.

My friend learned to be careful when using a SWOT. The problem she discovered is that underesti-

143

mating weaknesses can be more dangerous than overestimating assets.

An article by John Humphreys, associate professor of management in the College of Business and Technology at Texas A&M University in the *MIT Sloan Management Review,* agrees:

> "In fact, the notion of discussing weaknesses has become anathema to strategy formulation in many companies. Too many senior executives simply do not want to talk about them. Doing so is often seen as admitting defeat and appearing vulnerable. Organizational leaders must bear some of the responsibility for ignoring weakness. But many who consult in this area also share some of the blame by referring to everything the company lacks as an opportunity. We know managers recoil at the term weakness, so opportunity becomes a generic pit into which a broad continuum of true opportunities and veiled weaknesses are tossed. I've even witnessed a SWOT-analysis session where poor brand image was earnestly listed as an opportunity. Nonsense! Although the possibility for improvement may (or may not) exist, poor brand image clearly puts the company at a disadvantage when compared to competitors. Moreover, falsely labeling true weaknesses as opportunities actually puts the company at greater risk."[45]

This is not to suggest that iconic leaders or companies have what we would commonly call a "negative attitude." They *don't*. Instead, this should emphasize that iconic companies and leaders are not *afraid* of the negative. Rather, they *welcome* it as part of the process of creating, sustaining, or regaining iconic status. They are as intent on discovering customer dissatisfaction as finding out what pleases and satisfies those who do business with them.

WHAT INFURIATES YOUR CUSTOMERS?

Before we proceed, a bit of a confession. It took me a while to write this section because when I speak and write, I've always tried to use nonoffensive language. As the late great Zig Ziglar once told me, "No one will ever come up and say how much they loved all those times you cursed during your presentations. But people will come up after every one of them to tell you how much they appreciated that you kept it clean." I have always taken Zig's advice to heart.

While many have no problem with coarse language—and, I'll admit that I've been known to swear occasionally in personal conversation—others instinctively recoil at it.

When customers get bad service, are treated rudely, or are insulted, there really is only one way to describe their response: they are pissed off.

When you have terrible customer service, you probably don't find yourself saying, "The way you've treated me as a customer is an *affront*" or "I find myself *in a tizzy* over this situation with your company!"

My wife, Tammy, suggested I say, "ticked off," "grinds their gears," or "chaps their cheeks." While I appreciate her suggestions, I have to maintain that none of those phrases quite capture the intensity that a highly offended customer feels. I'm sorry if I offend you with that comment, but this isn't about mere irritation. It's more than friction that the customer experiences in the process of doing business. There's something about that term that connects with our deep-seated outrage and infuriation about having to deal with a problem that usually has no reason for existing.

I guess I'm saying that I hope I won't "chap your cheeks" because I'm using the term "pissed off."

However, I am also strongly advocating that if you don't know what is pissing off your customers—or your employees—you will never achieve iconic status.

Ask yourself what pisses you off when *you're* the customer.

Last night Tammy was at a dinner function, so I went to a local Mexican restaurant to dine alone. The place was packed, so I sat in the bar area. When a server finally approached me, she asked abruptly, "Know what you're having tonight?" I smiled and responded that a menu and water would be a great first step.

My dinner order took an exceedingly long time to arrive—and was a bit cold when it did. It obviously had been sitting in the kitchen for a while with no one to run it out to my seat. The person who placed the plate in front of me—I assumed it was the manager—vanished quickly before I had the chance to say anything. When I addressed the problem with the server, she said, "Well, it's not my fault. I turned the order in right after you told me what you wanted." When I asked to speak with the manager, she told me it would be a while; he was busy. To add insult to injury, the server made no adjustment on my bill. I was expected to pay full price for everything. There was no offer to "make it right."

While still in my seat, I went on Yelp and gave the place a scathing review.

My gears weren't just ground, my cheeks weren't just chapped—I was flat out pissed off.

Although the meal took a long time to arrive and was cold, not caring about it is the main issue. Problem in the kitchen? I may not like it, but I understand. Mistake in placing the order? It's not optimal, but it can be rectified with an apology—and maybe free dessert.

Not giving a damn? Now, you've crossed a line.

Every business has issues that are beyond their control. But, whatever the reason for poor service, *not caring about the customer* is at the heart of what *really* infuriates them.

I am sure that if a management consultant asked the team at that Mexican restaurant in a resort in the Green Valley area in Henderson, Nevada, if they cared about the customer, every employee and manager would respond with an enthusiastic, "Yes! Of course!" Their actions, however, said something different. And it was their response to the poor service that infuriated a customer who will never return and who shared his story with others. (My review had more than a thousand views on Yelp less than twelve hours later.)

> *The terrifying aspect is that there are customers and clients out there who feel the same way about your business and mine.*

Most businesses and leaders want to know who those customers are, so they can make it right and hopefully save the sale. Iconic companies are *obsessed* with learning what they did wrong, so they can change the behavior—or process—that created the unpleasant experience in the first place.

In chapter 4 we talked about how the genesis of disruption is dissatisfaction. Iconic businesses know that if they can eliminate the points of extreme dissatisfaction, they are taking steps that will erode their vulnerability to being disrupted.

How Do You Discover Points of Infuriation?

We all want to make our customers happy. The National Retail Federation released a survey indicating that among 418 executives across 137 companies in the retail industry, customer satisfaction currently is the top priority. Even if you're not in retail, there is no doubt the issue is high on your list too. Unfortunately, many leaders think it's just the behavior of employees that creates customer service issues. They tend to overlook it could be that the underlying culture of their organization isn't geared to creating iconic results. (We'll discuss that in the next chapter.)

Going negative or focusing on your company's weaknesses is not a sign of . . . well, *weakness,* but a sign of good leadership. Iconic companies view this level of introspection as a symbol of strength.

> *Don't be reticent to focus on the negative and ask the questions that lead to the answers we really need to move to the iconic level.*

In 2002, a top management consulting firm, Bain & Company, developed a short consumer survey to test brand loyalty. The survey consists of one brief, simple question: "On a scale of 1 to 10, with 10 being the highest, how likely is it that you would recommend our company/product/service to a friend or colleague?" This has been called the "ultimate question" for any business to ask.[46]

Customers responding with a 9 or 10 are deemed as Promoters. They will remain loyal customers, purchase more, and tell friends and colleagues about your organization. Detractors respond with a score of 0 to 6. They aren't coming back—and they aren't referring you. They even may be actively telling colleagues and friends to stay away (like me and the Mexican restaurant.) If you answer with either a 7 or 8, you are a Passive. Your behavior is determined to fall in the middle between Promoters and Detractors.[47]

The cumulative results to this question became known as the Net Promoter Score (NPS). You learn your NPS by subtracting the percentage of customers who are designated as Detractors from the percentage of customers who are deemed to be Promoters. Passives are naturally included in the total number of respondents, which serves to lower the net score. The NPS has been advocated as "the one number you need to grow" your level of customer engagement and satisfaction—and, therefore, your business.[48]

Scott McKain

Naturally, most organizations allow customers the opportunity to leave additional comments as they answer this short question. (This is commonly called the VOC, or "voice of the customer.") And many will follow up with those customers who respond with lower scores, so the company can "close the loop" and attempt to build a better relationship.

Some leaders and are skeptical of the simplicity of this evaluation approach. Opponents think that a single, basic question leads to overly simplistic evaluations and assumptions. They argue that NPS may not be all that accurate and that there may be a better question. Let's address these two issues.

Is NPS Accurate?

One critic of the Net Promoter Score asks: would you evaluate a student on the basis of just one test score? Or a baseball player on the basis of their batting average only? Or a car based only on its gas mileage?

These are valid and thought-provoking questions, no doubt. Yet, I have no problem with the single-question approach to customer feedback. My experience with thousands of companies over several decades is that if you make a customer survey too complex, you get no feedback. And some feedback is better than no feedback.

An obvious challenge, though, is that the NPS cannot tell you the customer's actual likelihood or influence in recommending or criticizing your business. What if meek customers are saying they'll advocate and extroverted customers are your Detractors? The end result will likely be that compelling opinion leaders will steer more people in their direction than those who gently promote your brand.

Another problem with the NPS question is that it does not tell you *why* your customers made their choice. For example: are customers saying they'll recommend you because they had a superior experience with your *product*—or because your *service* was exceptional? These are completely different aspects of your deliverables.

And what if they really aren't over the moon about a particular product or experience, but they are fans of your brand overall? That is something altogether different.

So if you aren't certain *why* they're recommending you, how do you know what specific aspects to accentuate and what needs to be improved? According to research from Stanford University, Intuit Corporation, and Harris Interactive, leaders

> need to understand whether more recommendations directly drive the growth of their business (in which case they would want to focus their efforts on directly increasing recommendations) or whether measures of likelihood of recommending are tapping into a gen-

eral attitude toward the company (which might require other efforts). In that context, it is also important to understand whether more recommendations are more important than preventing the loss of already attracted customers."[49]

There are numerous detractors that conclude that NPS is not a statistically accurate reflection of either the satisfaction of your customers or their willingness to refer you to others. Here are some key points they make:

- The standard NPS question is unipolar (willingness to recommend) but analysis treats it as bipolar (willing to detract versus willingness to promote). (Ken Roberts, Forethought Research Australia)
- NPS is attitudinal (what you say you will do) rather than behavioral (what you do) (Bird, Ehrenberg, and Barnard)
- "Satisfaction" and "liking" are better predictors of recommendations than "likelihood to recommend." ("Measuring Customer Satisfaction and Loyalty: Improving the 'Net-Promoter' Score" by Daniel Schneider, Matt Berent, Randall Thomas and Jon Krosnick)

My point here is not to be overly critical of NPS. It's to suggest that to achieve the iconic level, you must look at specific aspects of customer satisfaction and dissatisfaction to know how to improve.

> *With NPS, we know if they'd recommend us or not, but not what we are doing to infuriate our customers.*

THERE MAY BE A BETTER QUESTION

In chapter 4, we noted the high level of customer satisfaction scores for the Apple Watch. In addition, I outlined my personal complaints—even though overall, I'm a satisfied Apple customer.

However, as I wrote in my book *What Customers REALLY Want*, when you stop to think about it, satisfaction is a pretty low standard.

Imagine being a guy about to get down on one knee, holding a box behind your back. It contains a ring that cost four months' salary. Setting things up to pop the big question, you nervously ask the person you hope will become your lifelong partner how she feels about the relationship. "Well," she responds unenthusiastically, "I guess you could mark me as satisfied"?

Is that good enough? No! You want your engagement to begin with your fiancé being amazed, thrilled, and overjoyed with the relationship!

Don't be satisfied with satisfied customers. Seek to have amazed, thrilled, and overjoyed followers.

If *satisfaction* is such a miniscule standard in personal relationships, why is it so seemingly acceptable in professional ones? Don't we want loyalty and commitment there, too?

This may be an exaggeration, but I hope it makes the point. Satisfaction isn't really *that* significant, and we don't learn much from it either.

What we really need to do is to improve our "how" by going negative and getting to the core of our weaknesses.

What if you asked every customer something like, "What have we done in the course of our relationship that has pissed you off?"

No doubt it takes courage to ask that. Having that kind of courage, though, is what sets iconic companies apart from just differentiated or even distinctive companies. Iconic companies have the confidence to learn where their errors are because they have the conviction that their team can fix them.

155

You want to drill deeply into the specific points of infuriation.

Obviously you will need to customize what and how you ask your customers for honest feedback, but you should thoroughly explore where the friction is in your relationship with your customers and employees.

Apple would have received *much* more valuable information from me by asking, "What pisses you off about your Apple Watch?" than inquiring, "Would you recommend your Apple Watch to a friend?"

THE BITCH BOOK

Wanting to research this idea of customer feedback more thoroughly, I turned to social media. I asked my followers how they go about finding out what infuriates their customers about doing business with them.

One of the best ideas shared with me was from Jamie Morse, a health, wellness, and life coach who is on the volunteer leadership committee for the Relay for Life event of Queen Creek and San Tan Valley, Arizona. It's a fund-raising event for the American Cancer Society that is donation-driven and volunteer-administered.

Jaimie told me that the money raised at their event provided help to cancer patients in the community. If the event doesn't do well, they are letting down their neighbors who are battling cancer. (As someone who lost his spouse to cancer, I share her passion for this cause.)

The day of the event, Jamie placed a notebook in a central location and asked all the committee members to make notes in the book about areas where they could improve. She said if they heard anyone "bitching" about anything, they were to write it down. Thus, the notebook was dubbed the Bitch Book.

Jamie certainly wasn't afraid to go negative, but she also made it clear she wanted to know the positive, too. She asked people to also let her know if something went over really well. She finished her story with a great question: "The saying 'If it's not broke, don't fix it' is true, but how do we know if something is broken or not unless we ask?"

Customers are flocking to the Internet to voice their frustration. We've all heard of Yelp and Trip Advisor, but one website—PissedConsumer.com—reports over one million reviews of sixty-four-thousand companies from upset customers. The site claims to generate 3.5 million monthly visitors. Many customers—even those of iconic companies—are pissed off and are not reticent to share their opinions.

The question remains: *will you know who they are and have the courage to ask what caused their problem?*

POSITIVE NEGATIVITY

When I tell people they should go negative, often they have a knee-jerk response. They confuse a search for the negative *reactions* we may stimulate in others with having a negative *attitude*, which some researchers call "self-handicapping."

"Self-handicapping is a strategy with the primary aim of protecting self-esteem in the event of failure," according to researchers from the University of Rochester and Saint Mary's University.[50] We see this when leaders or organizations are so negative about potential outcomes they construct obstacles to success. This means that if—or when—failure occurs, it is attributed to the barrier rather than to any weakness of the company or management.

How many times have you heard a leader say, "There's nothing we could have done; it's the economy"? or "You just can't find good people to hire anymore"? Those are forms of self-handicapping. It's another way of saying, "It's not my fault! The economy is bad, and I have idiots working for me." Or, as we saw in the introduction, it can be executives who insist, "We didn't do anything wrong."

However, there is another form of a negative approach that researchers call "defensive pessimism." It sounds counterintuitive, but I consider it a positive approach to negativity.

For example, studies have found that in students who are apprehensive when taking important tests, it was discovered that "while pessimism is often seen as a negative trait, *defensive* pessimism can be a useful way for someone to harness their anxiety into positive results."[51]

At its core, defensive pessimism is examining what has gone—or could go—wrong, so you take the necessary steps to prevent it from occurring. This, naturally, assists in assuring a positive outcome. It is sometimes described as analyzation and overpreparation for negative outcomes to ensure positive results. Self-handicapping is expecting the worst—and being so negative that you'll prepare something to blame just in case it does.

"One thing that separates defensive pessimism from pessimism alone," researchers assert, "is that defensive pessimists...unlike true pessimists...also report a propensity to reflect about, or plan for, their performance."[52]

That's an important distinction. Defensive pessimists aren't just sitting around moping or fuming over the outcomes that have upset their customers and employees. After reflection, they are making plans to fix the problem.

Researchers identify the flip side of defensive pessimism as strategic optimism. Those employing this approach do all they can to avoid thinking about potential negative outcomes. They focus and plan for things to go right.

From observation and experience, the challenge that I often see is that those who identify themselves as strategic optimists can tend to minimize the impact that a negative experience can have upon the customer from an emotional standpoint. They find it easier to just paste on a smile and rely on the old, "We'll try harder next time" approach without directly confronting and solving the problem.

The aforementioned studies on pessimism found "Defensive pessimists show significant increases in self-esteem and satisfaction over time, perform better academically, form more supportive friendship networks, and make more progress on their personal goals than equally anxious students who do not use defensive pessimism."[53]

To be sure, defensive pessimism does not mean that we are playing defense. Rather, defensive pessimism is a method of evaluating what could go wrong—as we are on the offensive—so we can anticipate and prevent missteps.

THE MILLIONAIRE CHIMNEY SWEEP

Mark Stoner is a terrific entrepreneur. Starting as a teenager with a dream, Mark founded Ashbusters Chimney Service in Nashville, Tennessee. Mark has expanded and grown the success of his company to the point he was featured on CNBC as a "blue-collar millionaire." Yes, you read that right—a multimillionaire from his chimney sweep business.

Stoner has also founded SirVent Chimney and Venting Franchise and has served as the president of the Chimney Safety Institute of America. (He's also a member of our elite mastermind program, the Insiders Group of the Ultimate Business Summit.)

He attributes a significant part of his business success to specifically addressing the negative issues that create disconnections with customers. After every home visit by a chimney sweep from one of his companies, a preaddressed and prestamped "How Did We Do?" postcard is left for the homeowner. It specifically asks them to identify the issues where the customer might believe the performance of the chimney sweep fell short of the promise that they perceive Ashbusters made.

As they say on cheesy infomercials—but wait! There's *more*!

The day after a technician from Ashbusters performs the scheduled service in your home, you'll receive a personal phone call from them to inquire—*again*—if there were any issues or problems. It isn't enough for Ashbusters to have satisfied customers. They want to be certain that Ashbusters has delivered an Ultimate Customer Experience. They are defensively pessimistic to make certain they do it exactly right for every customer, every time.

This may be a bigger task than you might imagine. According to Stoner, "We service about two to three hundred customers a week." That means they make up to sixty phone calls every day from their Nashville office. "It's a lot of work," Stoner said, "but we feel it's absolutely necessary."

Stoner's website, MarkStoner.com, states a similar philosophy. "By studying his failures... remaining focused and dedicated, and continuously striving to improve and learn, Mark has gone from *being owned* by his business to *owning* his business."

LET'S DISRUPT OURSELVES

How do individuals, patients, and consumers want their health care delivered, and what is the expectation they place on anybody that's delivering health care? That is the core question that the leadership team at St. Vincent Health Care in central Indiana started asking. It's their version of "what's pissing off our constituencies about health care?"

The result? Instead of focusing on expanding their huge campuses, St. Vincent is introducing several small regional facilities to be closer to patients and families. St. Vincent is looking to proactively deal with the rising pharmaceutical costs that are hurting their customers, as well as with the challenges presented by changes to care delivery. In addition, they promise to dramatically enhance the level of consumer education regarding health care issues available in their marketplace.

St. Vincent CEO Jonathan Nalli said, "We feel that if we don't drive transformation in health care, we will be disrupted and so we believe *disrupting ourselves* is the most important way to evolve health care as an industry."[54]

If you fail to focus on what is infuriating your customers, you can easily ignore the dissatisfaction that is the genesis of disruption.

HOW TO GO NEGATIVE

Your three action steps are to:

1. Probe internally for areas of weakness—and do it constantly. *Don't view talking about organizational or procedural weaknesses as a sign of negativity or weakness in the employee discussing it. Don't "shoot the messenger!" Learn from the message.*
2. Aggressively seek negative input from customers. *Find out what pisses them off! Then, fix it!*
3. Become "defensively pessimistic." *Examine in detail everything that could go wrong in every point of contact with customers. You can't fix what's broken if you aren't actively trying to discover what's damaged.*

Tesla cofounder Elon Musk supports this approach as well. "Pay attention to negative feedback and solicit it, particularly from friends," Musk said. "This may sound like simple advice, but *hardly anyone does that*, and it's incredibly helpful."[55]

Add the aforementioned founder of Amazon to this group. The richest person in the world provides customers with his email address so he can always be watching for the negative.

"In his book *The Everything Store*, author Brad Stone recounts the reaction Jeff Bezos sometimes has when a customer emails him at jeff@amazon.com to complain. Namely, he forwards the message to his leadership team 'with a one-character addition: a question mark,'" reports Bill Murphy, Jr. on Inc.com.

"Getting a question mark email is 'a ticking bomb' that 'elicits waves of panic,' according to Stone, as Amazon employees scramble to explain what went wrong—and make it right." [56]

However, as mentioned earlier, customers don't want you to have to "make it right."

Customers want you to GET it right.

Iconic companies and leaders are confident and self-assured enough to go negative. They obsess over learning what is pissing off their customers in order to ensure they will develop what it takes to get it right for them.

However, the willingness to go negative to serve customers does not mean you have a negative approach to the culture of your business. That's the point we will explore in the next chapter.

- Have you done a SWOT analysis for your team, department, organization? If not, why not? If yes, did you experience the phenomenon when identifying "weaknesses" that were discussed in this chapter?
- Are your colleagues afraid to talk about how they couldn't discuss weaknesses—because it will be perceived as a weakness? (You need to have a conversation about this!)
- Do you welcome—or resist—discussions about negative aspects with your colleagues?
- Why would a customer recommend you to their friends or colleagues? What aspect of your organization (or team or department) do you want customers to be talking about to friends? (Product? Service? Brand?) How does your performance earn their referrals?
- Think about your approach. Is it:

  1. Self-handicapping?
  2. Strategically optimistic?
  3. Defensively pessimistic?

- What do you need to change to get your thinking (organizationally and individually) where you want it to be?

- And, finally: what pisses off your customers about doing business with you? What are you going to do about it?

CHAPTER SEVEN

#5 Reciprocal Respect

As my first wife and I were opening our wedding gifts many years ago, one stood out from the rest because of its uniqueness. It wasn't dishes or pots and pans—although starting our young lives together we were pleased with those too. Friends had gifted us with two tickets to see comedian Rodney Dangerfield. Our friends understood—quite correctly—that after the bustle of the marriage ceremony and reception and the time unpacking in our new apartment after our modest honeymoon in Gatlinburg, Tennessee, we would need a respite. Joining them for a night of laughter was just the thing we needed.

Rodney Dangerfield was a stand-up performer and actor who was a dominant force in the comedy scene in the 1980s and 90s. He won a Grammy for one of his comedy albums and starred in several films. He appeared on the *Tonight Show* over thirty times and sold out concert halls across the United States. It was just a year after Dangerfield's performance in the monster hit movie *Caddyshack*—perhaps the very height of his fame—and as we entered for the show, the theater was packed.

When Dangerfield walked on stage in his trademark black suit, white shirt, and red tie, the audience erupted in applause. He told a few great jokes for several minutes before he finally delivered his catchphrase all his fans were anticipating: "I get no respect—*no respect at all!*"

Oddly, later in the show, a man walked onto the stage carrying a pen and the program that was sold at the event. As Dangerfield was focused on his performance, the man walked almost up to his side. Dangerfield recoiled and shouted, "Get the hell off the stage!" The audience, assuming this was part of the show, laughed uproariously. Dangerfield shouted, "Where the hell is security in this dump?" At that point, three uniformed officers sprinted onto the stage, grabbed the man, and hauled him away. Still assuming this was all in the routine, the audience kept laughing—until it was obvious Dangerfield was very upset.

"Wow!" Sheri said as we strolled back to the car. "I can't believe that idiot just walked on stage and expected to get an autograph." She then thought for a moment and said, "I guess Rodney Dangerfield really *doesn't* get any respect!"

THE FORMERLY
TERRIFIC EMPLOYEE

"Ever had an incredible employee and thought, *This is the one!* They were smart, engaged, driven, and seemed to really love the job. You thought, *We're going to be together forever!* You could really see yourself promoting this person, mentoring them, watching them climb the ranks in your company. . . and then one day, they quit. They might give you the 'It's not you, it's me' speech, but what does it actually mean?" asks author and speaker Bernard Marr on CNBC.com.

"*No respect*" is how Marr answers his question. "There's an old saying that employees don't leave a company, they leave a manager. No matter how much you like, respect, or appreciate an employee, if they don't know it, they may leave. Make sure your interactions with employees are always respectful, and that you look for ways to actively value their contribution."[57]

According to a study by Christine Porath, professor at the McDonough School of Business, and Christine Pearson of the Thunderbird School of Global Management, more people than ever are feeling disrespected at work. "Of the nearly 800 managers and employees across 17 industries [we] polled, those who didn't feel respected performed worse."

How much worse? The study indicated:

- 47 percent of those who were treated poorly intentionally decreased the time spent at work.
- 38 percent said they deliberately decreased the quality of their work.
- 66 percent reported their performance declined.
- 78 percent said their commitment to the organization had declined.[58]

You can't build an iconic organization
or become an iconic leader when the
productivity of your team is declining.

Leaders in any organization need to be aware of how their people are treated. A full 12 percent of those treated poorly said they "left their job because of the uncivil treatment. Yet, those who quit in response to incivility typically *don't tell their employers why*. When employees are exposed to rudeness, they are three times less likely to help others and their willingness to share drops by more than half."[59]

When your team feels respected by leadership, the research clearly shows they perform better. How much better?

- 92 percent greater focus and prioritization
- 55 percent more engagement

- 56 percent better health and well-being
- 89 percent greater enjoyment and satisfaction with their jobs.
- 1.72 times more trust and safety
- 1.1 times more likely to stay with their organizations than those who didn't[60]

How do you stand out from—and defeat—a competitor that has a team with 92 percent greater focus and 89 percent greater enjoyment and satisfaction with their jobs?

You *can't*.

Disrespected employees, as you might imagine, create an additional problem. They, in turn, *disrespect your customers*.

TRICKLE-DOWN DISRESPECT

My wife Tammy and I recently took a trip to Maui, adding a few days of vacation between two speeches I was presenting on the island. When we checked into our hotel room, a room service tray evidently from the previous occupants of our room sat in the hallway. A part of our shower was broken. A lightbulb in the bathroom was out. A sign at one elevator in the lobby was broken and had what appeared to be exposed wiring sticking out. Housekeeping made our bed each day, but the room wasn't really cared for. The ironing board remained out and trash remained in the can.

On our first day at the resort, I accidently left my key in the room and walked to the front desk to ask for another. I gently reminded the desk clerk to be certain that I also had access to the Regency Club, for which I qualified.

"No, you don't," she loudly stated. "It's nowhere on your record that you have access."

I softly explained I had the gold sticker on my key, had already been to the club, and was an elite member of their points program.

"No," she argued. "It's nowhere in here that you qualify."

"Well," I asked as politely as I could, stumbling for some kind of satisfactory resolution, "then how do I know about the gold sticker on the key?"

"You must have seen someone else's," she replied with obvious disdain.

Here's my question: even if I don't qualify, why be so disrespectful to a customer? Why not give the customer the benefit of the doubt? The biggest downside is that you would be out perhaps a couple cups of coffee and some slices of pineapple.

I returned to my room, found my original key with the gold sticker, and—for the heck of it—went back to the front desk. I simply said, "I wanted you to see this so you wouldn't think I was being dishonest with you."

Believe it or not, her response was, "Well, I have no idea how *you* got *that*!"

The next morning at the Maui resort, I put laundry in the bag the hotel provided and delivered it to the bell desk. Rather than greeting me with a "Good morning" or "How may I assist you?" instead the woman at the desk blurted out, "We normally come to the room and pick that up."

Oh," I responded with a smile. "Well, I saved you the trip then." Her response? "Harrumph."

No "Thank you" or "You shouldn't have" or "I'm calling security on you!" Nothing but "Harrumph."

After we returned home, I received a call from Hertz asking when I was planning on returning my Maui rental car to their location. My problem was that as we were checking out of the hotel, the Hertz desk there was unexpectedly closed. I asked the bellman who was carrying our luggage to the airport shuttle if he would help return the keys to the Hertz desk for me. He told me he would take care of it and I tipped him for his trouble. Somehow the car was never returned. Hertz was holding me responsible, which, of course, is what you would expect them to do. They didn't have their car!

When I called the hotel and asked for the bell desk, wouldn't you know it, I got Harrumph Lady. When I explained that a bell captain said he would take care of our rental car, she jumped in and said, "That cannot be true. We don't have bell captains working at that hour!"

"You don't have bellmen working at that hour?" I asked. "Then who helped me with my luggage?"

"We have bellmen, but there are no bell *captains* on duty then!" Rather than debate with her about the relative titles of members of the hotel bell staff, I hung up and called the Hertz desk at the resort.

Finally, I was treated as a customer should be. The agent promised to figure out what was wrong—and make it right. Not long after that, he called me back. He hadn't found the car or the keys, but he just wanted me to know that he was still working on it. An hour later, he called with the good news. He found the car. The bellman (who isn't a "captain," evidently) for some reason had moved the car to the wrong spot—and had forgotten to return the keys. Since the matter was not my fault, Hertz didn't charge me for the extra days. That difference in experience is precisely why I always rent from Hertz—and have never returned to that Maui resort.

A lot can be learned from this unusual customer service story.

When a customer receives such consistently disrespectful engagement at all levels—front desk, bell desk, bellman, for example—what is your guess about how the employees at that resort are being treated by their respective managers? How are those managers being respected by the general manager or CEO of their hotel? I think we all know the answer to that.

Think back to the story about Jack Miller and the Fairmont Scottsdale Princess. Do you imagine he consistently displays respect for his team? The Scottsdale Princess has among the lowest employee turnover rates of any hotel or resort in the world. That is not a coincidence.

RESPECT MUST BE EARNED

At a job I landed right out of college, my new boss told me about all of the people who had previously worked under him. He proudly related the professional success that they went on to achieve. As this was the first major-market radio station where I had ever worked, I was inspired by the long list of legendary broadcasters—and their achievements were my goals.

Not long after working there, I realized that I was employed by a manager who was a screamer. Regardless of the severity of your error—or even if he only *thought* you might have made one—he would explode with loud, outrageous, demeaning profanity.

Previously, my experience was with bosses who set high standards and aggressively held you to them. I had certainly worked for people who were a bit prickly and difficult. This, however, was my first experience working for someone who displayed no respect for his team.

After working there a year, I marched in his office and told him, "I quit."

"I get it," he said, "you aren't under contract here and another station offered you a better deal. What does it take to keep you?"

"That's not it at all," I replied. "I can't work like this. I just can't be productive when I'm treated the way you're treating me."

"Yeah, right. How much?" He assumed it was all a ploy to get a raise. That's how little respect he had.

Later, I found out that of the impressive list of successful broadcasters he touted on my first day, all of them had quit because of his disrespect. Without exception, they found employment somewhere they were treated with dignity, which allowed their careers to blossom, as they became nationally recognized professionals. Rather than being their launchpad, that screaming boss had been an anchor to their careers they had finally escaped.

Employees and customers are constantly—both consciously and subconsciously—evaluating the level of respect that is displayed towards them. Respect, as with being iconic, isn't something you achieve through demands. It must be *earned*.

Iconic leaders and organizations understand it is their responsibility to lead by example.

The iconic company or leader does not give respect only *after* respect is shown. They must show respect first. You can't grow plants without seed and sunshine coming first. You can't grow people without investing respect in them first.

The Key Is *Reciprocal* Respect

Iconic companies have cultures of uplifting reciprocal respect.

You may be a bit surprised to learn the single most important word in that sentence is *reciprocal*.

The word *reciprocal* dates back to the 1560s and comes from the Latin word *reciprocus*, which essentially means "returning *in the same way*." In other words, reciprocal respect means that I will respect you in the same manner—and at the same level—as you display your respect for me.

"Professionals attract other professionals," Craig Huse of St. Elmo's Steakhouse in Indianapolis told me. "The people at St. Elmo have kept us successful and relevant through their passion for the restaurant. They are professionals doing something that most people treat simply as a job instead of a career. That's why many of our staff members have been with us twenty or more years." St. Elmo's has incredible employee retention and productivity because professionals who treat each other with respect attract other professionals who deserve and display the same.

This means that to develop iconic status, there are two particular aspects required for success:

1. How you display respect to others
2. Your unequivocal demand for respect at all levels

1) HOW YOU DISPLAY RESPECT TO OTHERS

After a decade of experience as a movie reviewer and commentator on the entertainment industry—and meeting more celebrities than you could imagine—there was one aspect that always left me befuddled: autographs. While I can understand why a fan would want a picture with a celebrity, I've never understood how getting them to sign on a piece of paper would thrill anyone. What I comprehend even less is why some stars refuse to do it.

In numerous situations, I've seen stars who refuse to sign anything or take pictures with their fans. This seems silly to me. The fan is responsible for your career. All of us should realize that we are beholden to our customers. If you're in show business and have no fans, we call you a waiter. I understand that some performers in show business are natural introverts—hiding behind a character or with a band and a song—and are reticent about personal engagement. But you can still be respectful and provide some "customer service." What I don't understand are the celebrities who are just jerks, pompously taking the time to condescendingly explain that they don't sign anything or ever take photos. The oddest part of this is that it takes them as long—or longer—to deliver the refusal than it would to just let their fan take the damn selfie.

In both cases, they deliver a degree of disrespect to their fans, or customers, that I find discouraging.

The nicest celebrities that I've ever been around?

- Arnold Schwarzenegger not only was engaging, he has booked me for presentations, including one at the White House with the president in the audience.
- Tom Hanks practically refused to talk about himself. Instead he enthusiastically praised others he had worked with on a project.
- My interview with Meryl Streep was delayed, so she asked if I'd like to go for coffee. We laughed and talked about our mutual connection to Indianapolis (her husband's hometown and my home for many years).
- John Travolta was late for his next appointment because we couldn't stop talking about men's suits. The next time we crossed paths, he

started with, "So, what designer am I wearing now?" With all the people that he meets—and as important as he is—I could not believe he remembered.

- The Oak Ridge Boys have been close friends for decades, and we still slip away from their concert halls to dine together several times a year.

Please don't read this and think it is an exercise in name-dropping! I'm not trying to impress you. I'm trying to express something important.

It's not that Schwarzenegger, Hanks, Streep, Travolta, and the Oaks became really popular and then said, "Well, we'd better start treating folks right, now that we're famous!" It's exactly the opposite. They displayed their respect first—and more studios, producers, concert promoters, fans, and journalists wanted to be associated with them.

How do you display respect to others? Most of this will—hopefully—come naturally to you. However, a simple reminder from time to time can be helpful.

Six Steps to Becoming Respectful

1. Don't just hear—listen
2. Display open body language
3. Don't nitpick

4. Show how you're following up
5. Don't withhold praise
6. Treat others equally and with sensitivity

Don't Just Hear—*Listen*

Hearing means you have the physical ability to turn the sounds expressed by others into meaningful language in your brain. *Listening* is a function of attention, the effort of taking the language and interpreting its deeper meaning. In a world with a myriad of distractions, focusing your attention and making the effort to hear customers and colleagues is a fundamental aspect of leadership.

Display Open Body Language

You can be taking in every word that I'm saying, but if your hands are on your hips or if your eyes roll toward the heavens, there's no script you can recite that will make me believe that you care. We all have sensors that tip us off as to whether or not someone is truly engaged. Your stance, your demeanor, and your tone of voice all register on our internal detection devices. Display openness in all you do—not just with the words you say.

Don't Nitpick

Have you ever worked with someone or been a customer dealing with an employee who argues about everything? If you said, "The sky is blue," they would disagree. "Haven't you been outside today?" these types might say. "The sky is gray! What the heck is wrong with you?" It seems as though they are waiting to correct something—anything. Does anyone ever want to be around these people? If you're always judging, criticizing, and dismissing others, they will eventually come to see you as a bully. We may believe we are merely offering "constructive criticism," but I challenge you. The next time you want to criticize or argue, ask yourself:

- Is it really "constructive"? Does it serve to help them or to make me appear as the authority?
- Do they desire the criticism? If they haven't invited your critique, then—from their viewpoint—all you are doing is bitching.

SHOW HOW YOU ARE FOLLOWING UP

After we have identified a problem, we are constantly told by everyone from our vendors to our kids that they will "get right on that." In many cases, we know that their comment is precisely where their effort ends.

It's a great sign of respect that you inform employees and customers that you will follow up. It's even more impressive when you demonstrate it. For example, notice how the Hertz employee picked up the phone and called to keep me posted. That's not only great customer service, it's a display of respect for the concern I was experiencing—worrying that the car had perhaps been stolen and I was going to be responsible. The follow-up was highly valued and appreciated by me, the customer. Every employee, every leader, and every organization can follow that model of respect.

Don't Withhold Praise

Here's another aspect that I personally find baffling. I know some people who act as though there is a limited supply of praise that they are granted to disseminate in their lifetime. They seem to hang onto it for fear that they'll exhaust their allocation. Or they might have other excuses like, "If I'm always praising my employees, they'll ask for a raise" or "If I keep telling them how good they are, they'll get a 'big head' and take it for granted." You know the routine.

Maybe they actually believe these inane ideas. Or maybe they aren't receiving enough praise themselves, so they refuse to provide it to others. Either way, it's never good to withhold validation from deserving customers or employees.

If you are not a millennial, it's even more important for you to understand why this aspect is so critical in achieving iconic status. Only 19 percent of millennial workers say they receive routine feedback at work, according to a study by Gallup. However, only 15 percent of millennials strongly agree that they *ask* for feedback they desire. "Millennials who meet with their manager on a regular basis are more than twice as likely as their generational peers to be engaged at work."[61]

Remember: you go first.

Millennials often aren't requesting your feedback. But they are silently hoping that you'll go first.

TREAT OTHERS EQUALLY AND WITH SENSITIVITY

It's terribly sad to me that anyone needs to be reminded of this—yet, perhaps all of us do.

I'd like to believe that no one ever goes to work thinking, *Today, I get to treat my team unequally and be insensitive to the needs of my customers!* Yet we probably have all observed that kind of behavior.

Hopefully, none of us would say that we want to pay women less than men for the same job or behave boorishly when it comes to our words and deeds toward other races, religions, and cultures. However, we know it happens.

Equality and respect are woven into the fabric of the conduct and performance of iconic organizations and leaders. Period.

SCOTT McKAIN

I also would hope that as individuals and organizations become more enlightened, those who are being proactive and truly trying to change are not given a "death sentence" because of past missteps. Don't misunderstand—I'm not suggesting that they should be instantly forgiven for all misdeeds either. (And we also know that some will sprint to the altar because they know they're about to be caught.)

What I am suggesting is that if there is no path to recovery, there's no incentive for wrongdoers to quell the problem. All of us who desire change in the workplace also have to be willing to allow space for people who sincerely want to correct what they've done wrong. It's often said that the only people who dislike smoking worse than nonsmokers are former smokers. Could this be true of formerly disrespectful people as well? Might it be possible that if offenders can see both the damage and the opportunity, they can become more forceful advocates for change? I hope so.

Just as in the teachings of my chosen faith, forgiveness is only possible through salvation. But if there was no chance to be forgiven, what is the incentive to seek redemption?

Start today. Follow up on *all* six steps.

187

2) Do Not Tolerate Disrespect

Disrespect is like a weed in a garden. You've got to *kill it* or it will multiply and take over.

Your organization does not have to be arrogant, and you don't have to be an ass. Expecting to be treated respectfully when you are being respectful is neither haughty nor contemptible.

A contractor friend of mine in northern California has shared all kinds of stories on the rich and famous in the exclusive area where his business is located. After he worked on remodeling a superstar's home, he told me one I'll never forget.

This superstar also owned a very exclusive country club. A multimillionaire businessman had just joined the club. On his first round, he played exceedingly slow and left his trash on the course for others to pick up. He was behaving contemptibly. To top it off, when he came into the clubhouse after playing golf, he was rude to the server.

Just then the superstar owner of the country club appeared holding a check made out to the member. It was the refund of his large initiation fee.

"We don't tolerate disrespect here," the iconic figure told the millionaire. "Our team members are as important as our club members. You're no longer welcome on the property."

I'm certain every single employee of that country club in northern California would agree their superstar boss had just "made their day."

While that's a good story, it's also an instructive lesson. The iconic entertainer didn't merely tell everyone how much he respected them—he demonstrated it. And how do you suppose the other members of the club now act toward the employees—and other club members as well?

The superstar owner killed the weeds of disrespect before they could take over.

DISRESPECTFUL BEHAVIOR SHOULD NEVER BE TOLERATED

An aforementioned friend—author and hall of fame speaker, Larry Winget—frequently talks about the importance of respect. He inspired me to make a list of the seven disrespectful behaviors that I won't tolerate. Your list may be different—here's mine:

1. *Dishonesty.* If I know you'll lie to me, what can you say or do that I can possibly believe?
2. *Disloyalty.* A variation of dishonesty. It's a betrayal of the trust that I've placed in someone.
3. *Apathy.* If we actively disagree, that's fine. It's hard to respect someone who just doesn't give a damn about anything.

4. *Stratification.* This is someone who respects people differently. They may be courteous to a colleague and mean to a waiter. You know the type—someone who will kiss up to the boss and kick anyone below them on the org chart. Disgusting.

5. *Selfishness.* It's not all about you—and it's certainly not all about me. If you can't recognize that, I don't want me to be around you.

6. *Inequality.* If you think that your gender is better, your race is preferred, and there are people lesser than you, we're done.

7. *Totalism.* That's the word I use to describe people who think their side is totally right—and those with other viewpoints are totally wrong. This is what has led to the lack of significant discussion and meaningful conversation on important issues in every nation around the world.

What if your organization made its own list of seven disrespectful behaviors that you won't tolerate and posted them prominently? How would that shape the behavior of your team—and your customers?

- The employees you want to attract will not work where they aren't respected. Therefore, aside from just being the right thing to do, it makes great economic sense to be respectful to them.

- The customers you want to attract aren't going to do business where they aren't shown respect. Therefore, aside from just being the right thing to do, it makes great economic sense to prove your respect for them.

As I mentioned in chapter 3, there are many annual lists touting the results of studies on the best places to work.

Fortune, for example, listed their top five in 2018 as Salesforce, Wegman's, Ultimate Software, Boston Consulting Group, and Edward Jones.[62] Glassdoor listed Facebook, Bain & Company, Boston Consulting Group (again), In-N-Out Burger, and Google.[63]

It should not escape our attention that these are all remarkably successful corporations. While some might suggest that it's easier for winning companies to treat their people right, I'd advocate that it's *because* they are treating their teams with reciprocal respect that they are so successful.

Note, too, that these companies do everything from serving burgers to offering financial services—from consulting major corporations to bagging groceries. There is no thread that unites them other than they are all great places to work. It's impossible to receive this extraordinary level of positive reviews from your employees without reciprocal respect.

- 95 percent of Salesforce employees agree that "people care about each other here."
- 96 percent advocate that "management is honest and ethical in its business practices."
- 48 percent of the reporting employees at Salesforce are millennials, 44 percent gen Xers, and just 8 percent are baby boomers.[64]

Wegman's Food Markets—where the job descriptions are highly different and baby boomers make up almost three times more of the workforce than they do at Salesforce—reports almost identical responses about their organization.[65] In other words it's not about the industry, or the job, or the employee's generation. It's about the reciprocal respect in the organization.

FIRE THEM!

If you have someone on the team who doesn't respect his colleagues: *Fire them.*

If you have someone in your organization who won't respect her customers: *Fire them.*

If you have a customer who will not respect your employees: ***Fire them, too.***

"Everyone deserves respect, but some clients think that rule doesn't apply to them. In a distorted sense of reality, some clients believe they can treat you like dirt because they are paying you," says Nathan Gotch, founder of Gotch SEO. "Think about it this way... would you continue being friends with someone who was rude or disrespectful? Probably not."

"So," Gotch continues, "why would you take that type of abuse from a client? Money is nice, but your sanity is what matters. If your heart races when you think about your rude client, then it's time to make change."[66] I couldn't agree more.

Why would your best employees want to continue in your organization if they are expected to tolerate customers or clients who disrespect them? That's obviously not iconic behavior.

What you tolerate is what you endorse.

What you tolerate is what you endorse. In other words, when you tolerate disrespectful behavior from some customers, you endorse that behavior in other customers too. The discourteous actions you fail to stop with one employee become the actions you have just endorsed among all employees. By not stopping the disrespect-fulness immediately and boldly, you are saying that you approve the behavior. It's all-inclusive. If you allow one person to do it, you are really saying that you're allowing others to do so as well.

My pal Larry Winget suggested I change the word *tolerate* to *endorse* when I speak on respect. I now pass that advice on to my clients.

Try it! When you're talking about a specific employee or customer's attitudes or behaviors, just change the word *tolerate* to *endorse*. It may change your perspective. For example, I can almost hear discussions that may have taken place about men who were making unwanted advances on women in the workplace. Somewhere, someone may have said that because of the man's position, power, reputation, sales success, or other achievements, the company would "have to tolerate" some of his bad behavior.

Some insiders—"off the record," of course—confessed that Miramax Films had "tolerated" Harvey Weinstein's behavior because of his status and track record. What if, instead, it was required that the board or other senior officers had to publicly announce that they had "endorsed" his repulsive actions? Could you imagine that? Absolutely not!

Once we switch the word *tolerate* to *endorse*, our perspective on bad behavior becomes better focused.

Iconic Levels of Respect

If you want to obtain, maintain, or regain iconic status, it's not going to be accomplished in a vacuum. You'll need a team of customers and employees who advocate for you in today's connected marketplace.

This can only happen when you extend to others the respect you desire for yourself and your organization. You must refuse to tolerate disrespect from those who are missing the confidence to engage without vitriol or unacceptable behavior.

You cannot grow your garden unless you're willing to kill the weeds.

Endorse the behavior you desire. Extend—and expect to obtain—high levels of respect from all. You're not Rodney Dangerfield. You can get—and give—respect. It's just part of who iconic people *are,* and what iconic people *do*.

The Five Factors of Iconic Performance

There you have it. Those are the five factors of an iconic performance:

1. Play Offense
2. Get Promise and Performance Right

195

3. Stop Selling
4. Go Negative
5. Reciprocal Respect

Our next important question is this: what happens when you've attained iconic status, have maintained it for a period of time, then lose it?

Can you ever get it back? Can you ever return to the highest level of distinction?

That's what we'll examine in our next chapter.

QUESTIONS FOR CHAPTER 7

- When do you feel like Rodney Dangerfield—and you get "no respect"? What do you do about it?
- How would you rate the level of respect that your organization delivers to your employees?
- How would you evaluate the level of respect that your colleagues share with you? What can you do to make the answers to both of these two previous questions even greater?
- How do you demonstrate that you are REALLY listening?
- Strike the pose! How would you stand (or sit) to display open body language?
- Are you a "nitpicker"? How could you respond to one in a manner that helps them?
- How do you demonstrate that you're following up?
- Name the last three times you praised someone—and the compliment wasn't coupled with anything negative!
- When have you failed to be treated with dignity?
- How can you make certain no one you come in contact with feels that way?
- What actions from others have you "tolerated" that you would not "endorse"?
- What are you going to do to stop tolerating/endorsing such behavior?

PART THREE

BRINGING IT
ALL TOGETHER

CHAPTER EIGHT

REGAINING ICONIC STATUS

If you remember at the very beginning of the book I mentioned a few market leaders in decline or no longer in existence: Sears, Nokia, HoJo's. We could add many more companies to our list:

Compaq, EF Hutton, Woolworth's (the US company), Arthur Andersen, TWA, Blockbuster, B. Dalton's Booksellers, Kodak, Service Merchandise, MCI WorldCom, Golfsmith, Radio Shack, Toys "R" Us, Western Auto, Tower Records, Circuit City, PanAm, Casual Corner, Bethlehem Steel, Lehman Brothers, Levitz Furniture, Border's Bookstores, Oldsmobile, Sports Authority, Mervyn's, Crazy Eddie's, Linens 'n Things, Dominick's, Waldenbooks, FAO Schwartz

You could probably name *many* more.

The question: if you lose your iconic status, can it ever be regained?

The answer is: it depends.

There are three critical factors that determine whether or not you can regain iconic status:

1. Where you are in your slide
2. Why the slide occurred
3. How the market perceives you now

WHERE YOU ARE IN YOUR SLIDE

Obviously, there is a point of no return. Maybe you're overleveraged and you cannot finance your future obligations. Or maybe some new technology has made you irrelevant and obsolete. For some, if you discover you are on the slide early enough, you still have time to prevent extinction.

"At Wells Fargo, CEO Tim Sloan admitted the bank had been slow to adapt to a changing financial landscape. 'Five years ago, we were the most valuable financial institution in the world,' said Sloan, before pointing out that the bank suffered some complacency. 'That will never again happen at Wells Fargo.. . .You can't rest on your laurels as much as we did.'"[67]

For example, why did companies like Spotify eventually destroy companies like Tower Records? Obviously, downloading tracks—like we did legally on iTunes or not so legally from other services—replaced buying CDs. Now, streaming music has replaced downloading tracks. So why didn't Tower do that first—or at all? They already possessed significant resources and industry relationships. It certainly wasn't that we all stopped loving our

---

music. The answer, to a great degree, is that by the time complacent Tower Records realized the marketplace and the desired delivery method had changed, it was too late. They were in the wrong business.

You've probably heard the stories of Netflix trying to sell their company to Blockbuster and the Wright Brothers attempting to get Union Pacific to acquire their patents on flight. The reason Blockbuster and Union Pacific didn't see the opportunity before them is because they were thinking small—about their specific business, but not the larger opportunities in their industry.

- Blockbuster thought they were in the retail business, *not the entertainment distribution industry.*
- Union Pacific thought they were in the railroad business, *not the transportation industry.*
- Tower Records thought they were in the album or CD retail sales business, *not the music distribution industry.*

By the time these companies recognized they were on the road to oblivion, it was too late to reestablish their distinctive status. Let's face it, everything goes faster when it's heading downhill.

If you're losing your iconic status, you must be brutally honest about where you are on the descending slide.

WHY THE SLIDE OCCURRED

The primary reason why a company's reputation and market share is sliding provides insight into whether or not the company will return to iconic—or even distinctive—status.

If your company is sliding because of ethical reasons, there is likely little hope of regaining iconic status. It is much easier to destroy a reputation than it is to rebuild one. Take Enron for example. It was a behemoth energy company in the late 1990s that got into the derivatives market trading all sorts of commodities, some of which did poorly. Enron hid its losses for as long as it could, but eventually it was found out. And when it was, all hell broke loose. The company went down and caused the demise of famed accounting firm Arthur Andersen along with it.

And remember Theranos, the biotech company I mentioned in chapter 4 that lied about contracts with the Department of Defense to boost its credibility? Would you ever again believe anything Theranos claimed? When unethical behavior is behind your decline, your goose is likely cooked.

Yet, for most, the slide occurs not because of deceit but myopia.

The slide generally happens because of the narrow-minded, shortsighted approach that many entrepreneurs, corporate executives, and sales professionals take.

Such an approach creates a blindness toward the marketplace and a bias about their product or service that practically ensures poor decision making about the future.

The good news is that if your approach or mindset is your problem—as opposed to unethical behavior—there may be a chance of recovery. But you need to act quickly. You must be brutally honest as to why the slide occurred.

To stop the slide, you must be brutally honest as to why the slide occurred.

Stating, "We didn't do anything wrong" simply assures the marketplace that you aren't going to be the one to fix the problem.

HOW THE MARKETPLACE PERCEIVES YOU NOW

Do good feelings remain in the marketplace for you? Could it be reestablished and expanded?

Remember my story about Nokia in the introduction? Nokia may have been down, but they weren't out. There remained a vast reservoir of goodwill for Nokia. Their current resurgence as a technology and software company specializing in network solutions, as well as cloud, artificial intelligence, 5G mobility, and IoT (Internet of Things) services holds potential.

Nokia's reputation was still intact enough to make a comeback. However, I don't think a new version of Radio Shack, for example, would hold any appeal. They had their chance for years and didn't deliver in a compelling manner for customers when they had the opportunity to do so.

In other words, how you treat someone the first time is how they assume you will treat them again. If you lost out because of reasons other than poor service, you may have enough goodwill left in the tank to restart your organizational engine.

HOW DO YOU REGAIN ICONIC STATUS?

If, after review, you've determined that

- you can stop the slide before extinction,
- the slide occurred for correctable reasons, and
- enough goodwill remains in the marketplace for customer reengagement—then it's time to get started reclaiming your iconic status.

While there is much to do—and many prospective approaches that you could take—my research and experience suggests these three primary principles:

1. Think start-up
2. Work from the inside out
3. Build performance before enhancing promise

THINK START-UP

Would a start-up announce that they were going to be "all things to all people"? Of course not. Uber didn't begin by proclaiming that they were going to deliver meals and transport patients to health care appointments. They started by specifically focusing on the dissatisfaction people had with taxicabs.

> *To reclaim iconic status, you're going to need a more innovative mindset—you need to start thinking like a start-up.*

The goal of the start-up is not to maintain the status-quo. The start-up seeks to destroy those "way it's always been done" procedures.

When companies want to rebuild their status, many seem to desire to do so without significantly changing how they think and approach the market. Trying to reestablish your position in the marketplace by holding on to your old way of business is essentially blaming your customers for your decline. It's akin to saying to customers, "Obviously, you didn't 'get it' when we tried this before.

Now, we're giving you another chance to see how terrific we are."

It used to be that we accepted the philosophy in business that *"the big eat the small."* This meant that size was the strategic advantage in the marketplace.

It used to be *"the fast eat the slow"*—meaning that speed to market and rapidity of change were the primary factors.

However, once again, the rules have changed. Now, for lack of better terminology, it is that *"the smart eat the dumb* (or perhaps, the "less savvy").

In other words, to recover your iconic status you must be more

- perceptive about where customer dissatisfaction is based,
- insightful about the opportunity that pro-vides, and
- shrewd in delivering on your promises.

This is what rules in today's market. This is why we often see the articles, books, and research on the methods and concepts of such brilliant start-up leaders as Gary Vaynerchuk (see chapter 5) and others like Leo Wildrich of Buffer, Jess Weiner of TTJ Consulting and Changemakers, Mark Cuban, Bert Jacobs of Life Is Good, and Julie Rice, cofounder of SoulCycle. It's not about their speed—it's about their smarts.

> Don't start by asking how you reestablish your current franchise. Ask how a start-up would erase the dissatisfaction that your customers face.

If you're having challenges coming up with the ideas and potential solutions you need, why not ask a start-up to assist? Tim Sloan, CEO of Wells Fargo, admitted at a conference that is exactly what the financial giant has done when it comes to making it easier for customers to get mortgages processed more efficiently. When Sloan realized Wells Fargo couldn't design the product itself, "it turned to Blend, a San Francisco startup, for help."[68]

WORK FROM THE INSIDE-OUT

No amount of television spots or online ads can overcome a negative internal culture. Yet, unfortunately, many companies that have an internal issue will launch outward efforts to recover iconic status. Until your culture is right *internally*—no matter the size of your organization—many of your external efforts won't help. Instead, they'll just draw more attention to your dysfunction and help speed your demise.

ICONIC

Until your culture is right internally, many of your external efforts won't help.

For example, United Airlines is a client of mine and I'm a Global Services member of their MileagePlus frequent flyer program. I have already put my tail in their seats for over one hundred thousand miles this year. I have great appreciation and respect for them. Unfortunately, because of several incidents that have attracted global attention, their reputation has been wounded. Until they get their internal culture better aligned and everyone on the same page to deliver a great customer experience, investing in a new "Fly the Friendly Skies" ad campaign is not going to help.

A strong internal culture is what enables your organization to align the promise-performance matrix we discussed in chapter 4. Deloitte is a $40-billion-dollar, multinational company specializing in audit, consulting, and tax services, among others. One of their executives in human capital, Anthony Abbatiello, defines *culture* as the "set of values and attributes that shape how things get done in the organization."[69] He proposes three steps to help align your culture with the strategy of your organization:

1. **Define who your culture carriers are.** These are often leaders. Define what leader behav-

iors need to be in order to live the culture. To increase courage, for example, leaders should support their staff when taking risks.

2. **Systematically reinforce the behavior.** Find important company events where culture comes out, such as sales process, annual budget process, and the performance management process. Rewarding or aligning those with attributes of behavior is important in monitoring culture.

3. **Have leaders tell stories.** "There's a power of storytelling in an organization that is really important for the culture and for connecting emotionally with your workforce," Abbatiello said. When communicating the importance of taking risks, employees will respond to a story about a risk the leader took, how they failed, and what they learned. This is more powerful than simply hearing a leader say, "Take risks."[70]

As a United customer, I wondered why they weren't taking quicker strides toward improving the customer experience. Then I realized—especially after seeing the awful video of the passenger being dragged off the plane in Chicago and reading of the death of a family pet in an overhead bin—the only way their management could make a change in the customer experience was to first change the internal culture. This is an effort that

1. takes significant time to successfully accomplish, and
2. is seldom readily apparent to those outside the organization.

After I had the opportunity to work for and with the airline—and meet several members of their senior leadership team—I walked away impressed by both their effort and the size of their task. Tens of thousands of United employees deliver the "friendly skies" experience every day. Yet, it is one gate agent in Chicago or a single flight attendant on a plane from Houston who makes headlines.

The flight attendant whom I saw comfort a scared little boy traveling as an unaccompanied minor—and the representative on the telephone who helps you—is privately appreciated. The one who is rude gets blasted on Trip Advisor and read about by thousands.

The challenge for every organization is that *every* team member needs to be on board with providing an excellent experience. In today's world of ubiquitous cameras and social media, all it takes is one single individual who does something wrong to garner you worldwide derision. Because iconic leaders understand this concept, there is *no excuse* for not pursuing the principles of reciprocal respect outlined in chapter 7 in order to achieve the goal of total employee engagement.

United's position, in my opinion, was diminished by a previous leadership team. Will they ever reclaim its iconic status as the "friendly skies" airline? There are no guarantees. However, I promise you that the current team, led by CEO Oscar Munoz, is working from the inside out—with enormous effort and grit—to make that happen.

Like United, the legacy telephone company in Australia (and client of mine), Telstra, has suffered from customer service challenges. One executive there told me that at one point Telstra's residential customer service was so inferior it was impacting sales in the corporate division and even their mobile telephone operations. Customers assumed if Telstra could not get their residential service right, why should they trust them with their mobile or business needs?

To combat these problems, Telstra's HR professionals worked with senior leaders to redevelop their vision and values. Working directly with the CEO, they recently articulated what "the desirable culture and values should be to establish a 'One Telstra' mindset and relevant behaviors towards customers."[71] Part of the beauty—and that's the right word—is that "One Telstra" recognizes that all components of the company have to be aligned internally before they can expect results externally.

It must happen throughout the organization!

"Turning customers into lifelong advocates requires companies to embrace the customer experience throughout the organization," Jason Bradshaw of Volkswagen Group Australia told me. "We've been working diligently to create a culture that embodies the following philosophy: *If I have a problem in front of me, my job is to get that problem fixed. If I have two problems, my priority is the problem that impacts our drivers and our owners.*"

Bradshaw is absolutely right.

BUILD PERFORMANCE BEFORE ENHANCING PROMISE

"Give us another chance!" sliding companies seem to be saying. "We will do better next time!"

But what if you *don't*?

If you are going to regain iconic status, it will happen because you have rebuilt a solid, dependable performance *before* you restate or enhance your promise to customers. Business relationships mirror personal relationships, and rebuilding trust with a customer is a lot like trying to regain the trust of a girlfriend or boyfriend. It takes a lot to be able to get a second chance—and a third or fourth chance is practically impossible.

If your company has fallen from its iconic status, there is a reason that customers have "broken up" with you. Getting them back is a monumental task because they assume if it didn't work out previously, it's not going to work out at all. At best you might get a mere second chance to reestablish any kind of positive relationship with your customer base. They have to see that you will do what you said you will do. You *must* deliver.

What tends to happen? Many organizations and leaders become so desperate to reengage, they make exaggerated claims in an attempt to capture the customer's attention—knowing that mindshare always precedes market share. However, you grow neither for the long run by making claims that cannot be supported. If you can't deliver on your promises, all you're doing is accelerating your descent into Fraud territory.

Volkswagen Group Australia is an example of how to do it right.

Given the well-publicized emissions scandal that Volkswagen faced recently, that statement may come as a bit of a surprise.

The leadership team for VW in Australia—led by Group Managing Director Michael Bartsch—has focused on what they can control. Over the past couple of years, resale values of the cars sold by Volkswagen Group Australia have not been impacted, suggesting that their efforts are successful. VW dealers in Australia remain more profitable than most. "The values of the vehicles reflect normal lifecycle and our dealerships are profit-

ICONIC

able," said Bartsch. "They're performing at a level above most franchises in Australia in terms of return on sales."[72]

This is not to suggest that VW Australia was immune to the challenges presented by the misdeeds of their corporate parent in Germany. However, the impact of this situation "down under" has been notably less than in the United States due to the strong initiative by the VW dealers in Australia to enhance the customer experience. When the scandal first hit, Chief Customer Officer Jason Bradshaw knew his team had to take action. Extensive training across all dealerships nationwide was not an easy sell because tangible results are challenging to quantify. Nevertheless, Bradshaw was determined to improve the customer experience.

The results of building performance first have been evident in VW Australia sales, growth in dealership profitability, and enthusiasm throughout the organization. It enabled VW Group Australia to go to market with the "Premium for the People" campaign discussed in chapter 5. "I think that's a real testament to how, as an organization, we want to be obsessed about continuous improvement and everyone taking accountability," Bradshaw told me.

If you are trying to regain iconic status, it won't be easy. Nothing in this chapter should be seen as a quick fix. You are facing difficult odds. Rebuilding trust with customers requires extraordinary effort and restoring the luster to an eroded brand takes immense perseverance.

However, what's the alternative?

There's no justification for giving up on formerly distinctive, iconic organizations that have faded from importance. Why wouldn't you fight to keep your status—or to reclaim your esteem in the marketplace?

In the final chapter, I'll close with some insight provided by an amazing restaurant—and with a challenge for you to reach the ultimate level of distinction.

QUESTIONS FOR CHAPTER 8

- Is your status in the marketplace on the rise or on the decline? If you're ascending, how do you sustain your growth? If you're declining, where are you currently located on the slide?

- Why has your marketplace position eroded? If it has not declined, identify a competitor that has and answer why they met that fate.

- Think like a start-up and come up with three "start-up" ideas for your business.

- What shifts, changes, additions, or subtractions need to be made to your organizational or departmental culture?

- Name a company that *talked* about how much better they had become but didn't deliver. How did that make you feel about them? Did you continue to do business with them?

CONCLUSION

YOU Can Become Iconic

To review, the Five Factors of Iconic Performance are:

1. **Play Offense**
2. **Get Promise and Performance Right**
3. **Stop Selling**
4. **Go Negative**
5. **Reciprocal Respect**

When you execute each of these five factors with excellence, you can move your organization—and your personal leadership abilities—from distinctive to iconic.

Although many of the examples of iconic companies in this book have been million-dollar businesses, you do not have to be big to be an iconic company. You don't have to be globally recognized like Mark Zuckerberg or Jeff Bezos to be an iconic leader. One example is an entrepreneur whose business is not iconic . . . yet.

THE VALET BREWER

On many occasions, I would pull my car to the valet stand at Green Valley Resort and Casino in Henderson, Nevada, to be greeted by a parking attendant whom I knew only as Dave.

After many occasions of friendly, generic small talk, Dave asked me what I did for a living. When I told him that I was an author of business books and professional speaker, he inquired if I had a podcast or other audiobooks he might download. I told Dave about my podcast, "Project Distinct." In all candor, I thought this extremely nice guy was just being kind to a regular customer. The next time I parked at Green Valley, Dave rushed up and commented on a recent podcast. Wow! He really had been listening! Then, Dave told me his job was at Green Valley Ranch for a steady income and the benefits. His business, however, was owning and running a craft brewery in Las Vegas.

Dave Forrest and his wife, Wyndee, had the idea for starting up Craft Haus Brewery while on a trip together through Europe. What they wanted to bring back home—"one pint at a time," as Wyndee says—is not just European beer, but a European beer experience.

Dave invited Tammy and me to the brewery for a tour. I was a bit reticent, because I don't know anything about beer. (I'm more of a bourbon guy!)

However, Dave's engaging manner made it impossible to say no.

Before visiting, I was at a local supermarket and noticed Craft Haus beer being sold there. For the heck of it, I picked up a six-pack of their Belgard Coffee Stout, because at least I know I like coffee. Imagine my surprise to discover that I absolutely loved their brew.

We toured the brewery during their annual Comrade Day. Craft Haus will brew a special Russian Imperial Stout for sale only on that day. Then, they throw an all-day party at the brewery to enjoy this special batch of beer. During this visit, I met many customers who were passionate fans of Craft Haus.

Dave and Wyndee focus on creating an experience for their customers. The brewery holds everything from yoga classes that are combined with craft beer tasting to hosting a sausage and beer festival complete with a European food truck.

It is truly amazing! This little brewery is

- bringing high quality products to a marketplace ruled by beer giants like Budweiser and Miller Lite;
- producing innovative products, such as the stout beer brewed with an elite coffee blend;
- developing creative customer experiences—from Comrade Day to yoga in a brewery.

What business—of any size—couldn't learn from a company that is delivering innovative, quality products wrapped around a unique, Ultimate Customer Experience?

From humble beginnings to selling craft beer in supermarkets and at fine dining establishments, the valet parking attendant who owns a craft brewery is on his way to developing an iconic business.

THE IMPACT OF SMALL ICONIC COMPANIES

While the story of Dave and Wyndee might sound like a nice anecdote about young entrepreneurs, it's also illustrative of how small iconic businesses can impact global leaders.

Billionaire Jorge Paulo Lemann, cofounder of 3G Capital—which owns several global food and beverage conglomerates, such as AB InBev (which includes all of the Budweiser and Miller beer brands)—recently called himself a "terrified dinosaur."

"I've been living in this cozy world of old brands and big volumes," said Lemann. "We bought brands that we thought could last forever"—and borrowed cheap money to do so, according to a report in *Forbes*. He added: "You could just focus on being very efficient (in the past). All of a sudden we are being disrupted."

SCOTT MCKAIN

"Craft took us by surprise," Lemann confessed.

Certainly, Lemann and AB InBev will respond to the challenge. What else would we expect them to do? And they are responding in a manner similar to the points suggested in the previous chapter. AB InBev and Lemann's team created a new business—Zx Ventures—with the goal of investing in innovations like craft beer, e-commerce, and home brewing. Lemann described this as "self-disruption."

"We hope this will be a model which we can build on," he said. "I'm not going to lie down and go away."[73]

By leveraging their unique connection to their customers—and by using their savvy understanding of the marketplace—Craft Haus can survive and thrive no matter what the AB InBev team chooses to do. Dave and Wyndee are small business entrepreneurs who think like iconic leaders.

THE CIRCLE CITY STEAK HOUSE

A smallish restaurant in a mid-sized city in the Midwest has proven you can go up against globally known competition and achieve iconic status.

Indianapolis, Indiana, has long been called the Circle City because the midpoint of the metropolis isn't a block like Times Square. Instead, the center of the city is Monument Circle.

In 1902, the Soldiers and Sailors Monument—a memorial 284.5 feet tall to honor Hoosiers who served in the Civil War—was dedicated in the middle of that circle. A few months later, Joe Stahr opened a tavern and buffet restaurant two blocks away and named it after the patron saint of sailors. He brought in a beautiful tiger-oak back-bar from Chicago. St. Elmo's was simply a small tavern with a standard menu. When the first Indianapolis 500 was held in 1911, St. Elmo's was already nine years old.

In 1946, Sam and Ike Roth purchased the restaurant and invited their brother Harry, who was an optometrist, to join them. Harry said he went from "eye glasses to bar glasses," and in 1956, when his brothers left the restaurant, Harry invited a lifelong friend, Isadore "Izzy" Rosen, to join him.

With Izzy's larger-than-life personality—a trait that served him well in his previous profession as a bookie—and Harry's quiet business skill, they made a terrific team. St. Elmo's became, according to their website, "a place where salesmen and tycoons came to seal the deal, where attorneys and politicians strategized and plotted, where coaches and players celebrated wins and lamented losses, where celebrities came to unwind from a show."[74]

It still is the place where those encounters occur in Indianapolis.

From 1947 to 1986, Harry and Izzy skillfully guided St. Elmo to continued success. They turned over the reins to veteran Indianapolis restauranteur Stephen Huse, who remains the present owner. In 1997, Huse partnered with his son, Craig, who is now the president of the corporation. Craig says his favorite quote is "A good restaurant serves its customers; a great restaurant entertains its guests."[75]

Local lore in Indianapolis has it that St. Elmo's is responsible for both a Super Bowl and a super concert.

The NFL holds its players combine—the event for scouting college players who are prospective pros—every year in Indianapolis. So many NFL owners, coaches, and executives loved dining at St. Elmo's during that event it helped Indianapolis secure that sport's championship game—one seen annually by a billion viewers around the world.

When the Rolling Stones were touring the United States a few years back, music industry veterans were surprised to see they were playing two consecutive nights in Indianapolis but only one show in much larger cities. Keith Richards is reported to have said the reason was they wanted to dine again a second night at St. Elmo's. (And they did!)

Celebrity appearances might be uncommon for most of the Midwest, but they're nothing new at St. Elmo's. The Wine Cellar Room is usually called the Peyton Manning Room because of his frequent visits there, even now that he's retired.

They also have a private dining area called the Card Room named in honor of Bon Jovi. "He and Cher dined with us many years ago and would play cards after their show," said Kirsten DeWitte, St. Elmo's private dining manager.[76]

Up on the second level of the restaurant is the private Huse Dining Room. Right outside the window is the iconic St. Elmo sign. Former Indiana governor and current United States Vice President Mike Pence often enjoys a good steak in the Huse Dining Room.

It's obvious St. Elmo's is a great place to eat in Indianapolis. *Forbes* named it one of the "10 Great Classic Restaurants Well Worth Visiting" in the world. And they've received the prestigious America's Classic award from the James Beard Foundation.

But what does this mean for your business?

Take a look at how St. Elmo's delivers on all Five Factors of Iconic Performance.

ST. ELMO'S *PLAYS OFFENSE*

Morton's, Ruth's Chris, and Fleming's make up three of the eleven steakhouses within a few of blocks of each other, all downtown in the Circle City. Yet you cannot get Craig Huse or his team to talk much about them. It's not that they are uninformed about their competition; it's that they are playing offense and choose not to focus on their "faceless opponents."

"There are fourteen other steakhouses operating just in downtown Indianapolis," Huse told me. "We focus inside our four walls—as there will always be competitors. Each new opening reminds us that we have to delight our guests each and every time. We cannot ride the coattails of our successful past into the future."

St. Elmo's *Gets Promise and Performance Right*

St. Elmo's makes a promise that is embodied in a comment from Craig Huse:

> Jim Nantz of CBS Sports, says that St. Elmo is his favorite restaurant in the world. Certainly, we are not the best restaurant in the world, but we are the best restaurant in Jim Nantz's world . . . and that is what we aspire to with each of our guests.

You can't be the favorite restaurant of such a well-traveled, experienced professional as iconic broadcaster Jim Nantz without *delivering exactly what you promise.*

Aspiring to be someone's favorite restaurant—and delivering the performance that's congruent with the promise—is a major element in what makes St. Elmo's iconic. And when your promise and performance are aligned in the right spot, customers can become your biggest advocates.

St. Elmo's leverages the willingness of their customers to recommend them through their Patron Saints program. "This recognizes some of our very best guests," Huse said. "These guests not only dine with us frequently, but they also have a sense of pride—they advocate for our restaurant to their friends, family, coworkers, and even the person sitting next to them on the airline."

Isn't it fascinating that this is not the typical loyalty program where points are accrued and exchanged for free meals? "A Patron Saint does not earn points or discounts because we don't want to devalue our relationship. We simply do the little things that prioritize these very special guests." Patron Saints have a special phone number for reservations, reserved table signs with their names on them, and "random acts of surprise and delight," as Huse put it. With that kind of recognition for guests, doesn't it make sense they would be vibrant advocates for St. Elmo's?

ST. ELMO'S *STOPPED SELLING*

When you visit Indianapolis, you may see reminders of the St. Elmo experience. However, you'll never see them hawking the restaurant in the manner that you'll observe from other local establishments and national chains in the city.

You don't become Jim Nantz's favorite restaurant, the place where Peyton Manning hangs out, where Jon Bon Jovi and Cher play cards, and the vice president enjoys a steak because you twisted their arms into coming and having dinner.

It's amazing that we've discussed St. Elmo's and I have yet to bring up their world-famous shrimp cocktail sauce! The amazing—and amazingly spicy, horseradish-laden—sauce is known around the world. It serves as a discussion point and conversation starter. Through this unique condiment, St. Elmo's has an element that engages customers. You might be asking: are younger professionals interested in a two-hour meal—typically with a hearty steak—in the restaurant's main dining room? After researching that issue, they opened the "1933 Lounge" above their traditional restaurant to ensure continued relevancy in a changing market. "We don't want to become known as your grandfather's steakhouse."

Younger professionals "want small plates and craft cocktails in an atmosphere conducive to relaxation and conversation, within sightlines of the bar. We tried to make this area a sexy juxtaposition to the black-suited service in the dining rooms on our main level," Huse said.

When combined with superior food and extraordinary service, they don't have to sell . . . because they *attract* customers of all generations.

ST. ELMO'S *GOES NEGATIVE*

Craig Huse—following in the tradition of his father—is committed to, and engaged with, his team of employees. He is constantly and aggressively seeking out

ICONIC

what is wrong so he can do what it takes to deliver for his customers.

Mark Sanborn, author of the best-selling book *The Fred Factor* and long-time friend of mine (who knows I am a big fan of St. Elmo's), was dining there on a recent trip to Indianapolis. My friend had a minor problem with his order. He texted me to say that while he loved almost everything about the experience to that point, there was just one slipup.

I immediately dropped Craig an email.

To Sanborn's (and my) surprise, before he could finish his meal, the St. Elmo's team leaped into action. Here's the text I received from my friend:

> Manager on duty came over and said the owner wanted
> to buy me some bourbon. Holy smokes. Btw, I just had
> the best bone-in ribeye I've ever eaten. Seriously perfect.

Certainly, every manager and every restaurant should jump to immediately fix any problem. However, my experience is that many don't want to hear the bad news. (Just look at how few owners or managers respond personally to complaints on social media. I have yet to receive any response to that negative review of the Mexican restaurant that I critiqued online.)

Because Huse encourages his team to look for the negative—and for others to share challenging feedback—they earn positive responses from customers like Mark Sanborn.

St. Elmo's Has a Culture of *Reciprocal Respect*

"My dad genuinely likes, respects, and values the St. Elmo staff—at every level, front of house, back of house, management—everyone," said Craig Huse. "Because of him, it's as natural as breathing for me."

"We provide an opportunity for service staff to earn a real income and we support them with training, business cards, making them the stars of the show—similar to professional sports and entertainment where the athlete or performer is highlighted. And we have group health insurance, short-term disability options, 401(k) plans, years of service recognition programs and events.

"Having seven-year old twins of my own (Sophia and Carson), I understand the sacrifices people in our industry make to work and provide for their families," Huse continues. "Nights, weekends, schedules constantly being adjusted to meet guest demand—all of these are taxing on the children and spouses of our service professionals. I'm certainly much more sympathetic to this reality and grateful for their commitment."[77]

My experience has been that the team at St. Elmo's—among the longest tenured staff at any restaurant I've ever visited—have great respect for Craig Huse because of the great respect he has for them.

ICONIC SUCCESS

Managers and staff have bad days and employees fail to deliver for customers on occasion. I'm certain that St. Elmo's is no different.

However, no small part of their achievements spring from the perspective that they bring to their business. "My father—Steve Huse—and I refer to all of us as *stewards*. We are here guiding this iconic steak joint through a period of time, with the goal of leaving it in a much better place than when we arrived. Stewardship versus a job or an investment leads to a lasting legacy. St. Elmo belongs to the city of Indianapolis. We are simply its stewards," Craig Huse told me.

Consider the thousands of elegant restaurants in the United States—hundreds alone in just in midtown Manhattan, for example. Yet, according to a report in *Restaurant Business Magazine,* this single location on Illinois Street in Indianapolis is the nineteenth top-earning establishment in America.[78] (Raking in $21.3 million in 2017, St. Elmo's had higher gross sales than New York City's Tavern on the Green or 21 Club.[79]) St. Elmo's isn't just a distinctive Midwestern restaurant. They're an iconic business that can teach any organization about the Five Factors that are the message of this book:

1. **Play Offense**
2. **Get Promise and Performance Right**

3. **Stop Selling**
4. **Go Negative**
5. **Reciprocal Respect**

NOT EVEN ICONIC BUSINESSES ARE PERFECT

Every business has problems. Even ones who proclaim—like Nokia's CEO—they "didn't do anything wrong" make mistakes. None of the organizations or leaders in this book are perfect.

Some, like the Fairmont Scottsdale Princess, are rapidly ascending. More, like St. Elmo's, are sustaining and enhancing their position. Others, like United Airlines, are trying to reestablish their status. However, they are all attempting to be at the forefront of customer attraction and loyalty. They have expanded profitability while positively engaging their employees. All must keep striving to enhance their execution in order to be considered esteemed and relevant organizations.

- It's not about longevity. Whether you are just launching your enterprise—like Dave and Wyndee Forrest—or you've been around since the early 1900s—like St. Elmo's Steakhouse, you can be an iconic organization.
- It's not about size. You don't have to be Amazon to become iconic. (Even *it* started small!)

- It's not about location. You don't have to have a pristine piece of property like the Fairmont Scottsdale Princess to attract customers.
- It's not about glitz and glamour. As we've seen, you can be a chimney sweep and establish an iconic business—and even became a millionaire.
- *It's all about what you **do**. . . and **how** you do it.*

When you create distinction in your industry and apply the five factors you have studied here, you can join the rare group of iconic leaders who are the future of business.

My wish is that you do.

Endnotes

Chapter 1

1 Rob Haskell, "Disney CEO Bob Iger on Taking the Biggest Risk of His Career," *Vogue*, April 12, 2018, https://www.vogue.com/article/bob-iger-disney-ceo-interview-vogue-may-2018-issue.

2 Jim Rohn, "Success Must Be Attracted, Not Pursued," *Success* Magazine, September 4, 2016, https://www.success.com/article/rohn-success-must-be-attracted-not-pursued.

Chapter 2

3 Serena Ng, "P&G to Shed More Than Half Its Brands," *Wall Street Journal*, August 1, 2014; https://www.wsj.com/articles/procter-gamble-posts-higher-profit-on-cost-cutting-1406892304.

4 Greg McKeown, *Essentialism: The Disciplined Pursuit of Less* (New York: Crown Business, 2014), 16.

5 David Edelstein, "Blockers Is a Raunchy Farce That's Fundamentally Sweet," *Vulture,* April 5, 2018, http://www.vulture.com/2018/04/blockers-review.html.

6 Cheryl L. Grady, Anthony R. McIntosh, M. Natasha Rajah and Fergus I. M. Craik, "Neural correlates of the episodic encoding of pictures and words," Proceedings of the National Academy of Sciences of the United States of America, March 3, 1998, http://www.pnas.org/content/95/5/2703.

7 "Mastering Omni-Channel B2B Customer Engagement," Forrester Research (commissioned by Accenture Interactive and SAP Hybris), October 2015, https://www.accenture.com/_acnmedia/Accenture/Conversion-Assets/DotCom/Documents/Global/PDF/Digital_3/Accenture-Mastering-Omni-Channel-B2B-Customer-Engagement-Report.pdf (emphasis mine).

Chapter 3

8 Liz Hilton Segel, in an interview for "Playing offense: What it takes to drive growth," McKinsey.com, March 2017, https://www.mckinsey.com/business-functions/marketing-and-sales/our-insights/playing-offense-what-it-takes-to-drive-growth.

9 Catherine Clifford, "How Amazon founder Jeff Bezos went from the son of a teen mom to the world's richest person," CNBC; October 27, 2017, https://www.cnbc.com/2017/10/27/how-amazon-founder-jeff-bezos-went-from-the-son-of-a-teen-mom-to-the-worlds-richest-person.html (emphasis mine).

10 Peter King, "His Career Forged in Darkness, Eagles Coach Doug Pederson Ready for Spotlight of Super Bowl 52,", *Sports Illustrated* MMQB, January 28, 2018, https://www.si.com/nfl/2018/01/29/doug-pederson-philadelphia-eagles-super-bowl-52-brett-favre-peter-king.

11 Laura Morgan Roberts, Gretchen Spreitzer, Jane E. Dutton, Robert E. Quinn, Emily Heaphy, and Brianna Barker, "How to Play to Your Strengths," *Harvard Business Review,* January 2005, https://hbr.org/2005/01/how-to-play-to-your-strengths.

12 Bob Glauber, "Super Bowl LII: Doug Pederson's aggressive coaching makes him the toast of Philadelphia," *Newsday*, February 5, 2018, https://www.newsday.com/sports/columnists/bob-glauber/super-bowl-eagles-doug-pederson-1.16548722.

13 Ibid.

14 Sophie Quinton, "The Economic Case for Paying Your Cashiers $40K a Year," Citylab.com, March 20, 2013, https://www.citylab.com/life/2013/03/economic-case-paying-your-cashiers-40k-year/5037/.

15 Ibid (emphasis mine).

16 Ibid.

17 Ben Parr, "7 Ways to Capture Someone's Attention," *Harvard Business Review*, March 3, 2015, https://hbr.org/2015/03/7-ways-to-capture-someones-attention.

18 Gordon Tredgold, "7 Truths About Accountability That You Need To Know," Inc. Brand View, Inc.com, September 14, 2017, https://www.inc.com/gordon-tredgold/7-truths-about-accountability-that-you-need-to-kno.html.

19 Peter Bregman, "The Right Way to Hold People Accountable," Harvard Business Review, January 11, 2016,

https://hbr.org/2016/01/the-right-way-to-hold-people-accountable.

20 Kim Harrison, "Why employee recognition is so important—and what you can do about it," "Cutting Edge," Cutting Edge Public Relations, https://cuttingedgepr.com/free-articles/employee-recognition-important/.

21 Tobias J. Moskowitz and L. Jon Wertheim, "Does Defense Really Win Championships?" Freakonomics.com, January 20, 2012, http://freakonomics.com/2012/01/20/does-defense-really-win-championships/.

22 Ibid.

Chapter 4

23 William J. McEwen, "Promises, Promises," *Gallup Business Journal;* November 19, 2001, http://news.gallup.com/businessjournal/169/promises-promises.aspx.

24 Christopher Koch, "Looks Can Deceive: Why Perception and Reality Don't Always Match," *Scientific American Mind*, July 1, 2010, https://www.scientificamerican.com/article/looks-can-deceive/.

25 Jenna McGregor, "Stepping out of Steve Jobs' shadow, Tim Cook champions the promise of Apple,"*Chicago Tribune*, August 15, 2016, http://www.chicagotribune.com/bluesky/technology/ct-tim-cook-apple-20160815-story.html.

26 Kevin Tofel, "Love it or hate it, 97% of Apple Watch customers are satisfied in product survey," ZD Net, July 20, 2015, https://www.zdnet.com/article/apple-watch-satisfaction-survey-results/.

27 Facebook posting from John T. Howard; used with permission

28 Julia Belluz, "The SEC charged Elizabeth Holmes, CEO of Theranos, with fraud," Vox, March 14, 2018, https://www.vox.com/science-and-health/2018/3/14/17120606/theranos-sec-charges-fraud-elizabeth-holmes.

29 Ibid

30 Zoe Kleinman, "Uber: The scandals that drove Travis Kalanick out," BBC News, June 21, 2017, http://www.bbc.com/news/technology-40352868.

31 "Our Story," Kasita.com, https://kasita.com/our-story/.

32 "The 25 Most Disruptive Companies of the Year",' *Inc.* Magazine, https://www.inc.com/profile/kasita.

33 Chris Weber, "Introducing Uber Health, Removing Transportation as a Barrier to Care," Uber Newsroom, March 1, 2018, https://www.uber.com/newsroom/uber-health/?state=V6IhuDwdOAL5idTuQnGDWQoZyw3XGZYD7aHb_S6OQeA%3D&_csid=iGbUjU7kRTc0zIwu-puGXg#_.

34 Ayelet Gneezy & Nicholas Epley, "Worth Keeping but Not Exceeding: Asymmetric Consequences of Breaking Versus Exceeding Promises," Social Psychological and Personality Science, May 8, 2014, http://journals.sagepub.com/doi/abs/10.1177/1948550614533134 (emphasis mine).

35 Ibid.

Chapter 5

36 Ian Altman, "How to Sell Like an Expert, Not Like a Salesperson," Inc.com, https://www.inc.com/ian-altman/how-to-sell-like-an-expert-not-like-a-salesperson.html.

37 Leigh Ashton, "Sales Is Not About Selling," NASP.com, http://www.nasp.com/article/B37B4EC2-D838/sales-is-not-about-selling.html (emphasis mine).

38 Philippe Aussant, "6 Stats That Show How the Customer Experience Impacts Your Bottom Line," iPerceptions.com, June 14, 2017, https://www.iperceptions.com/blog/customer-experience-statistics (emphasis mine).

39 Interview with Lynn Vojvodich, "The Customer Experience Journey," McKinsey & Company, December 2014, https://www.mckinsey.com/business-functions/marketing-and-sales/our-insights/marketing--sales-the-customer-experience-journey.

40 Ibid

41 Gary Vaynerchuk, "The One Thing I Didn't Clarify Enough in *Jab, Jab, Jab, Right Hook*," *Gary Vaynerchuk blog*, 2016 https://www.garyvaynerchuk.com/the-one-thing-i-didnt-clarify-enough-in-jab-jab-jab-right-hook/.

42 Ibid.

43 Daniel Cressey, "Brain Scans of Rappers Shed Light on Creativity," *Nature*, November 15, 2012, https://www.nature.com/news/brain-scans-of-rappers-shed-light-on-creativity-1.11835.

Chapter 6

44 Sarah Elizabeth Adler, "The Power of Negative Thinking," *Atlantic,* Jan/Feb 2018, https://www.theatlantic.com/magazine/archive/2018/01/the-power-of-negativity/546560/#2.

45 John Humphreys, "Weakness or Opportunity," MIT *Sloan Management Review,* Spring 2007, https://sloanreview.mit.edu/article/weakness-or-opportunity/.

46 Jennifer Kaplan, "The Inventor of Customer Satisfaction Surveys Is Sick of Them, Too," *Bloomberg News*, May 4, 2016, https://www.bloomberg.com/news/articles/2016-05-04/tasty-taco-helpful-hygienist-are-all-those-surveys-of-any-use.

47 Frederick F. Reichheld, *The Loyalty Effect: The Hidden Force Behind Growth, Profits and Lasting Value* (Boston: Harvard Business School Press, 1996).

48 Ibid.

49 Daniel Schneider, Matt Berent, Randall Thomas, and Jon Krosnick, "Measuring Customer Satisfaction and Loyalty: Improving the 'Net-Promoter' Score," June 2008, http://www.van-haaften.nl/images/documents/pdf/Measuring%20customer%20satisfaction%20and%20loyalty.pdf.

50 Andrew J. Elliot and Marcy A. Church, University of Rochester, and St. Mary's University, "A Motivational Analysis of Defensive Pessimism and Self-Handicapping," *Journal of Personality* from Blackwell Publishing, June 2003, http://persweb.wabash.

edu/facstaff/hortonr/articles%20for%20class/elliot%20self-handicapping.pdf.

51 Joaquín Selva, "The Upside of Defensive Pessimism: The Potential Benefit of Anxiety," *Journal of Positive Psychology*, August 14, 2017, https://positivepsychologyprogram.com/defensive-pessimism/ (emphasis mine).

52 Ibid.

53 Ibid.

54 Dan McGowan, "Nalli: St. Vincent Adapting by 'Disrupting Ourselves,'" *Inside Indiana Business*, May 8, 2018, http://www.insideindianabusiness.com/story/38142783/nalli-st-vincent-adapting-by-disrupting-ourselves (emphasis mine).

55 Jason Boog, "Elon Musk: 'Pay attention to negative feedback, and solicit it, particularly from friends'," *Adweek*, March 21, 2013, http://www.adweek.com/digital/elon-musk-pay-attention-to-negative-feedback-and-solicit-it-particularly-from-friends/.

56 Bill Murphy, Jr., "Why Every Leader Should Try Jeff Bezos's Infamous 'Question Mark Method'," Inc.com, June 1, 2017, https://www.inc.com/bill-murphy-jr/customer-service-jeff-bezos-question-mark-rule.html.

Chapter 7

57 Bernard Marr, "Why Great Employees Quit." CNBC.com, February 27, 2017, https://www.cnbc.com/2017/02/27/why-great-employees-quit.html (emphasis mine).

58 Christine Porath, "The silent killer of workplace happiness, productivity, and health is a lack of basic civility," Quartz.com, September 15, 2017; https://qz.com/1079344/the-silent-killer-of-workplace-happiness-productivity-and-health-is-a-lack-of-basic-civility/.

59 Ibid, (emphasis mine).

60 Ibid.

61 Amy Adkins and Brandon Rigoni, "Managers: Millennials Want Feedback, but Won't Ask for It," Gallup, June 2, 2016,

http://news.gallup.com/businessjournal/192038/managers-millennials-feedback-won-ask.aspx.

[62] "100 Best Companies to Work For" *Fortune*, http://fortune.com/best-companies/.

[63] Jessica Dickler, "These are the best places to work in 2018," CNBC.com, December 6, 2017, https://www.cnbc.com/2017/12/05/the-10-best-companies-to-work-for-in-2018.html.

[64] "Salesforce: Great Places to Work Review," Great Place to Work Institute, 2018, http://reviews.greatplacetowork.com/salesforce.

[65] "Wegman's: Great Places to Work Review," Great Place to Work Institute, 2018, http://reviews.greatplacetowork.com/wegmans-food-markets-inc.

[66] Nathan Gotch, "How to Fire a Toxic Client," Gotch SEO, https://www.gotchseo.com/how-to-fire-a-client/.

Chapter 8

[67] Antoine Gara, "Jorge Paulo Lemann Says Era of Disruption in Consumer Brands Caught 3G Capital by Surprise," *Fortune*, April 30, 2018, https://www.forbes.com/sites/antoinegara/2018/04/30/jorge-paulo-lemann-says-era-of-disruption-in-consumer-brands-caught-3g-capital-by-surprise/#4721bca51f9b.

[68] Adam Lashinsky and David Meyer, "Steel Twist, Facebook Privacy, Autonomy Conviction," *Fortune* CEO Daily, May 1, 2018, http://fortune.com/2018/05/01/steel-tariffs-whatsapp-privacy-autonomy-conviction-ceo-daily-for-may-1-2018/.

[69] Lauren Dixon, "3 Steps to Align Culture with Business Strategy," *Talent Economy*, August 31, 2016, http://www.talenteconomy.io/2016/08/31/3-steps-to-align-culture-with-business-strategy-3/.

[70] Ibid.

[71] Linden Brown, "10 steps for HR: how to build a strong customer culture," *Inside HR,* November 17, 2015, https://www.insidehr.com.au/10-steps-to-building-a-customer-focused-culture/.

72 Feann Torr, "'No reason' for dieselgate class action, says VW," *Motoring*, November 8, 2017, https://www.motoring.com.au/no-reason-for-dieselgate-class-action-says-vw-109733/.

Conclusion

73 Antoine Gara, "Jorge Paulo Lemann Says Era of Disruption in Consumer Brands Caught 3G Capital By Surprise," *Forbes*, April 30, 2018, https://www.forbes.com/sites/antoinegara/2018/04/30/jorge-paulo-lemann-says-era-of-disruption-in-consumer-brands-caught-3g-capital-by-surprise/#11bda62f1f9b.

74 https://www.stelmos.com/about/history/

75 Jill Phillips, "5 Questions: St. Elmo's Craig Huse strives to carry on tradition," *Indianapolis Star*, January 25, 2014, https://www.indystar.com/story/money/2014/01/25/5-questions-st-elmos-craig-huse-strives-to-carry-on-tradition-/4894795/.

76 Kyle Inskeep, "The Suite Life: St. Elmo Steak House," Fox 59 News, February 19, 2018, http://fox59.com/2018/02/19/the-suite-life-st-elmo-steakhouse/.

77 Ibid.

78 "The Top 100 Independents," *Restaurant Business Magazine*, 2017, http://www.restaurantbusinessonline.com/top-100-independents.

79 Liz Biro, "2 more steakhouses are coming to Downtown Indianapolis," *Indianapolis Star*, September 12, 2017, https://www.indystar.com/story/entertainment/2017/09/07/2-more-steakhouses-coming-downtown-indianapolis/641878001/.

ACKNOWLEDGMENTS

Extraordinary thanks to my friend and publisher, Jonathan Merkh. It was an honor to have worked with you through the years—and it's even more of a privilege to reunite under your imprint at Forefront Books.

Thanks as well to Geoffrey Stone. Your insight and gentle hand through the editing process has been appreciated from my first book to this latest one.

This book would not have happened without the dedication and belief of Shelley McKain Erwin, chief operating officer of the Distinction Institute and Distinctive Presentations. Shelley makes it all happen—from coordinating my crazy schedule to all things design and Internet-based. And the fact that she's the world's greatest sister is pretty cool too.

I also appreciate the others in our small organization—especially the work of Benjamin Amick, who edits video and audio, contributes to our website, helps keep the wheels on the business, and does an all-around great job.

Thanks, too, to Perry Cremeans for his diligent efforts for so many years.

Each year in Las Vegas, the Ultimate Business Summit is held to provide entrepreneurs the opportunity to grow their business and themselves. My partners and friends, Larry Winget and Randy Pennington, make this a professional privilege and personal delight. I'm grateful for the opportunity to work together with such terrific pals.

I am indebted to my clients at corporations and associations across the nation and around the world. In addition, I want to express my appreciation for the amazing people at the speakers bureaus who keep my calendar full.

Jason Bradshaw at Volkswagen Group Australia is an incredible client and remarkable friend. Thank you for the opportunity to share with your team and learn from your significant expertise.

Thanks, too, for the friendship and dynamic leadership I've experienced with Michael Bartsch, managing director of VW Group Australia. His innovative concepts—like positioning the service department at the front end of the dealership—have provoked much of the thought you see reflected here.

Jack Miller at Fairmont Scottsdale Princess is the epitome of leadership. You have endured tragedy, engaged your team, excited your community, and exuded the positive spirit the world needs. Thank you for allowing me to be a small part of that.

Craig Huse of St. Elmo's was kind to share his insights about my favorite restaurant in America. I appreciate both his willingness to participate and the extraordinary experiences I've enjoyed as a customer of his for many years.

Thank you to my colleagues in Speakers Roundtable. It is such an honor to join you as a part of the most esteemed association of individuals in professional speaking.

There are so many pals in the world of professional speaking and publishing that I'm reticent to name any individuals for fear of accidentally excluding someone! I will make special mention of Scott Stratten in thanks for our Speak and Spill group of speakers. Scott's friendship is extraordinary—and he has brought together a highly diverse and remarkable group of professionals who have become great friends. Thanks, Scott, for adding so much to the texture of my life through these wonderful associations.

I would like to extend a special note of gratitude to the great guys and consummate professionals that I am so honored to call friends—the Oak Ridge Boys. I first met these amazing men in my teens, and they still inspire me to this day. Joe, Duane, William Lee, and Richard—and road manager, Darrick—I am grateful for your friendship.

Heartfelt appreciation to the best buddies a guy could have—my pals in the band, Diamond Rio. Thanks to Brian Prout, Dana Williams, Gene Johnson, Jimmy Olander, Dan Truman, and Marty Roe. You guys rock! (But not too much—you're a *country* band!)

My gratitude as well to the many authors and speakers who have given me ideas and assisted in the development of the concept of this book.

My deepest appreciation, too, to my two stepsons, Corbin and Faron, and Corbin's wife, Amber, and their newest additions to our family, young Calvin and Lydia!

Finally, my heartfelt gratitude to my wonderful wife, Tammy, for being such a loving and gentle presence in my life. It's great being teammates through life together with you.

Finally, last but certainly not least, thanks to *you,* the reader, for taking your time to absorb *Iconic*. I sincerely hope it will be of value to you.

DEDICATION

In chapter 3 of this book, I recounted the story of how I was wowed by my friend, Gerard Mauvis, who devoured my book *Create Distinction* and then asked, "What's next?" That was the question that inspired the writing of this book.

Gerard was an enthusiastic supporter—and implementer—of the principles of creating distinction and growing into iconic status. Alongside his leader and close friend, Jack Miller, Gerard gave his all into growing the Fairmont Scottsdale Princess from a respected resort into a globally iconic property.

Gerard also delivered to my wife and me some of the greatest customer experiences that we've ever had. He truly "walked his talk" and was one of the most consistent leaders whom I've ever had the privilege of knowing.

In September 2016, Gerard Mauvis tragically lost his life in an accident. He left behind a wonderful wife, Marlee, and sons, Will, Harrison, and daughter, Demi.

Following the tragedy, Jack Miller said, "Gerard's zest for life, his love of family and friends, and his contributions to our resort, community, and industry will be missed. I personally feel a loss of partnership as he was so much a part of what we have created over the past five years. Although we are saddened, we have the deep joy of remembering his love of life and adventurous spirit. Rest in peace, dear friend." These are my sentiments exactly.

With deep appreciation and humble respect for his memory, I dedicate this book to Gerard Mauvis in thanks for his integrity and his inspiration.

Scott McKain
May 1, 2018
Las Vegas, Nevada

About the Author

Scott McKain's experiences have been diverse and remarkable.

From playing the villain in a Werner Herzog movie that esteemed film critic Roger Ebert named as one of the fifty great movies in the history of the cinema, to being inducted into the Professional Speakers Hall of Fame, from having been chosen (along with Zig Ziglar, Dale Carnegie, and Seth Godin) to be one of about thirty members of the Sales and Marketing Hall of Fame, to a decade as a globally syndicated television commentator on the entertainment scene, it's not a stretch to say Scott McKain's life has been distinctive.

He has spoken on platforms in all fifty US states and twenty-one countries. His audience members have ranged from a president on the White House lawn to farmers in a small hut with a dirt floor in Brazil. His clients include the icons of global business: SAP, Cisco, Apple, VW, Fairmont, CDW, Canyon Ranch, and many more.

He is the founder of the Distinction Institute and is one of the most requested and iconic professional speakers in the world.

He and his wife, Tammy, live in Las Vegas, Nevada.

For More Information

We would love to hear—and share—your stories about iconic organizations and leaders! Visit IconicBusinessBook.com and join our community!

If you would like more information on creating distinction and becoming iconic, access our resources at: DistinctionNation.com. You'll find videos, white papers, and even a free audio training course on how to create personal distinction. It's all there for you.

Join leading companies like Apple, SAP, BMW, Cisco, CDW, Lilly, and many more—have Scott McKain speak to your next event!

Contact Shelley@ScottMcKain.com for more information — go to ScottMcKain.com — or, call us at +1-800-838-6980. We would love to work with you to make your next meeting iconic!

OTHER BOOKS
BY SCOTT MCKAIN:

ALL Business Is Show Business!

What Customers REALLY Want

Create Distinction
(originally published as *The Collapse of Distinction*)

Seven Tenets of Taxi Terry

ALL Business is STILL Show Business!
(15th Anniversary Edition)

The New Americans
Recent Immigration and American Society

Edited by
Steven J. Gold and Rubén G. Rumbaut

A Series from LFB Scholarly

Ethnic Identification among Urban Latinos
Language and Flexibility

Rosalyn Negrón

LFB Scholarly Publishing LLC
El Paso 2011

Library of Congress Cataloging-in-Publication Data

Negrón, Rosalyn, 1978-
Ethnic identification among urban Latinos : language and flexibility /
Rosalyn Negrón.
p. cm. -- (The new Americans : recent immigration and American
society)
Includes bibliographical references and index.
ISBN 978-1-59332-468-1 (hardcover : alk. paper)
1. Hispanic Americans--Ethnic identity. 2. Hispanic Americans--
Languages. 3. Hispanic Americans--Cultural assimilation. I. Title.
E184.S75N44 2011
973'.0468--dc23

2011021130

ISBN 978-1-59332-468-1

Printed on acid-free 250-year-life paper.

Manufactured in the United States of America.

Table of Contents

List of Tables

List of Figures

List of Maps

xi

Acknowledgements

My deepest appreciation goes to the eleven men and women whose stories and conversations I share in this book. The advice and feedback of several supportive individuals have helped this book along at various stages of its development. I am especially grateful to Drs. H. Russell Bernard, Christopher McCarty, Gerald Murray, Diana Boxer, Tim Sieber, Stacey Giroux, Mark House and Amber Wutich. I am indebted to Emily Wandrei for her research assistance and keen editorial eye. Many thanks also due to Nathaniel Murray and Sanja Martin for their research assistance. Finally, thank you to the National Science Foundation for funding this research.

CHAPTER 1

Latinos & Ethnic Flexibility

INTRODUCTION

Some of the liveliest discussions I have had in my classes at the
University of Massachusetts Boston have been on the topic of ethnic
flexibility. Ethnic flexibility is the use of distinct ethnic categories or
distinct levels of a category across social contexts. I usually broach the
subject by asking my students, "Who among you have found yourself
switching your ethnic identification depending on where you are and
who you are talking to?" Though many hands shoot up, many remain
un-extended. Of the students who don't raise their hands, most are
unaccustomed to thinking of themselves as ethnically distinct. Perhaps
their family histories in the U.S. go back hundreds of years. Others,
whose great-great and great-grandparents immigrated to the U.S. from
Europe at the turn of the 20th century, have never quite thought of
themselves as anything other than white and American, and hence as
"having no ethnicity." But the possibility of developing a fluid ethnic
identity is an attractive one, particularly because of the opportunities
for diverse human connections that it seems to afford. One student,
who hadn't seen herself as having multiple ethnic identifications, once
asked, "I would love to be able to do that. How does someone become
more ethnically flexible?"

In this study I explore this question, further examining the contexts
and ways in which ethnic flexibility is exercised in daily interactions.
My discoveries during these explorations reflect parallels in my own
experience as a Latina who came to the U.S. as a nine-year-old child. I
did not necessarily set out to explore these parallels, as on a personal
quest, but was certainly informed by my own experiences, as well as
those of my family members. I was born in Puerto Rico, to a Puerto

Rican father and a Dominican mother. My mother has admitted that she identifies as Puerto Rican for her own reasons. Ethnicity for me has always been a matter of context and flexibility: Puerto Rican, Dominican, both of these, Latina, American, and a cosmopolitan embodiment of all of these.

Quite often I am asked to explain my ethnicity and appearance to others. Colombian, Egyptian, Pakistani, Venezuelan, Brazilian, Moroccan; I have been different things to different people. Undoubtedly, this quality, to be for others what they want to see in me, has helped me in my research. My ethnicity is not easily identifiable by my appearance alone. When I speak English my Spanish accent is barely detectable and when I speak Spanish my Puerto Rican accent is lost in the phonological mix that it has become, with the adoption of non-Puerto Rican elements of stress and intonation. Only the keenest ears can hear me transform /r/ into /l/ or delete intervocalic and syllable final /s/ as is characteristic of the Puerto Rican dialect. I have acquired aspects of my speech, my style, my behavior, and even my perceptions from my many encounters, purposely sought or otherwise, with diversity. Indeed, this seems to be key to developing a flexible ethnic identity: the more culturally, linguistically, and ethnically diverse our interactions and relationships are the more likely we will develop fluid ethnic identities.

It is something of a sociological fact that people possess multiple identities or identifications that are invoked situationally. Context determines which of several social categories people make salient to achieve interactional goals. The same applies to seemingly uniform, deeply sentimental identities like those based on ethnicity. We know for example that through language crossing, a person may take on an out-group ethnic identification (Bucholtz, 1999; Cutler, 1999; Rampton, 1995). Such moves are often viewed with suspicion or derision because they flout shared concepts about who the 'authentic' members of such categories are. For example, Sweetland (2002) documented one white woman's expert use of African American Vernacular English (AAVE) in her daily interactions. AAVE was the code that she felt most comfortable with and reflected her close, life-long relationships with African American friends, neighbors, and significant others. Because boundaries between presumed in-groups and out-groups are situationally activated, it is problematic to think of any one group as an essentialized, bounded set (Bailey, 2001).

Today, an increasing number of people regularly switch from ethnicity to ethnicity in normal discourse, in an attempt to maximize their economic and political interests. If the 2000 Census is any indication, more and more Americans are rejecting the notion that only one ethnic category can best describe them (Morning, 2003). So while the situational use of ethnicity has long been recognized in the literature on ethnicity (Barth, 1969; Cohen, 1974; Gluckman, 1940,1958; Kaufert, 1977; Mitchell, 1974; Nagata, 1974; Okamura, 1981; Paden 1967; Padilla, 1984; Patterson, 1975), never before has the potential for developing broad ethnic repertoires been available to so many. Considering the international scale of countless interactions and the incredible ethnic diversity of many local contexts, it is clear that developing a fluid ethnic self has its advantages in the age of globalization.

Ethnic flexibility involves an awareness one's ethnic repertoire and knowledge about the rights, privileges and duties linked to each identification. Ethnic flexibility also involves an understanding of the ways in which ethnic markers like language or the use of ethnic labels elicit responses in others in particular contexts. While ethnic flexibility is increasingly relevant in today's ethnically mixed societies, it is not necessarily something that everyone does or is aware of. That some (or how some) become more adept at this than others will be explored in this study by focusing on the experiences of New York City Latinos. The choice of Latinos was both methodologically and theoretically driven. Because language use is a key way in which people invoke their ethnicity, my Spanish-language fluency allowed me access to the ethno-linguistic identifications of Spanish-speakers. In addition, the U.S. Latino pan-ethnicity includes at least nineteen dialects (Lipski, 2004), socio-historical roots in nearly every continent, and distinct immigration histories within the U.S. - placing Latinos in an especially advantageous position to manipulate ethnic and linguistic categories, expectations, and assumptions, and making Latinos an ideal group for examining the salience and negotiation of multiple ethnic identifications and the development of ethnic flexibility.

Frequently, when I talk about ethnic flexibility in presentations and conversations, people wonder how it is possible for a person to switch their ethnicity. How can anyone meaningfully switch "who they are," their *identity*? Ethnic identity is a multi-dimensional construct, which in past studies has been described as ways of 'being,' 'feeling,' 'doing' and/or 'knowing.' Here I emphasize the 'doing' and 'knowing' dimensions of ethnicity. In other words, I am most interested in the perspectives and behaviors associated with ethnic flexibility. These ways of knowing and doing can often act independently of non-instrumental self-understanding. Therefore, ethnic flexibility should not be understood as some sort of mysterious intra-psychic transformation. At the individual level, it can be an automatic shift between multiple, situationally appropriate frames of reference, or ways of *seeing*. I also refer to this shift as *cross-cultural fluency*. Other times, it is the willful manipulation of categories and markers, or ways of *doing*. Kinesics, dance, music, athletics and other embodied and expressive performances of ethnicity are important ways of signaling ethnic belonging and cultural competence. So too are those practices associated with particular trades, crafts, cooking traditions, and games. Interwoven throughout all of these activities, and assisting their performance, is language. Knowledge of multiple linguistic codes makes accessible multiple sources of cultural knowledge and creates opportunities to develop multi-cultural competence. Thus, along with cross-cultural fluency, linguistic flexibility – which entails knowing multiple languages, dialects, and speech styles – is crucial for cultivating and performing ethnic flexibility. *Doing* ethnicity can also include the discursive expression of ethnicity, through invocations of ethnic frames of reference, or the use of ethnic labels to describe oneself or others. Thus, cross-cultural fluency and linguistic flexibility are crucial for cultivating and expressing ethnic flexibility.

Like all skills, ethnic flexibility benefits from both practice and predisposition. However, this statement comes with an important caveat: Waters (1990) has pointed out that European Americans have ethnic options not available to African Americans and other under-served ethnic groups in the U.S. – such as the option to not make their ethnicity relevant at all. Dark skin, and other racialized physical features, limits the extent to which some individuals can develop broad ethnic repertoires. On the other hand, without linguistic flexibility and limited cross-cultural fluency some European Americans' options may also be limited – particularly for those who do not see themselves as "having an ethnicity". Still, Waters' insights point to another important dimension of ethnic flexibility, physical appearance, or *image*, which can enhance or hinder ethnic flexibility.

In this research I will consider these three dimensions that best describe and explain ethnic flexibility: cross-cultural fluency, linguistic flexibility, and image. In so doing, I will highlight the case of

Roberto,[1] a person with an exceptional penchant for ethnic flexibility. Roberto, a bilingual and multi-dialectal Venezuelan born resident of Queens, was a 36-year-old entrepreneur when I met him during my fieldwork in New York City. He had lived in the U.S. for most of his life, and forged relationships with people from a range of backgrounds, including a multi-ethnic wife of Puerto Rican and African American descent. Roberto also had an ethnically ambiguous physical appearance. In other words, on first impression, and without hearing him speak, one could not easily guess his ethnic background. This ambiguity enabled him to tailor his ethnic self-identification depending on with whom he was talking, the context, and interactional goal. While Roberto habitually used the Venezuelan label when asked about his ethnic background, his social network and language use reflected important Puerto Rican and American influences. His case raises important questions about the reliability of habitual (biographical) ethnic labels as meaningfully descriptors of individuals, and especially as a means of predicting loyalties and behaviors. Clarissa, a young woman I met during my research, provides another example of how unreliable biographical ethnic labels can be. When I questioned how she identified herself, Clarissa, a fair-skinned woman of Euro-Puerto Rican descent stated, "I'm black." Clarissa supported this claim by describing how many of the people in her life were African American: her closest friends, the men she dated, her neighbors from childhood onward, etc.

It is clear, then, that the company we keep has important consequences for how we self-identify. A key argument I make here is that social networks reflect the ethnic identifications people adopt throughout a lifetime and influence the identifications they invoke during interaction. I propose that ethnic flexibility is more common among individuals with ethnically diverse social networks. Not only are social networks the sites in which people attain the cultural knowledge that informs their sense of belonging to an ethnic group, they are also "crucial environments for the activation of schemata, logics, and frames" (DiMaggio, 1997: 283) associated with specific ethnic identifications. I will illustrate this for Roberto and for Abel, the second key collaborator whose case I will examine in-depth here. Ecuadorian-born Abel was a 37-year old satellite TV salesman when I

---

[1] All names have been replaced with linguistically approximate pseudonyms to preserve the anonymity of research collaborators.

worked with him. His social network reflected his relationships with Latinos from various Latin American countries. Having lived and worked with immigrants from Argentina, Brazil, Colombia, the Dominican Republic and Uruguay, Abel had developed a certain cross-cultural fluency that connected him to people of different ethnic backgrounds. He had also learned phonological and intonational features of a few Spanish dialects – a skill he applied to his advantage during many interactions. Abel's cross-cultural fluency and linguistic flexibility made it possible for him to cross multiple ethnic boundaries, going beyond what he perceived to be the limits of his Ecuadorian ethnicity. While he felt strong sentimental attachments to his biographical ethnicity, he was keenly driven by instrumental goals to flexibly present his ethnic identity.

Ethnicity and Ethnic Identity

Ethnicity arises from the cognitive, human need to create conceptual categories and groupings in order to simplify and comprehend environmental complexity. The earliest classifiable *ethnic* differences likely arose between spatially isolated human groups, with each developing cultural patterns uniquely suited to their environment. To this day, ethnicity as a construct overlaps with cultural, regional, linguistic, and religious distinctions. Cohen (1978) argued that the emergence of ethnicity as an analytical construct in the field of anthropology marked the decline in usage of terms such as *tribe* for describing the groups anthropologists studied. While tribes were previously isolated and bounded units, in contemporary times these same groupings have *become* ethnic groups in the sense that they have become interrelated not only with other groups, but also with the state. Thus, ethnicity emphasizes the non-isolated, shifting nature of group boundaries. Barth (1969) argues that because ethnic distinctions persist even in the face of group boundary change, what defines the ethnic group is cognitive self-ascription and ascription by others.

Using this conceptualization as a platform, in its most basic sense, ethnic identity refers to the *self-ascription* part of ethnicity. It does not preclude that people can and may make multiple self-ascriptions, and it does not assume that any given person will have a *core* self-ascription or ethnic identity. Brubaker (2004: 44) argues that *identity*, has been employed to describe how individual and collective action is driven by *both* instrumental "structurally determined interests" and non-instrumental "particularistic, understandings of self." Rather than use the ambiguous identity term to do this conceptual and explanatory heavy lifting, he offers *identification* or *categorization* and *self-understanding* or *self-location* as alternatives. Following Brubaker, most of the behaviors described in this study are best described as *ethnic identification*, which denotes instrumental uses of ethnicity. As the data will show, in identifying or categorizing oneself to others, a person can act independently of any non-instrumental self-understanding. Without dismissing the importance of emotional attachments people have to symbols, networks, practices, etc. associated with an ethnic group the findings presented here shows the ways ethnicity is used situationally to achieve instrumental aims and forge social bonds.

Situational Ethnicity in the 20th Century

The concept of situational ethnicity (Paden, 1967; see Okamura, 1981) traces to the work of Max Gluckman and his students in urban Africa. In his work with the Zande of Sudan, Evans-Pritchard (1937) had observed that beliefs in witchcraft were invoked according to situational convenience. Building on this observation, Gluckman (1940, 1958) described what he called *situational selection*, in which people claimed membership in a group depending on the situation. Cohen (1974) also observed this phenomenon during his research in Africa, noting situations in which two or more people from different ethnic groups wished to signify the differences between themselves, especially when the groups represented different socioeconomic scales. These classic studies theorized ethnicity as a contextual process with both structural and cognitive dimensions. In cognitive terms, ethnicity is concerned with the categorization process by which people ascribe ethnicity to others based on their behaviors and cues. I would add that this also involves an element of performativity according to models and schemas associated with particular categories. Conversely, the structural aspect of situational ethnicity recognizes that ethnic group membership comes to index a predetermined set of actions and is constrained by local conditions. Situational ethnicity allows people to structure the meaning of relationships and interactions with others, as they determine which of various identities are most appropriate within a given social context. Therefore, a person may change or switch their ethnic identity with changes in social context. With these contextual changes in ethnic identification come changes in the ethnic markers used.

Owing in large part to this work, we now understand ethnicity not as static and bounded, but as both flexible and negotiated. However, the foundational research on situational ethnicity emerged from particular historical conditions and theoretical agendas. Indeed, much of that research was developed in plural societies of Africa and Asia at a time when globalization processes were not yet at the forefront of anthropologists' thinking on ethnicity. In the contemporary US, this backdrop of intense and intensifying globalization, significant and steady immigration, increasing inter-racial and inter-ethnic unions, and rising numbers of multi-racial people urge a refining of the situational approach to ethnicity. The definition of a *situation*, as bound to particular local structures, has ceded to a de-territorialized view of ethnic enactments (Appadurai, 1996). Where ethnic shifts were theorized as trans-situational or trans-local, we must now consider transnational, or even cyber-transnational ethnic negotiations. Where in past research there was an emphasis on vertical situational selection (e.g. African > Ghanaian > Accran > Asante), today it is increasingly common to hear of individuals who can move horizontally across multiple ethnic boundaries (e.g. Colombian / Puerto Rican / American).

In addressing such complexities, anthropologists have moved away from the old structural-cognitive view of situational ethnicity in favor of more holistic and interpretative approaches that posit ethnicity as "socially constructed." For the constructivist, ethnicity exists only insofar as it is co-produced and made relevant during social interaction. In this vein, ethnicity is not a thing in the world but rather an invented and imagined discursive product. While agreeing that ethnicity is not an ontological reality, scholars have pointed to the limits of this approach (Brubaker, 2004; Gil-White, 2001; Levine, 1999). In his own critique of the state of constructivism within anthropology, Levine (1999) notes, "The news is full of ethnic cleansing and genocide while the anthropologists stress that ethnicity is 'invented' and set out to 'decentre' the notion (1999: 165)." Brubaker (2004) suggests that constructivism has become so banal as to yield little of the theoretical friction from which new questions and directions emerge. He calls for constructivist scholars to go beyond "simply asserting that ethnicity, race, and nationhood are constructed... [and] help specify how they are constructed (Brubaker, 2004: 18)." Both Levine and Brubaker argue for a reaffirmation and expansion of the cognitive approach that characterized early research on situational ethnicity.

In contrast to previous research on situational ethnicity, this study pays special attention to the *ethnically flexible person* engaged in everyday acts of situational ethnicity. Situational ethnicity relates to "the significance of the concept of the social situation for analysis of the structure and process of ethnic relations" (Okamura, 1980: 452). Ethnic flexibility, on the other hand, highlights the significance of personal histories, relationships, goals, abilities, and cognitions for understanding how ethnicity is used as a resource in everyday life. Thus, I explore how people become adept at situational ethnic self-identification. By focusing on individuals and their everyday practices I hope to contribute to an understanding of how globalization processes take place *on the ground* in what Brubaker calls the 'rank-and-file construction of racial, ethnic, and national realities' (Brubaker, Loveman & Stamatov, 2004: 53).

Ethnic Flexibility and Switching of Ethnic Identification

Three dimensions best describe and explain ethnic flexibility: linguistic flexibility, cross-cultural fluency and image. Ethnic options are constrained or enabled by each of these dimensions, which work in combination to direct choices of ethnic identification and patterns of ethnic identification switching, henceforth EI switching.

Linguistic flexibility

Linguistic flexibility, including multi-lingualism, multi-dialectism, and multi-sociolectism, offers speakers exceptional control over ethnic self-presentation. People use language varieties at their disposal to signal a number of ethnic identifications. Code choice, including dialects and distinct styles within one language, emphasizing or hiding an accent, variations in intonation, and even accompanying speech with select kinesic cues, may all be used to indicate or invoke ethnic identifications.

In multi-ethnic settings language may be the least ambiguous criterion used to categorize people into ethnic groups. Even among those who share a common language, lexical, grammatical and phonological variations are important ways to distinguish between various national or regional populations. Among all the criteria that may determine membership in an ethnic group, language, then, is potentially the strongest cue to a person's ethnic identity (Fishman, 1977; Giles & Johnson, 1981). As Fishman and others explain, because a person's accent, style of speech, and language choice is learned and acquired, in contrast to inherited characteristics such as phenotypic appearance. Similarly, writing about Puerto Ricans, Rosario (1983, cited in Zentella, 1990a) writes: *"el ser puertorriqeño envuelve el conservar vivo el idioma corriente de nuestro pueblo"* ('being Puerto Rican entails the live conservation of the common language of our people'). The loss of knowledge of a native language is even thought to result in the loss of one's original group identity (Pool, 1979 in Eastman, 1981). For some, claiming the right to identify with a group - despite a lack of knowledge of the group's language – has been labeled *pseudo-ethnicity* (Seda Bonilla, 1975). These claims are problematic, of course, as many U.S. -born, non-Spanish speaking Latinos demonstrate when they assert culture and ancestry to defend their claims of membership in the Latino pan-ethnicity. But whether language is a person's primary ethnic marker or not, people continue to use the presence, or absence, of language markers as a clue to the strength of a person's ethnic identity. In fact, LePage & Tabouret-Keller (1985) see language as an *act of identity* and suggest that linguistic behavior involves *shifts of identity* by the speaker. Through these identity shifts during interactions, speakers affiliate with or disaffiliate from particular groups.

LePage and Tabouret-Keller were particularly interested in bilingual and multi-lingual (or bi-dilective) interactions, and how acts of identity were accomplished through the choice of lexis, grammar, pronunciation or code. However, as Sebba & Wooton (1998) point out, monolinguals can do this as well, albeit through different communicative resources, such as style-shifting (Bell, 1997; Wolfram & Schilling-Estes, 1998). A distinction of bilinguals is their ability to invoke ethnicity through a more varied range of linguistic strategies. Perhaps the most studied of such bi- or multilingual identification strategies is codeswitching (CS), the use of two or more linguistic varieties in an interaction (Bailey, 2000a, 2000b; Bucholtz & Hall, 2005; Cutler 1999; Gafaranga 2001; Greer 2005; Lo 1999; Rampton 1995; Sebba & Wooton, 1998; Williams, 2006; Zentella, 1997). One case of CS that is especially relevant to the study of flexible ethnicity proposed here is code crossing. This is characterized as the unexpected switch to an out-group code – which is often viewed as "illegitimate" or "inauthentic" (Rampton, 1995).

Ochs and Schieffelin (1982) explain that becoming a competent speaker of a language is inextricably linked to becoming a competent member of a culture. Access to different languages means access to different vocabularies and frames of reference for describing and understanding the world. Accordingly, linguistic flexibility and cross-cultural fluency go hand in hand.

Cross-Cultural fluency

In discussions of cross-cultural fluency, the related term, cultural competence, is frequently used. (Betancourt, et al., 2003; Campinha-Bacote, 2002; Lynch, 1992). The term and concept of cultural competence has developed in, and become crucial to the healthcare field, where cross-cultural misunderstandings can have critical consequences. In an increasingly globalized business, effective cross-cultural communication has become vital to international and multicultural business settings (Johnson, et al., 2006). The culturally competent person has successful interactions with people of different cultures not only because they understand the behaviors and practices of other cultural groups, but because they are also aware of their own culturally determined actions. Likewise, cross-culturally fluent individuals have the cultural knowledge needed to establish common frames of reference with members of multiple cultures. Using Goodenough's (1957: 167) definition, the sort of *knowledge* I refer to is "whatever it is one has to know…in order to operate in a manner acceptable to" others. Related concepts include *communicative competence* (Gumperz, 1972) and *habitus* (Bourdieu, 1977). Knowledge of the rules governing particular contexts is necessary for determining the appropriateness of an identification. Furthermore, knowledge (represented by schemas, models, and other knowledge structures) guides interpretations and makes it possible to "pick up on" subtle cues. Knowledge and performance are closely linked. Thus, successful performance (e.g. linguistic) is grounded in knowledge.

People acquire the cultural knowledge that makes ethnic flexibility possible through their participation in social networks. I propose that the more diverse a network is, the more opportunities there will be for learning diverse ethnic markers, models, etc. Therefore, while a single ethnic identification *can* be dominant as a reflection of network composition, it does not preclude the development of other identifications.[2]

The importance of social networks for ethnic identification cannot be overstated. As sites of socialization, through interactions with network members people learn network-normative behavior and the cultural knowledge that guides such behavior. It is within their immediate social networks that people first come to think of themselves as part of "us" and distinct from "them." But social networks can correspond with multiple *social locations*. Work networks, family networks, recreational networks, neighborhood networks: each is associated with particular social identifications. Similarly, a network can reflect multiple ethnic group ties. Interaction in different social locations within a social network often requires the use of distinct frames of reference and behaviors.

Image

Two elements of image relevant for ethnic identification are: those traits that we are born with and cannot easily alter (phenotype), and those that are acquired and easily changed (style, dress, adornment). Successful performance of an identification is equally linked to self-image (perception of ourselves) and outward image (the perception of others). Awareness about how one's physical appearance is read is a first step to working with aspects of one's appearance to meet certain interactional goals. At the same time, stereotypes about how certain ethnic group members are *supposed* to look inform the judgments and guesses people make about a person's ethnic background. For some groups, image and behavioral stereotypes are so intertwined as to render a person ethnically inflexible. On the other hand, while members of some ethnic groups may resist image stereotypes, others may work image stereotypes to their advantage.

In addition to socio-historically pervasive stereotypes, social context determines how image cues are translated to estimate others' ethnic background and interpret their behavior. Therefore the range of possible translations available for negotiation can be extensive; particularly for those who can project an ambiguous or universal image.

---

[2] This dominant identification is likely the one to which people attach the most affective value. Or in other words, it may be another way to conceptualize "self-understanding" or "self-location."

In other words, social context in combination with aspects of a person's phenotypic appearance may result in myriad ascribed identities across contexts. People with ambiguous physical appearances may find that they can become different things to different people depending on the context in which they find themselves. I personally have found that because my ethnicity is not immediately obvious from my image alone, people see in me the ethnic background they most identify with. In an Indian neighborhood I am approached in Hindi. In a Middle Eastern enclave I am spoken to in Arabic. In a Jewish temple I am assumed to be Jewish. And among Latinos encountering me for the first time I could just as well be Colombian as Puerto Rican - as a result not only of my appearance, but also because my Spanish is unmarked with the accent of any particular Spanish dialect.

The most ethnically flexible individuals in this study played on the advantages given to them by their physical appearance. For some, the assumptions others made about their ethnic identity were simply left contested, even if those assumptions were incorrect. Of course, this was generally limited to contexts in which immediate advantages were sought - such as making a sale - and long-term interactions were not expected.

Why Do People Switch?

While EI switching is a multi-layered process that can depend on psycho-social, interactional, economic and political conditions, the reasons and results of EI switching fall under four main categories: 1) for expediency (i.e. to achieve immediate advantage); 2) as a consideration of social status (this refers to the *comparative reference group principle,* which stems out of a desire for positive association, particularly when questions of socio-economic status arise); 3) to express social distance; and 4) to express solidarity (Nagata, 1994). In this study, my ethnographic collaborators reported or were observed using ethnic flexibility in job interviews, to defend citizenship claims, make "the sale," acquire special privileges, strengthen social bonds, and to avoid rejection or threat.

Expediency and social status considerations

In a city like New York, ethnic networks, and the trust-based transactions circulating through those networks, are crucial to the economic advancement of ethnic groups. To the extent that people invoke an ethnic identification to create and maintain bonds with others who share a similar identification, they capitalize on the business partnerships or job opportunities that materialize from these interactions (Bonacich, 1973; Hannerz, 1974; Ooka & Wellman, 2003; Patterson, 1975; Sanders & Nee, 1987). For some Latinos, economic advancement means invoking a more inclusive, pan-ethnic identification (i.e. "I am Latino", rather than "I am Dominican") (Padilla, 1984).

Economic advantages occur at the intersection of state policies and personal goals. A number of state regulations exist that confer economic resources on the basis of ethnic affiliation (Nagel, 1994; Fenton, 1999). On a national level, this includes affirmative action legislation and policies regulating the distribution of aid and incentives to Native American tribal members. With the omnipresent debates over immigration policy, the ability to claim American identification is at a premium. In this research, some subjects reported highlighting their American citizenship when applying for work or when re-entering the United States from a trip abroad. As a result, the American identification marker *par excellence* is the American passport. One of my interviewees reported identifying himself as Dominican in most situations - except in an international airport. While he considered his nationality to be "100% Dominican," he acknowledged that his "legal nationality" was American. The substantial transnational movement of people is making international frontiers less significant. State tools for marking citizens and controlling the flow of people through borders, such as the passport, have become a marker and symbol of the flexible nature of citizenship, and less a means of claiming citizenship (Ong, 1999).

More minor invocations take place in daily life. Multi-linguals may recall moments where a language switch was used to hasten or smooth a transaction at a restaurant, store, or when traveling. EI switching is not unlike this process - as I will later show they can even go hand in hand. Consider, for example, a Dominican-Puerto Rican woman who reported rarely using the Dominican identification - except, in her words, "To get free drinks at a cruise once because our waitress was Dominican. I think it was like six drinks."

Expression of social distance

People can also use ethnic identification to distinguish themselves from others, especially those perceived to be economically disadvantaged. Waters (1994) writes of a second-generation West Indian teenager living in New York City who asked her mother to teach her a West Indian accent. She planned to use the accent when she applied for a job or a place to live. The teen's strategy was to emphasize aspects of herself that set her apart from African Americans, who she perceived to be less economically successful. It is also not uncommon for people to invoke an identity associated with more visible ethnic groups in the broader social context (Alba, 1990). For some Latinos in New York City, this has meant identifying as Puerto Rican, for political and social expediency and not from a personal or ancestral connection to the island. Conversely, there are cases in which people choose to distance themselves from the ethnic group into which they were born. One man in this study shared that after identifying as Mexican, and subsequently being rejected by Puerto Rican men at a gay club, he later allowed potential dates to assume he was Puerto Rican. Another Dominican interviewee indicated that to avoid being "judged" he rarely used Dominican identification. He explained that as a "Euro-Latino" who left the Dominican Republic with his family for political reasons, he did not think that the associations made of dark-skinned Dominicans – who he felt were more likely to arrive for economic reasons – applied to him.

Expression of solidarity

As a basis for forging bonds with others, invoking different ethnic identifications is a way of both strengthening and broadening ones social support network and improving social relationships. Among ethnically-mixed Latinos, or those whose parents belong to different ethnic groups, Stephan & Stephan (1989) found that respondents reported identifying with one distinct ethnic identity when with the closest members of their social network, while more than one identity became salient in various other contexts. Spickard & Fong (1995) have observed that individuals will often adopt the ethnic identity of a spouse or partner. Similarly, Kaufert (1977) found that Ghanaian university students reported switching to a more inclusive ethnic identity that de-emphasized their ethnic ties to a particular town or dialect in order to facilitate their adjustment as newcomers to university life. Their more exclusive kin-based identity, on the other hand, was most frequently invoked to mobilize the resources of their family to help them through their studies.

What Are Some Ways that People Switch?

Here I present some distinctions between various ways that people switch their ethnic identification in interaction. The boundaries between each of these types are by no means unyielding. They may best be understood as gradations of ethnic self-presentation.

Crossing / Passing

This refers to the act of presenting oneself according to the behavioral and/or appearance-related norms and expectations of an ethnicity other than one's biographical ethnicity (Bucholtz, 1999; Cutler, 1999; Lo, 1999; Rampton, 1995; Sweetland, 2002). Sociolinguists have conducted much of the best work on this sort of boundary crossing. Crossing is an important form of ethnic flexibility because it can be a tool for forging bonds with a broader, more diverse group of people. For individuals who are not multi-ethnic or multi-racial in the usual senses of these terms, ethno-linguistic crossing may serve as an entree into multiple cultures and multicultural relationships with diverse codes providing the means to transcend a mono-ethnic identification. Ethno-linguistic crossing is said to require little competence, (Rampton, 1995; see also Sweetland 2002) but it is clear that highly competent crossers are able to expand their ethnic identification repertoires through the use of out-group codes. Actually, in such cases it seems inaccurate to use the word "out-group" in reference to a group for which a person feels a personal connection despite not having biographical ties to it. A more apt word might be adoptive-group. Both Roberto and Abel, the focal informants in this study, did this sort of situational switching.

Returning to Clarissa, the fair-skinned Puerto Rican woman, who listed "black" as one of her identifications because, as she explained, "I just feel like I fit in with everyone else! To me it's just...it's like a feeling. It feels like that's where you belong." It is certainly possible that Clarissa had internalized the U.S. black/white racial binary in which Latinos are automatically not white. However, in another moment of her interview, when talking about the racial identities of her

Latina friends, she acknowledged, "we are a mixed race, that's why we have the different tones of skin color." Yet, in the part of a survey (prior to our interview) that asked her to identify the race of each of her network members, Clarissa clearly differentiated between those contacts who were "black" because they were dark-skinned (mostly African American), those who she labeled as "*morenita/ito*" because they were mixed-race or brown-skinned, and fair-skinned contacts like herself, which included members of her immediate family. When elaborating on her identification as black, Clarissa noted that she grew up in a black neighborhood among mostly black friends. Thus, she felt a special connection to black identity not quite as a racial identity, but rather a relational one.

The expected duration of the encounter is an important factor in crossing. Short-term encounters, in which actors are unlikely to come in contact again, allow more possibilities for flexibility in ethnic self-presentation. Indeed, risky ventures like crossing or passing are most effective in contexts in which being challenged or exposed is improbable, limiting effective usage in repeated or long-term encounters. During the course of my research, I never witnessed the women in this study's ethnographic phase cross - and most did not independently report having done so. Lisa, a 28-year old Salvadorian-American Astoria resident, was the exception. While Lisa's parents were from El Salvador, she had found she was able to pass for Southeast Asian. Despite an avowed dislike for questions about her ethnic background, she reported teasing curious strangers with this ambiguity by claiming to be Asian ("just to mess with them"). However, unlike the men of this study, Lisa did not expect to be taken seriously when passing.

Accommodating

Ethno-linguistic accommodation is manifested discursively (although here I extend the term to include kinesics and ornamental acts of self-presentation), and involves strategies that invoke ethnic identifications in order to achieve social approval, distinctiveness, or communicative efficiency (Giles, et al., 1987). In this research I link it to ethnically germane contexts, but the concept has been applied to other areas (Aronsson, et al., 1987; Coles, 1992). Ethno-linguistic accommodation often occurs in contexts where passing would be impossible or inappropriate, but where ethnicity is prized as a means of achieving the acceptance of others. Achieving acceptance by one group at times happens vis-à-vis differentiation from another group.

Signaling familiarity with the norms and expectations of a particular ethnic group is often an important motivation for accommodation - without the heavy commitment or potential humiliation, for example as a result of mis-performing, associated with other types of switching. In this way, people can identify with an ethnic category, at least indirectly and temporarily. In addition to codeswitching and accent accommodation, participants in my research invoked ethnic affiliations through references that signaled their (in-group) knowledge of categories including Puerto Rican, Colombian or African American. Making references to in-group knowledge may serve as a subtle means of negotiating multiple ethnicities. It is a way to *imply* affiliation without necessarily committing to an identification. In this way, the ethnically flexible people in this study declared "I am *like*_____" rather than "I *am*_____."

Accommodation is an efficient, mostly automatic, way to make a favorable impression on others during fleeting encounters. However, for some, accommodation is a persistent practice that blurs the line between full identification and mere situational adaption. Julia, a U.S.-born Colombian-American ethnographic participant, had grown up in a black community, among mostly black friends, and was heavily influenced by African American culture. Unlike Clarissa, Julia did not assert a claim to black identity. Rather, she unequivocally identified as Colombian, Latina, or American. Still, she reported that African American sensibilities came naturally to her and adhered (or accommodated pervasively) to the behavioral norms and expectations in the African American social spheres she frequented. She preferred this to identifying strictly with other Latinos:

> **Julia**: Like, there was a lot of other Spanish people too [in my old neighborhood], there was a lot of Dominicans, Puerto Ricans a lot of Africans but I never felt at home with them because, I don't know, like I never felt like that at home with like the Dominicans and the Puerto Ricans because to them I wasn't Spanish enough because I would still hang out, I've always been around black people. You know, it's easier for me to speak English. I think in English, I'm gonna speak in English. I only speak Spanish to my parents. So, I wasn't

Spanish enough! I already was, you know, accustomed to my way of doing things.

Rosalyn: So, how did you start that way of how doing things? How did you get into the [African American] scene?

Julia: I don't know, like my older cousins like I said, they were always into hip-hop and I would always want to chill with them and I could see their friends and how they were and I'm like, oh, so and so is like that too, you know what I'm saying? I'm going to chill with them, I think that's cool. You know, and I had no problem with it. Like I learned how to braid, I learned how to do all that stuff from their culture and I like doing it. So, that was it. I know what I am though I'm proud of what I am. I tell anybody what I am but that's just the lifestyle that I'm accustomed to, I feel comfortable with it.

In my observations with Julia, I watched as she used mostly Standard American English (SAE) with her professors, her parents, and with me. African American Vernacular English (AAVE) seeped into these various interactions but never to the extent that it did when she spent time with her African American friends. Just as her use of SAE was a form of speech accommodation especially relevant to interactions with certain authority figures, AAVE marked her accommodation to decidedly African American interactional contexts and a member of a friendship network sharing African American cultural orientations.

Featuring

This strategy refers to the contextual act of shifting between multiple biographical ethnicities or different categorical levels of inclusiveness (Bailey, 2000a, 2000b; Eschbach & Gomez, 1998; Nagata, 1974; Waters, 1990). As I suggest by the name, featuring entails highlighting a facet of an ethnic repertoire. The key difference between featuring and other types of EI switching is that the identifications used correspond more directly with ethnic self-understandings (usually preceded by "I am ___"); in other words, such ethnic identifications are viewed as more "authentic." Thus, featured identifications are rarely called into question, whether by self or others, because they are deeply grounded in personal experience and history. This sort of ethnic flexibility is often found among mixed-heritage people who explore family histories, develop multi-in-group allegiances, and/or spend considerable time in more than one homeland. As such, multiple ethnic markers and models are readily available to them for presentation and/or activation.

Conclusion

My work in New York City was guided by three main research questions. First I wanted to better understand the factors that lead some people to be ethnically flexible. Secondly, I sought to understand the conditions under which NYC Latinos switched their ethnic identification. Finally, I was interested in how people actually switched. The literature on ethnicity provides numerous examples of people invoking (or hiding) their ethnicity to strengthen or weaken their ties to kin, community and the state and thereby to improve access to economic and political resources (Barth, 1969; Horowitz, 1975, 1985; Kelly & Nagel, 2002; Patterson 1975). However, less is known about *how* people go about doing this in their daily lives. Beyond the potential for this work to make such contributions, I was heartened to find that my ethnographic collaborators felt my research would be personally relevant to their own lives. Several thought that the everyday experiences of urban Latinos were under-represented, and were excited about contributing to work that would document urban Latinos' lived experiences. With several issues related to Latinos playing prominently in the national stage, from immigration legislation to bilingualism, my research documents intimately how these political themes play out in people's everyday lives.

CHAPTER 2

Research Methods

INTRODUCTION

The study of ethnic flexibility poses a number of methodological challenges. This is due, in part, to the fact that ethnic invocations often occur unselfconsciously. There were times at which, I thought I may have observed an instance of ethnic identification only to learn that my informant had little awareness or explanation for the act. But even when ethnicity is invoked consciously, it is hinted at and alluded to rather than spoken aloud. While efficient, the use of ethnic labels ("I am Hispanic") are usually reserved as responses for the curious, serving less as spontaneous declarations. How then can researchers distinguish between those behaviors used to invoke an ethnicity and others serving purely communicative functions? Which linguistic behaviors can be classified as ethnic self-presentation and which serve purely linguistic functions? Arguably, the relationship between language and identity is not so clear-cut. Researchers point out that linking social identity with behavior, (in this case language), is complex and despite refined methods and theoretical developments, not a straightforward endeavor (Fishman, 1999; Milroy, 1980). For instance, a person may have two or three languages or dialects available but a multiplicity of social identities – therefore the relationship between these is not one-to-one (Sebba & Wooton, 1998). In some cases, the language a person knows and uses and the ethnic identification they claim may be unrelated, for example an immigrant may know American English quite well but not think of themselves as American. Similarly, ethnic groups are not the only groups with distinct communicative styles (e.g. Yorkshire). And so, how do researchers determine which of several social identities or ethnic categories is invoked in communication? What evidence do researchers need to conclude that an ethnic marker used by one person is received and understood by another? What if no clean, unambiguous category can be used to tag a purportedly ethnic behavior?

Issues such as these complicate the use of conventional ethnic categories for classifying research participants and their behaviors and point to the need for methodologies that go beyond the standard survey or interview approach (Keefe, 1992). Waters (1990) argues that while Census data supports the notion that ethnic identity continues to be a salient form of self-identification, it is not clear how and why people choose among several ethnic options, how ethnicity is used in everyday life or what the significance of these identities are to the individual. This suggests that long-term ethnographic research that captures the process of contextual ethnic self-identification in various natural social contexts is an ideal approach for the study of modern ethnicity. The vexing research questions and challenges inherent to studying ethnic flexibility call for methodological innovation. Studying situational ethnicity in the 21st Century defies researchers to try multi-disciplinary approaches, be daring data collectors and avail themselves of new research technologies.

Previous research on situational ethnicity has not detailed the individual, micro-level, quotidian processes involved in situational ethnic identifications. Many of these studies were particularly concerned with group-wide shifts in identification (cf. Barth, 1969; Haaland, 1969; Nagel, 1994; Patterson, 1975). Of the ones that focused on individual acts of situational ethnicity, self-reports (Kaufert, 1977; Waters, 1994), surveys (Eschbach & Gomez 1998; Nishina, et al. 2010), and field notes (Nagata, 1974) were used to document shifts. In this study I took a multi-tiered, multi-method approach that made special use of digital recorders to capture instances of ethnic flexibility in action.

My task early on was to design a research protocol that would better my chances for observing and recognizing naturally occurring instances of EI switching while working within a limited time frame. I also needed to incorporate methods that would yield data crucial to the accurate classification of ethnic identification behaviors – to be more certain about the meaning and significance of ethnic markers participants would use. Finally, recognizing that with ethnographic observations alone I would not be able to account for most factors contextualizing ethnic identifications, a survey phase allowed me to test the ethnic identification response in a range of scenarios. The research was designed to collect data about the proximate and ultimate conditions that contextualize ethnic identification. Data on the ultimate conditions included participants' socio-demographic circumstances, their physical environment (the community where they lived), social environment (their social network), and their ethnic identification. Proximate conditions would be those observable in the naturally occurring social context, before, during, and after an act of ethnic flexibility. The research design involved two main phases of data collection and took place between February 2005 and May 2006. Only the results of the first phase will be covered in this monograph.

In Phase 1 I gathered in-depth ethnographic information from a small group of participants. To correctly identify instances of ethnic identification, I accompanied eleven Latino women and men, each for one week, in the variety of their daily routines and both observed and recorded their verbal interactions. While I participated in many of their activities, I mostly continuously monitored in the hopes of witnessing subtle and sometimes fleeting presentations of ethnicity. Shadowing entailed constantly shifting research roles: between direct observer, participant observer, and sometimes, unobtrusive observer. But just as informants negotiated their ethnicity in NYC's diverse ethnic milieu, so too did my observations demand my own ethnic negotiations as I moved with my informants throughout the city.

Observations took place in all five boroughs of NYC, but Astoria and Jackson Heights/Corona in Queens served as my research bases. I became familiar with NYC as a system of neighborhoods, socioeconomic regions, and series of encounters. I was not, as in Philippe Bourgois' (2002) work in El Barrio, entrenched in one neighborhood, one community, or one zone of city blocks. I did not wake up every morning in a neighborhood where its residents would be subjects for my research. Instead, I commuted to my informants and they in turn served as my guides of the city. With each person I explored a different aspect of the city, a different network of relationships, different locations, different socioeconomic segments, different uniquely urban activities - different individual NYC worlds. I did not embed myself in their communities, but rather in their immediate social networks and their daily routines. Therefore, just as I vacillated between engagement and detachment when observing my informants, so too did my experience of the city shift between feeling like I belonged – one of its deeply committed dwellers – and, at other times, feeling like a wandering visitor.

Astoria, Queens

I first entered the field in February of 2005. To be exact, the field was a three- by-nine block section of Astoria, Queens (see Map 1). Since the 1960s, Astoria has been the site of New York's largest Greek community (Williams & Mejia, 2001). To this day, the neighborhood has maintained a distinctly Greek feel, with its restaurants, cafes, Greek orthodox churches, community organizations, and numerous Greek-owned businesses ranging from butcher shops, to bakeries and laundromats. In more recent years, and even since I entered the field in 2005, Astoria has received a large number of immigrants from Russia, Mexico, Colombia, Bosnia, Brazil, and Bangladesh. In describing Astoria, one participant said, "You know how they say New York is the melting pot of the world? Well, Astoria is the melting pot of New York."

Map 1. Main Astoria, Queens NY Field Site

© 2010 Google

The small section that I selected for the initial weeks of fieldwork is one of the busiest neighborhoods in Astoria, particularly because of its dense concentration of small- to medium-sized businesses. The borders of this dense commercial and residential area are four of the most active streets in all of Queens (see Map 1). To the north and south are 30th Avenue (Grand Avenue) and Broadway. Broadway is commercially and residentially similar to 30th Avenue; though when I first started fieldwork Broadway was less densely packed with businesses. This has changed. That I have observed this change over my two years in Queens attests to Astoria's rapid growth and importance. Recently, the neighborhood has experienced a frenzy of apartment seekers, mostly young professionals for whom Manhattan's consistently rising rent prices and living costs are not an option. Astoria is a ten-minute subway ride into midtown Manhattan. The N and W line – now the N and Q – runs along 31st Street, the western-most boundary of my Astoria field site. This proximity, relatively low rent prices, and reputation as an up-and-coming, ethnically diverse community, are all factors leading to changes in Astoria's demographics in a very short time. To the east and west are Steinway Street and 31st Street. For nine blocks, starting at Steinway Street and ending at 31st street, 30th Avenue is a shopping attraction. A five minute walk down 30th avenue will present observers with Thai, Italian, Colombian, Brazilian, Indian, Mexican and, of course, Greek eateries, Latino-owned money wiring centers, international meat and fish shops, news stands selling Bosnian and Croatian magazines and newspapers, supermarkets announcing halal selections, and real estate businesses whose outdoor signs display names hinting to the major ethnic groups in Astoria.

I first entered Astoria intending to unobtrusively observe and record life in a mixed NYC immigrant neighborhood. I paid particular attention to interactions within and between members of Astoria's many ethnic populations. My goal was to familiarize myself with the area, meet potential research participants or people who could help me find them, and get a sense of the neighborhood's ethnic group relations. My first field notes document early impressions about ethnicity in the everyday life of Astorians. The notes also detailed some methodological issues I had not fully considered until actually beginning observations.

Today is the first day of me sitting down, like a tape recorder, video recorder to absorb and capture the web of words, interactions, activities that surround me here, in a small park (Athens Park on 30th Street) in Astoria Queens. What am I thinking? First, about the process, about how I will come to feel completely at ease with holding a pen and paper taking notes from life's dictations. At once conspicuous and unseen. I'm also thinking about this observation process itself. What am I waiting to hear and see? What am I missing while I write? What do I note and what do I leave to dissipate into the air? I am sitting in a park, close to sundown, among small children, adolescent, and old alike. Of course, as with many descriptions of ethnically diverse communities I am compelled to write down what I see and hear around me that can capture the worlds, lives, spaces, thoughts, that come into contact in immigrant communities like Astoria.

Across from me I see a pizzeria and Janata Grocery (a halal meat shop and grocer, etc.). I see Acapulco Café. Beyond, I see a supermarket, no doubt one of those where ethnic food varieties are thoroughly offered and where a mix of people, Latino, Asian, European, shop. Among the pedestrians are those whose ethnicities I can venture a guess at and those that I cannot. The children in the playground, probably junior high school students, speak in English, but among them is a mix of Latinos and South Asians. I see Muslim women with their headdresses and young blacks, whites and Latinos on their skateboards. The skateboard kids are interesting...they sport grungy, skateboarder looks, unkempt hair and speak in unaccented English.

It seems true, at least on the surface, that ethnicity does not enter into the routine movements of life, the lives that I see around me; as parents take their children to the park, as couples walk together, as businessmen talk business. How then to get under the surface and understand what role ethnicity has for structuring interactions.

Some difficulty also lies in the subject matter. I am not interviewing people involved in a certain subculture that I can easily target and ask relevant questions to. I am not interviewing people about an activity that is tangible and easy to remember or understand. I am not asking questions about responses to an event that occurred in the community. Instead I must ask first about their own perceptions of their ethnicity...something which as I walk about Astoria I feel does not seem to enter into surface parlance, but rather looms in the background or remains covered underneath daily routine or daily understanding for those in the community. Ethnicity seems at once all encompassing and irrelevant. This I must confirm. All encompassing in the sense that in an immigrant community, with multiple languages, cultures, national backgrounds blending, merging, meeting, clashing it seeps into the very character of the community, it becomes what the community attracts, it defines it. Yet it is perhaps wholly taken for granted and un-contemplated.

From these initial unobtrusive observations I went on to conduct informal interviews with community members. Whenever possible I spoke with people who sat in the neighborhood parks or loitered on street corners. Usually, I staked out businesses that had steady customer traffic and asked the owners if I could inconspicuously station myself in their stores. The most memorable establishment, one that I would visit on repeated occasions, was the International Meat Market on 30th Avenue. A successful Greek-owned (though one of the owners was also Venezuelan) meat shop, the business also employed workers from Mexico and Argentina. The owners, two men in their mid-30s, and the other butchers had learned key words and phrases (and in some cases spoke fluently) in several languages, including Spanish, Italian, Croatian, and Greek. Because of its clientele and staff, the shop truly lived up to its name. The shop's consistent current of customers and alluring mix of languages and nationalities made it an ideal place to observe EI switching.

After Astoria, I eventually moved on to the slightly more daunting second field site: Corona/Jackson Heights, Queens. I chose Astoria because of its ethnic diversity, but also because Latinos were a visible part of the community. To assess whether the community where a person lives affects the development of ethnic flexibility, I chose Corona as a counterpoint to Astoria. It is also very diverse, but a place where Latinos are the considerable majority.

Corona / Jackson Heights, Queens

My observations in Corona / Jackson Heights (CJH) began in late May 2005, after I had already recruited some of the key collaborators whose stories fortify this monograph. While my initial observations in Astoria happened as I worked independently, I got to know CJH with research participants as my guides. I had actually traveled to CJH on several occasions before May and found it a challenging place to approach people in the streets or enter businesses to just sit and watch. The traffic of pedestrians is denser along CJH's main thoroughfares, like Roosevelt Avenue and Junction Boulevard. Businesses along Roosevelt Avenue are cramped. Many of them (including retail stores) are situated in small windowless suites in second and third floors. Most of my research was concentrated at the predominantly Latino intersections of Corona Plaza and Jackson Heights between Northern Boulevard and Roosevelt Avenue. These two neighborhoods lie about 2 1/2 miles east of Astoria in northwest Queens. At the northern most border of the CJH field site is Northern Boulevard. This important, highly commercial boulevard connects Flushing in the east, with Astoria and Long Island City (Astoria's sister neighborhood) along a 7-mile stretch of road. Running parallel to Northern Boulevard, four long blocks to the south, is Roosevelt Avenue. Roosevelt Avenue connects Flushing to Woodside, Queens, historically an Irish enclave southwest of LIC/Astoria (see Map 2).

The 7 train runs along Roosevelt Avenue. Dubbed the "immigrant express," the 7 train starts at Times Square in Manhattan, passes through LIC, Woodside, Jackson Heights, Corona, eventually ending in Flushing Chinatown, the site of a rapidly growing Chinese immigrant community. The train travels though a series of contiguous ethnic enclaves. Picture a train densely packed with women and men from more than 50 countries, speaking dozens of different languages, the working-class and the poor, middle-class professionals, citizens, residents, and undocumented immigrants. At Woodside, Irish constructions workers and Filipino nurses unload. First stop in Jackson Heights, Punjabi business owners and Colombian high school students enter and leave the train. At the next stop in Jackson Heights, Colombian, Ecuadorian, and Mexican salesmen, laborers, and office workers join the mix. Once in Corona, Latino passengers from all of Latin American, especially the Dominican Republic, Colombia, Ecuador and Mexico, disembark to shop, work, eat, or wait. By the time the 7 train makes its final stop in Flushing, most of the passengers are Chinese and Korean.

Astoria and Corona / Jackson Heights capture those qualities that make NYC an exceptional place to study ethnic flexibility in complex plural environments. Both neighborhoods are growing, densely populated, major commercial centers and quickly navigable by foot. Most importantly, they are part of the most ethnically diverse county in the U.S. (Business Wire, 2001; Roberts, 2006). They present ideal environments for understanding how the 'situation' in situational ethnicity has changed in the 21st Century.

Map 2. Main Jackson Heights/Corona, Queens NY Field Site

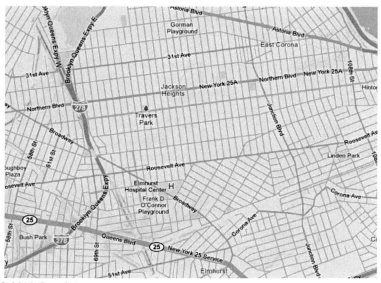

© 2010 Google

Continuous Monitoring / Shadowing Ethnography

The eleven men and women who participated in Phase 1 were selected through short screening interviews from a pool of potential participants who responded to online and newspaper advertisements, flyers or word of mouth. I looked for people who represented a range of backgrounds and experiences and whose daily routines cut across at least three domains of social interaction (e.g. work, home, social gatherings). Recruitment was carried out in four monthly cycles, starting in April and ending in July of 2005. At the beginning of each month, I placed an ad in the employment and community activities sections of New York's Craigslist, as well as posting flyers along busy streets in both Astoria and CJH. I also placed ads in the employment section of Spanish-language newspapers, *El Especialito*, a free bi-weekly newspaper, and *El Diario,* the New York metro area's largest Spanish language newspaper. Finally, contacts at Catholic Charities in Astoria and Forest Hills Community House in Jackson Heights agreed to spread the word about my research.

The most effective recruitment tool was Craigslist. While I received responses from all the recruitment channels I used, in the end, 9 out of the 11 ethnographic participants learned about the study through Craigslist. Of the two non-Craigslist participants, one called after being informed by an ESOL program supervisor, the other after seeing a flyer at her school. Craigslist was self-selective for a certain type of participant. They tended to be women, in their early-20's to mid-30's, spoke English, had access to computers and the Internet, and were born in the U.S. or had lived in the U.S. most of their lives. Initially I was concerned that Craigslist would also be self-selective for unemployed people, given that I posted mostly in the employment section. However, many of those who responded were looking to supplement their incomes (my ads offered monetary compensation) and had at least a part-time job. As advertised, the final ethnographic participants were given $200 for their participation.

Of the approximately 100 responses that I received about the study, I met with 22 people in person and selected 11 out of those 22. Potential participants were narrowed down from the initial pool based on their strong interest in participating, availability, neighborhood of residence, gender, age, nationality, and unique life circumstances. The 22 people who cleared the initial email and phone screenings were scheduled for face-to-face screening interviews. The purpose of these short, informal meetings was to explain more in-depth the purpose of my study and to learn about the daily routines of each participant. I sought participants whose daily routines were varied and cut across multiple domains of social interaction. Therefore, I asked each participant to take me through a typical week. Those who were not selected reported having few daily interactions or activities (usually because of unemployment) or had daily routines that would make it difficult to for me to be present. The 11 men and women who were selected worked, and/or attended school, maintained regular contact with family and friends, and had some unique life story highly relevant to the topic on EI switching (e.g. maintained a transnational lifestyle or had an ethnically diverse family history).

I sought a sample of 6 people from Astoria and 6 from CJH, equal parts men and women. I also sought a mix of immigrant and U.S.-born participants. Early on, I filled my quota for women, U.S.-born Latinos, the working-class, and people in their 20's. At about the midmark of the ethnographic phase (June/July) it became increasingly difficult to find people who were middle-aged or older, men, foreign-born, professional, Puerto Rican, Mexican, or from Astoria. Two participants in the final sample lived in neighborhoods other than Astoria or CJH. Because of the difficulty in finding willing Latino participants in Astoria, I had to substitute Astoria with neighborhoods having similar demographic characteristics. They had to be neighborhoods with Latino representation but great ethnic heterogeneity. Therefore, I accepted responses from potential participants who lived in Elmhurst (the most ethnically diverse neighborhood in the country) and Woodside, both in Queens.

In general, my screening was successful in leading me to participants with whom I experienced and documented a range of activities. However, one young man, Adalberto, had an inconsistent work schedule as a hairdresser and few interactions outside of work. I had to end observations with him after two days. The eleven participants in the ethnographic phase were (* denotes the two focal subjects in this monograph):

Esperanza: 26-year-old, Astoria resident, Argentinean biochemical engineering student who identified only as Latina and Argentinean. Esperanza was quite uniform in her expressions of ethnic identity and language use. When speaking in Spanish she was unchanging in accent and lexicon. Her difficulties with English limited her ethnic self-expression in that language. Esperanza admitted to preferring interactions and relationships with other Latinos.

Alfredo: 41-year-old, Corona resident, Dominican maintenance worker at a major Manhattan university. Alfredo was born and raised in the U.S. and is married to an African American woman. He identified first as Dominican, then Latino, and sometimes as American. He spoke Spanish well but did not have as extensive a vocabulary as many native speakers. Despite his Spanish-language limitations he had perfected a *stereotypical* Dominican accent and shifted between the use of this and standard Spanish. Alfredo had a teenage son from his previous marriage to a Dominican woman. He encouraged his son to maintain ties to his Dominican heritage and sent him to the Dominican Republic every summer.

Mildred: 36-year-old, Woodside resident, Dominican marketing executive for a small start up company. Mildred's discourses on ethnic identity where intermingled with her experience with obesity (she had undergone gastrointestinal weight loss surgery). She admitted that before anything else about her identity, people saw her weight. Mildred was born and raised in the U.S. and spoke fluent Spanish. She has made frequent extended trips to the Dominican Republic throughout her life. Mildred used her ethnicity to her advantage in her professional life. Her boss admitted to me that he encouraged Mildred to emphasize her Latino identity when calling potential Latino clients. He also stated that Mildred's bilingualism was one of the reasons she was hired.

Adalberto: 28-year-old, Astoria resident, Mexican-American hairdresser originally from Texas. Adalberto spoke very little Spanish and seemed the least Latino-conscious of all the participants. In fact, ethnicity entered very seldom into the few interactions I was able to observe him in. Adalberto spoke frankly about his strained relationship with his father. He explained that his father was attached to traditional notions of Latino masculinity and so did not accept Adalberto's homosexuality.

Alma: 48-year-old, Jackson Heights resident, Colombian sales woman trained in Colombia as an industrial engineer. When I met Alma, she had been in the U.S. for about 10 years and spoke limited, heavily accented English. While she identified strongly as Colombian, she did not see herself returning to Colombia because of the lack of job opportunities for middle-aged women there. Like Esperanza she tended not to switch. For her work she drew on an extensive network of Colombian friends and acquaintances. Alma is in a long-term relationship with a Greek man and the mother of two girls from a previous marriage.

Julia: 19-year-old, Jackson Heights resident, Colombian fashion design student. Julia was born in Colombia and moved to the U.S. before age two. She grew up in a predominantly African American housing community in New Jersey and had adopted styles of dress and speech often associated with black youth culture. Her network of school and neighborhood friends was largely African American. While she knew Spanish she rarely spoke it, not even for brief switches, in the week that I was with her.

Roberto*: 36-year-old Venezuelan-born Astoria resident. Raised by a Haitian stepmother in a Puerto Rican neighborhood, his friends growing up were mostly black and Puerto Rican. Roberto was persistently entrepreneurial: he rented canopies at street fairs, sold cologne and Italian ices on the street, and shoveled snow in the winter. In all his business ventures he unabashedly used his ethnicity and language skills to gain an advantage.

Abel*: 37-year-old Corona resident, Ecuadorian salesman. Abel entered the country illegally from Ecuador (through Mexico) and had worked as a construction worker, taxi driver and pimp at various stages of his struggle to make it in the US. When I met him he identified as a born-again Christian, was married to a Mexican woman and worked on the streets as a satellite television salesman.

Luis: 40-year-old Elmhurst resident, Ecuador-born children's tennis instructor who moonlighted as a casino dealer. He belonged to a local soccer league and played under an Argentinean coach with teammates from Peru, Ecuador, Mexico, the Dominican Republic, Korea and Colombia. He lived with his Chinese-American girlfriend and had a son with an Ecuadorian woman.

Anthony: 29-year-old Corona resident. Born in Puerto Rico but brought to the U.S. as a toddler, Anthony's mother is Cuban and his estranged father is Puerto Rican. As a teenager he submerged himself in NYC's graffiti-art subculture. When I met him he was a semi-pro wrestler (the WWF type) and made extra money by wrestling in exhibition matches at world-renowned Gleason's Gym in Brooklyn. Though raised by the Cuban women in his family, he grew up in predominantly Puerto Rican and Dominican neighborhoods and as a result learned to identify himself (and was identified by others) as Puerto Rican. Anthony does not speak Spanish fluently.

Lisa: 28-year-old Long Island City resident, Salvadoran-American yoga instructor who interchangeably identified as American or Latina but rarely as Salvadoran. Lisa spent much of her time practicing or teaching yoga. Within the community of yoga instructors she has used her Latina identity to differentiate herself from other yoginis and to appeal to the potential (though largely untapped) Latino market. For example, she has taught classes in Spanish. While she acknowledges the advantages brought to her by her identity, she is sensitive to having her ethnicity be the subject of scrutiny or fascination.

Pre-observation interviews

Participants agreed to provide additional detailed narratives about themselves and their lives before we embarked on the observation. The insights gained from the pre-observation interviews helped me to properly classify and contextualize observed behavior. First I carried out life-history interviews, and then I questioned them about their social networks.

Life-history interviews (see Appendix A):
These 3 to 6 hour interviews, conducted in both English and Spanish, identified life experiences that contributed to the formation of each participant's ethnic identity. Starting with childhood and ending in the present (at the time of the interview), participants were asked questions ranging from early family relationships and traditions, experiences with racial and ethnic discrimination, workplace diversity, pastimes, political and community participation, romantic relationships, immigration stories, and language use.

The life history interview was something of an icebreaker, a bonding prelude to the potentially awkward observations that would come. With the printed interview questions in hand as a guide, I encouraged respondents to take the discussion where they wanted. In this way, they opened up intimate details about their life that made the intensive observations seem less intrusive.

Personal social network interviews (see Appendix B):
Using Egonet (McCarty, 2003), I collected data on each participant's social network composition (e.g. percentage of network that is of a particular ethnic background) and network structure (e.g. the percentage of people in a participant's network who know each other). Beside network data, Egonet allowed me to collect socio-demographic information from each participant. These included gender, age, income, education and occupation, as well information about the ethnic background of parents and spouse / partner. The purpose of these data

was to first, lay out their social environment in a way that would help me recognize interlocutors during observations, understand aspects of their social network that would affect their ethnic identification, and provide visual data that I could refer back to when reviewing observation notes.

The computer-assisted egocentric network questionnaire was structured in four parts. The first part asked socio-demographic questions about each participant, or *ego*. The second part was the *name generator* that elicited the names of 40 people that the ego *knew*. A *known* person was defined as someone the ego recognized by face and by name and who in turn recognized the ego by face and name. I further asked that they only list people they had known for at least two years and who they could contact if they had to. In the third section, participants had to indicate the age, gender, nationality, race, relationship and closeness to each network member (*alter*) listed. Finally, participants had to rate the likelihood that alters would talk to each other in their absence. The software enables this task by displaying alter names in pairs, beginning with the first name on the 40 name list and going in the order that the names were listed. Participants had to evaluate a total of 780 ties, indicating whether alter A and alter B were *very likely*; *somewhat likely*; or *not at all likely* to talk in ego's absence. For purposes of this research, a tie existed in cases were alters were *very likely* to talk.

Egonet has a feature that will visualize the results of the network questionnaire. Alters are displayed as nodes. Socio-demographic or attribute data for each alter are displayed using color, size, or shape. Each alter attribute can be displayed one at a time or in combination, depending on the needs of the researcher. For example, during network visualization interviews in this research I first displayed the nationality of each alter using color (red = Puerto Rican, yellow = Dominican, green = Colombian, etc.). Then I displayed gender using shape (circle = woman, square = man). In this way I could view the gender and nationality of each alter simultaneously. Finally, using size, I displayed the level of closeness the ego felt to each alter. The larger the node the closer the ego felt to that alter. Examples of these visuals will appear in later chapters.

Egonet uses algorithms developed within the field of social network analysis to calculate the relative distance and positioning of nodes based on the presence or absence of ties. Ties are displayed using lines between nodes. One of the benefits of this feature is that it displays the nodes and ties in such a way that it reflects visually the actual (or at least reported) patterns of relationships in the participant's immediate social environment. Thus, a tightly connected ball where all or most nodes are tied indicates a very dense social network. Displays with three or four clusters, or *compartments*, suggests that the ego maintains several sub-groups that have little or no contact with each other (e.g. a family group, work group, or school group). Each participant's visual can provide insights challenging to discover with standard survey questions or even formal interviewing alone. When I used these visualizations to interview the eleven principal participants, I was able to gather clues about their isolation or gregariousness, friendship-making practices, daily routines, satisfaction with social life and relationships, and sense of belonging to different ethnic groups.

Shadowing Observations

Quinlan's (2008) description of shadowing is apt – "conspicuous invisibility." In the following section I will discuss the unique opportunities and challenges associated with this sort of observation. Conspicuous invisibility highlights the ways that shadowing observers must constantly negotiate distance and engagement with informants. Distance / detachment made it possible to closely and continuously attend to note-taking and close observation right as informants were "doing being ethnic." Participation / engagement, on the other hand, was an inevitable and welcome aspect of being "close and personal" with informants for a week. In writing about the seeming paradox of participant observation, Benjamin Paul (1953: 69) wrote: "Participation implies emotional involvement; observation requires detachment. It is a strain to sympathize with others and at the same time strive for scientific objectivity." As I will show, shadowing ethnography involves emotional attachment, while affording the researcher the freedom to gather evidence for behaviors of interest systematically.

Observations began on the day after each of the participants completed their life history and social network interviews. The observations of these busy urban women and men alternated between the tediously rote and exhausting, to the deeply moving and exciting. I explained to each person that the purpose of the research was to document their everyday lives and to better understand how ethnicity figured into various aspects of their daily life. To minimize self-monitoring of speech, I did not bring special attention to the sociolinguistic dimensions of my research. In the first week we scheduled five- to eight-hour periods of daily intensive observations. These scheduled observations took place in every area of their life that they felt comfortable with me observing. Domains included work, school, at-home interactions, church, shopping, and recreational social gatherings. While a digital audio recorder was ever present during these observations, I always carried a small notebook, collecting field notes as metadata for the audio recordings. I selected small (4" x 1 ½"), high-end, lightweight recorders that fit easily into cell phone cases and were able to be clipped on to participants' belts or pockets. Remote-control microphones were attached to the recorders and clipped on to shirt pockets, collars or lapels. The remote-control feature on this particular microphone model was invaluable to the participants. All became adept at pausing or stopping recordings on the fly - for example, during trips to the bathroom, when needing privacy, or during silent moments of activity not discernable in the audio recording. However, a consequence of having these recorders on for hours at a time was that they often remained on, unnoticed and forgotten, even during bathroom trips and idle points.

The audio recorder was as a second "observer" capturing small (e.g. phonological variation) and big details (e.g. background noises indicating place). The recorder freed me to focus more on observing. But depending on the situation it allowed me to be more engaged, more of a participant, without worrying about what might be missed if I could not take notes. A key benefit of doing continuous recordings of naturally occurring interactions was context. With continuous recordings (as with continuous ethnographic observations) I was able to more broadly capture information about the rhythms of daily life: the web of interactions, environments spanned, actions' antecedents, and the ways that talk affects the course of a day's activities.

I had planned to accompany participants in their daily activities for seven straight days (5-8 hours each day) in the first week and have them record on their own in the second week. I changed these plans once I realized that participants had at least one day in which it would be impractical for me to be present: days that involved resting at home, inaccessible or confidential work areas, or romantic dates. Instead, I asked that they let me observe for 6 days, at least 5 of them in sequence, with the option to reserve one day of observation for a later date. For example, Julia opted to reserve one of her days for me to attend the Puerto Rican Day with her. Roberto, who I observed in late

April / early May, suggested that we trade one of his idle days for an important June street festival he was to due to work at. This worked out fine, as it gave me more varied situations to observe.

Of the eleven informants, most were incredibly open and cooperative with the observations. After just a few days with each I was included in a host of unique and intimate moments, though there were numerous impractical situations in which observation stopped as a result of access or privacy concerns. However, this rapid familiarity seems to be one of the key benefits of quick shadowing ethnography versus more prolonged rapport-building ethnographic techniques. Building rapport is thought to be both a precursor to participant observation and a goal of participant observation (DeWalt & DeWalt, 1998). But what happens to rapport under time constraints? What if you only have a week to observe? Is it possible to build genuine goodwill and a mutual sense of commitment between researcher and informant in less than a week? My work suggests that rapid-rapport is possible and meaningful. The scheduled, short-term, and intensive nature of this method expedited trust- and relationship- building.

Another interesting benefit of establishing this quick rapport was that my identity as a woman was less problematic in observing men's worlds. There was a way in which the research arrangement pre-disposed the informants to all sorts of intrusions, and the fact that I was a woman often did not pose a significant obstacle as I observed and participated in male-dominated activities and networks. Of course, each of the informants accepted the 'intrusions' the moment they agreed to participate – and knowing that they would be compensated – so they were ready to shed some boundaries. Therefore, while Mildred did not ask me to accompany her on a first date with a man she met online, Anthony included me in his first face-to-face meeting with a woman he met online. Luis and Alfredo rarely scheduled me to observe on days when they did seemingly boring and routine tasks like laundry or food shopping. Esperanza, Julia and Lisa, however, allowed me to tag along when they ran these errands. I witnessed family conflicts, business negotiations, dating service phone interviews, undocumented immigrant labor recruitment, and other sensitive areas of interaction. I believe that for some of the respondents, rapid-rapport was also facilitated by my framing of the research experience as life documentation. Consider, for example, the following excerpt of my field notes during Anthony's meeting with a romantic interest he met online:

Field notes excerpt, August 23, 2005:
We've arrived at the go-go club in Elizabeth New Jersey, interestingly in the same town where I went to the first and last go-go club with Julia. When we entered there was one woman dancing and the music playing was dancehall reggae. The crowd when we entered consisted only of two white young women on one side of the bar and two young African-American men on the other side of the bar. Within 30 minutes more men had entered including two other women that may be dancers. The men who are in here are all black except for one white Latino. On the mirror walls are flyers in neon orange and yellow, advertising drink specials and special nights. One reads: "come see our hot Latina dancers." Anthony is about to take his shirt off to show off the tattoo on his back. She was expecting a bigger tattoo and keeps making faces and rolling her eyes. I suppose partly trying to be funny perhaps out of awkwardness or perhaps out of not exactly feeling psyched about Anthony. At times it seems like she's interested and into him and flirty and other times she jokes with a slightly mocking tone. While they talked the dancer came by to work the tip from Anthony. Then the bartender that Anthony is talking to, told her that she doesn't have to work him because Anthony is with her. Then Anthony told her to come by me, which she did, unfortunately, and I kept my head down in the notebook.

I was not there to take part in their interaction – in fact, I would have preferred not to be there at all. Anthony was there to get to know the bartender, as she was someone that he had been flirting with online on a few occasions. It was a date of sorts and he was comfortable enough about it that he let me tag along. Still, there was no pretense that I would take part in their conversation to any meaningful extent. I was there to see what things were like, to give him a ride, and as a companion to help him assess how the date was going. I was there with a notebook and he was there with a recorder. My participation consisted of being *there*. To take in the music and other sounds, the clubs' sights – a truly foreign place for me within the city. Anthony tried to pull me in to participation by suggesting that one of the strippers come to me for tips. I set myself deeper into the role of detached observer and note-taker. My observation had to be done subtly because on the one hand, I did not want to seem like an eavesdropper on his conversation with the bartender – although the recorder was my eavesdropper – and on the other hand I did not feel comfortable watching the women. In a space where all of the visitors were men and all of the dancers and some of the bartenders were women, I felt uncomfortably like a co-participant in the sexual objectification of women. Oddly, I also felt shed of my sexuality – as I was neither an object of the men's interest nor a consumer of the women's performance.

This research encounter was partly made possible (I had only just met Anthony a few days earlier) because of the "documentary" aspects of my work that drew people to the study. I suspect that my collaborators, particularly the young, second generation ones felt more comfortable with the process if they explained to themselves and others that they were opening up for a documentary of their lives. In fact, Anthony had sent me more than 100 photos from his earlier days in semi-pro wrestling in the hope that it would lend further source material for my documentation of his life. Because participants thought of and explained the experience to others as a documentary of their lives they were more open to being watched in situations that were very personal. Some of my informants used reality TV programs as referents for how such up close and personal observation could go. In fact, it reminded Lisa of MTV's "The Real World," a show in which young men and women are selected to live out their lives for 3 months under the merciless gaze of video cameras. Her "Real World" approach to the observations meant that I was best served to stay in the background and keep up or lose her in a crowded street or store (which I did on occasion). Like Anthony, Julia told her friends and family that a researcher was "doing a documentary" of her life and introduced me accordingly. I argue that popular *reality* media – whether on TV shows, You Tube, or personal blogs – has an interesting effect on how people submit themselves to observation. There is greater awareness and acceptance of life exposure among would-be research informants. Reality television, the mainstream success of documentary films, and Web 2.0 technologies in which users display various aspects of their personal lives for public viewing, have made it less threatening, and indeed, desirable to expose mundane aspects of private life.

I also had to protect the privacy of those who my collaborators encountered during observation. An inevitability of continuous recording was that the recorder would capture the voices of anonymous passers-by. Prior to embarking on the research, I consulted New York State laws that applied to recording brief periods of conversation without consent. I found that if persons engaged in a conversation reasonably expect that their conversation is private, recording without consent is illegal. Conversations in public spaces within earshot of others – such as at a restaurant or street corner – are generally not considered private, and so recording in such situations is protected by law. Furthermore, United States federal law allows for "one-party consent" statutes. This permits a person to record her/his conversations without the consent of other parties.

To these ends, I took a tiered approach to protecting non-key informants' privacy. Close family and friends who informants interacted with regularly for extended periods of time were fully aware about my research prior to starting observations and recordings. For some informants their participation in the research depended on both the consent and the support of those closest. Once research had commenced, relatives, friends, co-workers, classmates, and others with whom informants interacted frequently were told about the recorder at the first encounter. Typically informants took responsibility for sharing this information, but on occasions when they forgot or neglected to do so I would point out the recorder to their contact. In encounters with distant acquaintances or strangers I used a one-minute rule. If the encounter went on longer than a minute I would announce the presence of the recorder or signal for informants to do so. For brief interactions lasting less than a minute I deferred to informants' discretion about whether or not to bring attention to the recorder. Informants also had the choice to pause the recorder if they could not comfortably gain consent, and so they sometimes did. Beyond these privacy safeguards, the recorder was never hidden from view. The recorder's lavalier microphone, with its blinking lights, was always visible. Therefore, all interlocutors had a reasonable chance to become aware of the recording in progress. Even still Abel had many brief encounters with strangers in which personal information was exchanged. Understandably, he was reluctant to interrupt these sales encounters to announce the recorder. As an added measure, I provided Abel with a nametag reading: "Research participant. Recording in progress." And of course, my steady presence with a field notebook in hand provided further evidence that research was in fact in progress.

When informed of the recorder and research in progress, the reactions of those with whom my informants interacted ranged from outright enthusiasm to downright defensiveness. Take, for example, the case of an acquaintance of Alba. The acquaintance, a seamstress Alba visited for a business referral, discovered the blinking lights of the recorder before it was announced. Her response was immediately suspicious. She looked at me squarely, considering me as she ascertained in seconds whether I was trustworthy or not and asked what was going on. Before Alba, who stood blushingly by, could explain, I quickly clarified why the recording was being used and apologetically suggested that the recorder be turned off. Even though she was still slightly apprehensive, she went along with the interaction and consented to the recorders' use. Because she trusted Alba she allowed the recorder to remain on. Now and then, my NYC collaborators voluntarily paused recording when their interlocutors discussed health problems, relationship troubles, and other highly personal topics.

Given the continuous monitoring conditions of my research, much of the time I played a hands-off role in the activities in which informants were involved. I was often in the background to informants' encounters with others, documenting the interactional contexts and communicative behaviors. "It's time to put your notebook down," or "Are you going to write down all of this?" were common appeals. My steady presence and low level of intervention in informants' activities meant that, at least initially, they were highly aware of and uncomfortable with being observed. Alma, Abel and Adalberto were periodically reluctant and embarrassed to admit to others that they were research participants. Their approach was to integrate me more into their daily routines as a friend to lessen the awkward distance between them and me. This granted me more flexibility to participate in their conversations. Lisa and Luis tended to keep me at a distance and sometimes did not introduce me at all. So while I tried to keep a balance of both engagement and detachment, this was not necessarily a methodological choice made in the planning stages, but an adjustment to the actual observation circumstances I encountered and the informants I was with. When I was fully engaged as a participant it became difficult to keep the desired detailed, itemized notes about behavior. While as a participant there was less reactivity to my presence or monitoring. Discussions of such observer effects tend to focus on the effect on the person being observed. Shadowing observation also has an effect on the observer. At times I felt awkward, out of place, uncomfortable, prying, etc. This surely affected my body language, the things that I said, and how I said them, which in turn affected informants. Eventually this reactivity tapered off for both myself and my informants.

Monitoring and note-taking from a distance affected participants differently depending on how many people were involved in an interaction. As expected, the more people in an interaction the more easily I was ignored and the more unselfconsciously the informants interacted with others. I also found that the effects of my presence and the recorder tended to differ depending on informant characteristics, like age, but also, on relational factors. The youngest participants – less than 30 years old – tended to have interactions with younger people who were in turn less adverse to the idea of being followed around and recorded. In general, relational factors trumped the benefits of youth such that the weaker their relationship to an interlocutor the more uncomfortable they felt with the recording and observation. For example, the more unfamiliar informants were with someone, the less they knew about how s/he would react to the presence of the recorder. The comfort of non-focal speakers – like a focal subject's acquaintance – was an important factor affecting observer effects. In talking with the men and women about their experiences in the study I learned that if they sensed discomfort in their interlocutors because of the research situation, they because more self-conscious and uncomfortable.

Gumperz (1964) and Labov (1984; see also Labov, et al., 1968), two pioneers in the study of naturally occurring speech, reduced reactivity through participant observation and group sessions. Both Gumperz and Labov had tape-recorded informal conversations with groups of people that already knew each other. In this way, speakers' awareness of being recorded was counteracted by the pre-existing group dynamics of the speakers. Interestingly, I found that in the presence of friends during early recording sessions, some informants over-performed certain behaviors. Rather than becoming more formal or measured – as can commonly happen with reactivity – some informants overplayed a certain outgoing or hyperactive persona as a way to be more interesting for me to observe. Anthony confessed his concern that I would find his daily routine and behavior not interesting or useful enough for the research. Despite clear indication to the contrary in the Informed Consent forms, a couple of the participants viewed the research arrangement and compensation as something akin to a contractual agreement. In this view, compensation connoted an expectation of appropriate returns. Anthony was concerned that his level of participation would not warrant compensation. Because I understood that reactivity is an important concern in continuous monitoring research, the second week was designed to capture naturally occurring conversations without my presence. I met daily with participants in the second week. Typically, I saw them in the mornings before they started their day to download the previous day's recordings onto my laptop. When needed, I also replaced batteries. Since the recorder had a memory capacity of 8 hours and 56 minutes, it had sufficient space for a day of uninterrupted recording or two days of recording with stopping and pausing. Based on recording times, participants collected a total of 288 hours of recordings. This was about the same amount of time I spent observing them in the first week (290 hours). That means that in those two weeks with each participant I collected a total of 578 hours of recording.

Analysis of Linguistic Data

This study draws on discourse analysis (DA) approaches. DA describes a broad range of methods and orientations used to study language use, both in its spoken and written forms. In general, discourse is understood to be anything beyond the sentence level. Here I have also attended to phonological and prosodic variation that marked changes in dialect or style. Excerpts of participants' naturally-occurring interactions were descriptively transcribed using conversation analytic conventions (Sacks, et al., 1974; see Appendix C) and primarily analyzed in the interactional sociolinguistics (IS) tradition developed by Gumperz (1982). A fundamental concern of IS is shared and non-shared interpretations and the background knowledge needed in the interpretative process. IS takes non-linguistic factors, such as setting, and participant attributes, like gender, age, and ethnicity into account and is therefore regarded as micro-ethnographic in its approach to the analysis of interaction. Gumperz (1972) suggested that the analysis of language use and speech events involves the analysis of a significant and representative range of different contexts. Only through systematic and painstaking fieldwork can regularity in the activities bound to ethnic group identities be discovered. IS is particularly concerned with miscommunication in ethnically diverse environments. Advancing this agenda, Gumperz introduced the concept of *contextualization cues*. These, usually, prosodic triggers work with lexical material to establish the context in which messages are interpreted and understood (Gumperz, 2001; Levinson, 2002). Beyond lexical misunderstanding, cross-cultural miscommunication occurs when speakers do not understand each others' indirect allusions. Gumperz argues that such background knowledge is learned through our direct contact with close network members (Gumperz, 2001). The very same indirect signaling mechanisms that helps us be understood by our network members, allows others to assess our social identities. These signaling mechanisms include accents, intonation, and stress patterns. Codeswitching is one important *non*-prosodic contextualization cue (Gumperz, 2001). Representing shifts in contextual presuppositions, codeswitching as an interpretative tool makes sense when speakers share the same or similar presuppositions. Therefore, like accents, codeswitching functions to signal shared cultural/ethnic models and frames.

Some excerpts were examined using conversation analysis (CA). CA of bilingual interactions is a more recent development (see Auer 1998), following in the tradition first developed by Gumperz (1982). Gumperz described bilingual conversations as consisting of socially ordered discourse strategies. But where Gumperz (1983) see these strategies as symbolic action (i.e. they index localized norms and values), proponents of CA see language as *practical social action* or an activity in its own right. The CA approach emphasizes interpretation based on participant actions that have demonstrable effects, rather than on "context free symbolic" social categories external to the interaction.

CA has its roots in the field of ethnomethodology. Developed by Harold Garfinkel in the 1960's, ethnomethodology is concerned with the techniques that people use to accomplish their everyday tasks. Uncovering these techniques requires the fine description of interactions, specifically in a conversational setting. CA is carried out through the careful analysis of turn-taking between speakers (Sacks, et al., 1974) and relies on what can be gleaned inductively from detailed transcripts of conversation. In CA little attention is paid to variables like speakers' identities, relationships, and setting. Only when speakers can be shown to invoke these categories in the course of the conversation are they of interests to the conversation analyst (Li, 2002).

Conclusion

The key strength of the research design was the significant variety (and quantity) of data collected: interviews, social network surveys, ethnic identification surveys, naturally occurring conversations, observation data, and linguistic data. However, the research was limited by some sampling challenges. Finding Puerto Ricans (especially first generation), Mexicans, and first generation immigrants in general was problematic. I had not expected this given that Puerto Ricans and Mexicans are two of the largest Latino populations in the city. However, it was not difficult to eventually pinpoint the reasons. The rate of undocumented immigration among Mexican immigrants in New York is thought to be high and many are understandably wary of strangers identifying themselves as *investigadores*. Lack of Internet access among this and other Latino communities may also have contributed to low response rates. One of the reasons for the low response rate of Puerto Rican participants in the ethnographic phase was that I limited the phase to specific neighborhoods in Queens. While there are thousands of Puerto Ricans in Queens they are not concentrated in one area. Thus, I had no area to target with flyers and newspaper ads. In the ethnographic phase there is also an over-representation of young voices. Although I sought participants older than 50 years old, the recruitment methods I used did not reach out to enough older Latinos. Whatever the methodological challenges, documenting the everyday lives of my collaborators was a rewarding process for both them and me. It attuned me to the stuff of thick descriptions (Geertz, 1973). Those daily acts –flirtations, asking for the time, quick calls to say hello, humming a tune, laughing at casual humor, agreeing, complaining, comparing shoes sizes, discussing plans for a trip, asking for an opinion, reporting to a supervisor, being still – that can go unperceived or disregarded for their very commonness. I also become more explicitly aware of the ways that ethnicity is made relevant in many mundane acts. For informants, the opportunity to be recorded and observed was an opportunity to see their lives as exemplary cases of the human experience.

CHAPTER 3

Ethnic Identification in the NYC Context

INTRODUCTION

Latinos share a common language, similar geo-political histories, intertwined political destinies, and in some cities, neighborhoods where their lives overlap on a daily basis (Ricourt & Danta, 2003; Suárez-Orozco & Páez, 2002). Yet the similarities between Latino groups arguably end there. A number of scholars have reflected on the various intra-Latino pan-ethnic contrasts (see for example Padilla, 1984; Portes & Truelove, 1987; Rumbaut, 2006; Stepick & Stepick, 2002; Suárez-Orozco & Páez 2002; Torres-Saillant, 2002). Additionally, generational and background differences exist even between members of the same group. Scholars argue that many of these differences are, in fact, significant enough as to preclude all Latinos from being grouped together for analysis or policy treatment (Portes & Truelove, 1987).

A case can be made for either grouping or splitting. Antecedents to migration are strikingly similar across certain groups. Certain periods of Mexican, Puerto Rican, and Dominican migration were triggered by a shift from diversified, subsistence economies to capitalist agriculture and industrialization, pushing rural communities to urban zones and eventually abroad in search for work. Upon arrival in the US, Spanish-speaking immigrants are ascribed a shared group identity with normalized internal differences – consider the U.S. Census ethnic category as an example. This has partly served to engender a sense of political mutuality. Yet the socio-historical circumstances of Latino sub-populations are significantly variable. For instance, the forms of reception for each migrant group entering the U.S. have been quite different (Portes & Böröcz, 1989). Differences in the process of insertion into a host society and the set of conditions confronted by immigrants upon entrance can predict trends in economic and occupational mobility across immigrant groups. Such differences also help explain divergent patterns of ethnic identification among immigrants.

Ethnic identification and not merely economic and political integration is critical to immigrants' advancement. In the months surrounding the immigration rallies of 2006, debates about whether protesters should have displayed American flags or Mexican flags, "We are American too!" proclamations, along with collective praise of *latinidad* point to some of the ways that ethnic identification has consequences for Latinos' progress – individually or collectively. Such debates also underscore that ethnic identifications are not ideology-free. To the extent that specific ethnic identifications are associated with particular structural advantages and disadvantages, their invocations say much about where individuals position themselves (or wish to be positioned) within social hierarchies. Those differences that complicate the forging of a politically effective *latinidad* also reflect differences in the relative socio-economic and political standing of Latino sub-groups. My conversations with hundreds of Latino research participants in NYC revealed that many have an implicit sense of where various Latino groups stand in NYC's ethno-racial hierarchies. Patterns of ethnic identity invocation and EI switching – which identifications people emphasize and which they avoid – suggest how informants perceived Latino groups to be ranked. Race, wealth, education, immigration status, the size of the stateside community, and degree of political mobilization are among the most important factors comprising a certain calculus for conferring status upon a Latino subgroup.

Latino Demographic Profile: NYC, Astoria & Corona/Jackson Heights

The U.S. Census' 2005-2009 American Community Survey estimates show that 2,273,447, of the over three million Latinos in New York State, reside in NYC alone. Latinos, then, comprise almost one third of the total population of New York City. The Latino population in NYC experienced a steady increase from 2000 to 2006, growing by 5.8 percent. Puerto Ricans remain the largest Latino group in the city, at 35 percent of the total NYC Latino population, or 790, 097 individuals. The 552,155 Dominicans in NYC account for an additional 24 percent of the total Latino population. While Mexicans are the fastest growing Latino population, with an increase of 43.6 percent from 2000-2006, they are currently the third largest Latino group with 12 percent of the total Latino population and 277,151 persons. Ecuadorians and Colombians are the fourth and fifth largest subgroups of the Latino population, with 175,525 and 100,605 members respectively, though the Colombian population actually decreased between 2005 and 2006 and totaled 100,605 in the 2005-2009 ACS estimates.[3]

A comparison of this study's two main field sites, Astoria and Corona/Jackson Heights (CJH), show two highly ethnically diverse neighborhoods with notable social and economic differences. Astoria and CJH[4] have comparable population sizes with 184,083 and 182,868 respectively (U.S. Census American Community Survey 2006-2008). However, in a statement of neighborhood needs submitted to the NYC's Mayor's Office for fiscal year 2011, community board members for CJH's Community District (CD) 3 speculate that the true current total is more than 200,000 citing severe undercounts of the neighborhoods growing immigrant population (NYC Department of City Planning, 2010). A foreign-born majority lives in CJH (62.5%) while in Astoria the figure (45.3%) is on par with the overall percentage in Queens (46.7%). The foreign-born percentage for all of NYC is 35.9%, underscoring Queens' distinction as a major immigrant residential destination. For Latino immigrants, CJH is a particularly popular destination. Sixty-three percent of the population in the CJH Public Use Microdata Area (PUMA) is Latino versus 28% in the Astoria PUMA. Tables 1 and 2 show the five largest Latino populations in each of the neighborhoods. While the proportions in the list of the largest Latino groups would be quite different in other parts of NYC, Astoria and CJH are notable in that no one Latino population

---

[3] Unless otherwise indicated, all data in this section were obtained from the U.S. Census Bureau 2000 Census and U.S. Census American Community Surveys 2005-2009. This period period by the American Community Surveys overlap with the period of the study.
[4] Totals based on data for the Public Use Microdata Areas (PUMAs) corresponding to each of the two neighborhoods where I spent the most research time. Other data given in this section correspond to the overlapping but not identical community district (CD) delineations. Astoria is PUMA 4101 and CD 1. CJH corresponds to PUMA 4102 and CD 3.

predominates in either neighborhood. Still, in recent years Ecuadorians and Mexicans have come to play a more prominent economic and cultural role in CJH, a distinction once enjoyed by Colombians. Despite their majority in the overall NYC Latino population, Puerto Rican cultural and entrepreneurial influences are less marked in Astoria, and especially in CJH. While Puerto Ricans are Astoria's second largest Latino population, they are not concentrated in any one residential zone. This is also the case for CJH's Puerto Rican population.

Table 1. Top 5 Latino
Nationalities in CJH

	%
Ecuadorian	28
Mexican	18
Dominican	18
Colombian	14
Puerto Rican	5

Table 2. Top 5 Latino
Nationalities in Astoria

	%
Mexican	22
Puerto Rican	20
Ecuadorian	14
Dominican	10
Colombian	8

A closer look at the racial self-categorizations of Latinos in both communities shows a strong tendency towards identifying as white. As shown in Tables 3 and 4, this identification trend was most prevalent in Astoria. At 60% Astoria's rate of white self-identification is higher than Queens' rate of 53.5% and that in the NY-NJ-Long Island Metropolitan area more generally (40%). Given that the same Latino groups predominate in both CJH and Astoria, Latino Astorian's higher rate of white self-identification is suggestive – this in a community where 48% of the non-Hispanic population identifies as white[5]. It may be that the smaller overall Latino population in Astoria relative to the non-Hispanic white population exerts pressures or provides incentives to identify as white. The literature suggests that the level – and type – of diversity in a given context can influence self-identification. For example, in less ethnically and racially diverse schools, more students will identify with the majority group (e.g. "American") than with their own ethnic group (Nishina, et al. 2010; Rumbaut 2005). A similar pattern may be at play in Astoria. CJH was notable for the higher percentage of Latinos that identified as "Other race", which may reflect

---

[5] Compare to CJH's non-Hispanic white percentage - 13%.

CJH's larger Dominican population and/or greater variety of Latino groups, many with *mestizo* or indigenous heritage.

Table 3. Racial identification among Latinos in CJH

	%
White only	53
Black only	2
American Indian or Alaska Native only	1
Asian only	0
Native Hawaiian or Pacific Islander	0
Other race	42
Two or more races	2

Table 4. Racial identification among Latinos in Astoria

	%
White only	60
Black only	3
American Indian or Alaska Native only	1
Asian only	0
Native Hawaiian or Pacific Islander	0
Other race	32
Two or more races	3

The socio-economic status profiles of each of the neighborhoods show similarities in overall levels of educational attainment and key differences in occupational distribution. Twenty-two percent of Astoria's population holds a Bachelor's Degree, compared to CJH's 12.6%. Slightly more CJH residents have less than 9th grade education and a high school diploma (18% versus 13%). However, in all other educational categories, including graduate or professional degree holders, distributions are comparable. The slightly higher levels of post-secondary education in Astoria reflect the neighborhood's increasing importance as a home for young professionals working in Manhattan. These young professionals also contribute to the higher percentage of Astoria's population working in Management, professional, and related occupations (37.1%), which is almost double that of CJH (19.6%). In CJH service, production[6], and construction[7] occupations led the neighborhood's occupational distribution. A comparison of the two communities' household income distributions point to a curious pattern. Astoria had more households making $50,000 – 99,999 (42.4% to CJH's 34.8%) but CJH had a markedly higher percentage of households making $100,000 – 199,999 (13.4% to

---

[6] The full classification name as it appears in the U.S. Census American Community Survey (ACS) is "Production, transport, and material moving".
[7] ACS occupational classification: "Construction, maintenance, and repair".

Astoria's 3.9%). This may suggest more households with multiple income earners in CJH versus Astoria, or hint to the success of small business owners in CJH. Community Board #3's district needs statement to the Mayor's Office paints a clear picture of the importance of immigrant entrepreneurship in CJH:

> During the past thirty years, our community has experienced significant out-flows of population. This hemorrhaging of population and the negative consequences for the overall economic health of the community has been offset by the influx of new immigrant populations. Many of these new ethnic groups have added to the total mix of business establishments by initiating a wide-range of commercial start-ups... In effect, these small family-based businesses have expanded the local tax base, generated rapid growth of local labor markets, and revitalized the wide-range of commercial corridors found throughout Community Board #3. Moreover, this largely spontaneous mode of economic development has been carried out by entrepreneurs who seriously lack adequate access to technical business resources, formalized capital markets and knowledge of City regulations (Department of City Planning, 2010: 47-48).

The newest immigrant groups in CJH – and among the most entrepreneurial – include not only Mexicans and Ecuadorians, but also South Asian groups, and most notably a growing population of Bangladeshi immigrants.

If ethnic identity emerges through a process of sustained interaction between two or more ethnic groups (Barth, 1969; DeVos & Suarez-Orozco, 1990), then these two neighborhoods can produce unique ethnic identification outcomes. On the one hand, the diversity of ethnic groups available for comparison may strengthen the salience of a primary ethnic identity (Turner, 1985). On the other hand, sustained interaction can create opportunities for inter-group relations (through marriage or joint business ventures, for example), potentially weakening the salience of a primary ethnic identity (Eschbach & Gomez, 1998). I propose that a third possibility is the emergence of multiple ethnic identities. I argue that both neighborhoods offer opportunities for making the sort of inter-ethnic connections that encourage ethnic flexibility. Astoria, with its mix of European, Asian and Latin American immigrants and young professionals of many backgrounds promotes both English language abilities and a certain extra-Latino cosmopolitanism. As suggested by the distribution of racial self-categorization, day-to-day life in Astoria may also encourage identification as white. Those who live and work in CJH, where the significant majority is Latino and foreign-born, can get by with limited English proficiency and benefit from pan-Latino alliances. In addition, Mexicans, Ecuadorians, Dominicans and Colombians have sizeable numbers in CJH that help to reinforce home country cultural and linguistic practices. These various possibilities for ethnic identification vary in the advantages and disadvantages that they confer to individuals. Let's consider, then, how various ethnic options are configured in hierarchies of privilege and prestige.

Ethnic Identification and Latino Hierarchies

New York City's neighborhoods continue to be segregated according to class and race. In fact, it is one the most unequal cities in the country – containing among the richest and poorest neighborhoods in America within its boundaries. Decades after the decline of the manufacturing sector in NYC, service and knowledge-based fields – many requiring at least a high school education – drive the economy. Some Latino immigrants enter the U.S. as professionals, with both the economic means and cultural capital to enter in to and position themselves favorably within existing social structures. However, millions of Latino immigrants enter both the United States and the economy of NYC with few marketable skills and limited English proficiency.

Racial inequality has been a persistent threat to progress for Latinos, who tend to be racialized as non-white according to the American racial binary (Rumbaut, 2009). This happens regardless of whether Latinos identify as "white" themselves. However, some groups suffer more than others. Indeed, some groups experience racism before their arrival in the US, given the legacies of slavery and colonialism and histories of conquest and erasure of indigenous populations in Latin America. In the U.S., the darkest Latinos, those with African and indigenous heritage, experience a racial double-whammy – discriminated against by their whiter compatriots and fellow Latinos and subject to disadvantage in America's institutionalized racial hierarchy (Córdova & Cervantes, 2010). Indeed, as Torres-Saillant (2002) points out, black and indigenous Latinos have been the victims of a sin of omission in media and marketing discourses about both the composition and appearance of the greater and collective Latino population in the US. The binarism of America's racial system ensures that the integration of dark-skinned Latino immigrants will differ from that of light-skinned Latinos as individual and institutional race-based discrimination restricts socioeconomic mobility (Frank, et al. 2010). Beyond the economic consequences of this, ethnic identity formation is also affected. Some Latino immigrants have used American racial categories to their advantage. For example, lighter-skinned immigrants may find that emphasizing a white racial identity – as perhaps some Latinos in Astoria do – allows them greater social and economic mobility. In contrast, because the American racial binary stigmatizes dark skin, black Latinos are at a disadvantage. Therefore, dark-skinned Dominicans and Puerto Ricans may choose to emphasize a pan-Latino identity in order to mitigate the effects of non-white skin.

The American racial system produces varying self-identification patterns as it interfaces with those categorization systems immigrants bring with them. Perhaps optimistically, but not unrealistically, the meeting of incongruous ethno-racial categorization schemes, will yield new, more complex systems consonant with the lived experiences of Latino and other groups. Dominicans, who are perceived as the darkest of New York's Latinos, provide an illustrative case (Torres-Saillant, 2002). With a per capita income lower than Puerto Ricans, Ecuadorians, and Mexicans (NYC Department of City Planning 2007) the socioeconomic status of Dominicans in NYC demonstrates the negative effect of racial categorizations on advancement. However, the seemingly contradictory racial preferences among Dominicans in NYC also illustrate the process of racialization on identity formation. Dominicans enter the U.S. with notions of blackness that differ markedly from American racial conceptions and come to think of themselves in terms of a black racial identity after living in the U.S. (Bailey, 2001; Duany, 1998; Torres-Saillant, 1998).

Bailey (2001) argues that second-generation Dominicans are resisting both the contradictory racial self-conceptions of their parents and the rigid U.S. racial binary. Instead, many young Dominicans develop ethno-linguistic repertoires that reflect their daily interactions with both African and European Americans, as well as other Latinos. As a result of the common practice of sending Dominican children for extended summer visits to the Dominican Republic, many young

Dominican women and men grow up with strong ties to the Dominican Republic. These trips have also served as a way for second-generation Dominicans to maintain Spanish proficiency. As engaged transnational actors, second-generation Dominicans grow up strongly grounded in Dominican cultural and linguistic referents. On the other hand, they are also full-participants in NYC's multi-cultural milieu. Given access to multiple ethno-racial frames of reference, second-generation Dominicans help to contest facile racial classifications. Consider, for example, the following anecdote by Mildred, a 35-year old second-generation Dominican woman:

> So I like playing the guess game, just to fuck with people's heads. And sometimes, they'll say, "Oh. Where you from?" And I'll say, "Well, where do you think I'm from?" And they're like, "Hum? Are you this, are you that?" And they'll guess every nationality, except Dominican...typically they'll say, "Are you Puerto Rican?" and I'll say, "No." "Are you Colombian", and I'll say, "No." "Are you mixed—black with white? Or are you South American?" because I'm fair-skinned. Or lighter than most Dominicans, quote, unquote, because I think that's bullshit... Then I say to them, well, my parents are Dominican and I was born and raised here. And they say, "Dominican, wow. I thought that most Dominicans are like, darker complexion. You know like Sammy Sosa." And like at that point, I just got to take a step back and like, hold my emotions, because at that point, I could potentially say a lot of things. I get offended at the fact that they're bringing it up as an issue...it's this constant reminder; I'm neither here nor there.

The "neither here nor there" state Mildred describes is equally that space between "black" and "white" in the American racial binary and between "authentic" and "inauthentic" Dominican. Thus, in expanding the boundaries of what it means to be Dominican, members of the second-generation, including Mildred, must constantly push on multiple fronts. At the same time, these ambivalent ethnic spaces open up possibilities for developing ethnic flexibility. Puerto Ricans in the U.S. have gone through a similar over-simplifying racialization process. In the early years of their immigration history Puerto Ricans tended to settle near historically African American communities in

NYC and as a result have been subject to similar discrimination patterns. Both Dominicans and Puerto Ricans in New York, and particularly young men who face limited economic and social upward mobility, have embraced African American culture, identity, and language (Wolfram, 1974; Zentella, 1997). Roberto provides an apt example of how this association between Puerto Rican and blackness may be exploited. As a fair-skinned, blue-eyed Latino Roberto has at times accessed and performed dialects and styles indexing Puerto Rican identity to become "less white" by drawing on the historical associations made between NYC Puerto Ricans and NYC African Americans. Roberto is indistinguishable from other white Americans, except perhaps when he speaks in Spanish. As Roberto related to me in an interview, he had traveled to a historically African American NYC neighborhood to buy drugs though it was known that undercover police officers roamed this neighborhood. In the following excerpt, Roberto describes how he appropriated Puerto Rican (*Boricua*) identity to be seen as "more Latino" and less white:

> You know one thing when you are in a black neighborhood, right? You don't want these motherfucking *molletos*[8] to think you're white-white! Fuck that! *Me hago boricua* ('I make myself Puerto Rican')...instantly! Like I remember, the last time I got high I was on my way to cop [buy] and I knew these niggas was not even gonna look at me. You know what I did? I turned the phone to vibrate so it won't ring and I had the thing *y me pongo hablar* ('and I start to talk'), "*Mira que si este, que si lo otro, cla, cla, cla...*" ('"Look, this and that, blah, blah, blah"'). *Hablando una conversacion con el aire* ('Having a conversation with the air')! *Pero en español* ('But in Spanish'). *En boricua* ('In Puerto Rican'). *Y los tipos ahí* ('And the dudes there'): "*Bueno* ('"Well"'), you're not white!" (Roberto, life history interview, April 25, 2005)

As this example illustrates some Latino immigrants have used American racial categories and associations to their advantage, thus affecting patterns of ethnic identification. It further points to how Latino ethnicity has been conflated as a non-white racial identity. The

---

[8] A disparaging word for a black person.

significant heterogeneity of the Latino pan-ethnicity has made Latino identification into a universal key of sorts. In contexts in which blackness is valued or expected, as in the narrative above, it can be used to position oneself closer to black. Historically, immigrants who could pass as white (or would otherwise be classified as white) found that emphasizing a white racial identity allowed them greater social and economic mobility. Today, Dominicans, Puerto Ricans and other Latinos with African ancestry, may choose to lessen the impact of their skin color by emphasizing a more pan-Latino identity.

For some of the participants in my research, frequent and sustained contact with members of different Latino subgroups meant that they were able to acquire ethno-linguistic knowledge needed to relate with other out-group Latinos or even access or adopt an out-group Latino identification. Ricourt & Danta (2003; see also Sanjek, 2000), who conducted their study among women in Corona, argue that through *convivencia diaria* ('daily co-existence') a new pan-ethnic Latina community has emerged in Queens. The authors suggest that this web of informal alliances is mobilized to address pan-Latina concerns, without weakening any particular ethnic group identity. My own research indicates similar patterns of emerging pan-ethnic identification among men, especially for political and economic convenience or expediency. Though his workplace was almost exclusively Ecuadorian, and Ecuadorian ties were important to his economic advancement, Abel identified strongly with other Latinos – and had in the past roomed and worked with men from several Latin American countries:

> Since I've been here many years, I have lived with many nationalities. I have lived in an apartment where Uruguayans, Argentines, Dominicans, Brazilians live. I've gotten together with many different nationalities. Except with Ecuadorians.

Through daily contact with Latinos of different backgrounds Abel picked up various Spanish accents, greetings and idioms common in different Latin American countries, and knowledge about music and other expressions of national popular cultures. He deployed this knowledge in his daily pan-Latino interactions as a way to connect with others and express his friendly disposition - but it was Colombian identification that he would come back to time and again with more instrumental intentions. In an interview, Abel remembered one of his first jobs in the U.S. - working in construction for Portuguese contractors in New Jersey. He described his Portuguese bosses as racists who overworked and dehumanized the Ecuadorians who worked under them. Abel had learned from this to limit his identification as Ecuadorian:

> **Abel**: I didn't say that I was Ecuadorian, they have to treat me the same as them, the same as other people. I said I was Colombian.

> **Rosalyn**: And they believed you? People believed you?

> **Abel**: Because I changed my accent.

Abel had learned a Colombian accent[9] and picked up on common Colombian words and colloquialisms as a result of his many, mostly work-related, interactions with Colombians in Queens. Colombians in Queens tend to have middle-class standing and high educational attainment relative to other Latino groups. The visibility of numerous successful Colombian businesses throughout Jackson Heights adds to their prestige as a community. In the interview excerpt above the *"them"* refers to the stereotyped poor, brown-skinned *indios* of Ecuador, Mexico, Central America, etc.

Roberto and Abel drew on stereotypes of Latino subgroups that generally held the highest prestige as evaluated by Latinos in New York City. Their choices reflect the hierarchical arrangements of the various Latino subgroups in the city. As evinced by Roberto, Puerto Rican identity is both accessible and desirable. Were Latino groups' relative standing in NYC's ethnic milieu based solely on socioeconomic status, Puerto Rican's favorable position would be unexpected, especially given the history of economic marginalization of Puerto Ricans in NYC. On the other hand, Nuyorican bi-culturalism has been described as a neither here nor there dilemma. During my research, I spoke to one native-born Puerto Rican young man who contrasted his circumstances with that of Nuyoricans (he was a professional who had come to the U.S. to study and work). He saw the

---

[9] Abel did not specify which accent he used among several regional Colombian accents, which include inland and coastal varieties.

Nuyorican situation as "sad because they are rejected by both Americans in the mainland and Puerto Ricans on the island." The biggest problem, he said, "was that Nuyoricans do not speak Spanish." Thus they could not adequately comprehend and reproduce authentic Puerto Rican cultural practices and traditions. Ramos-Zayas (2004) argues that Puerto Rican authenticity – as defined by Puerto Rican islander elites like the young man above – is tied to implicit social knowledge and cultural capital gained from life on the island. Thus, Puerto Rican islanders reject mainland Puerto Ricans claim to Puerto Rican authenticity. It is interesting that Roberto identified with and performed a Puerto Rican identity rejected by Puerto Rican islanders as "exaggerated" and out of touch with current cultural practices on the island – hence closer to Nuyorican identification (see also Ramos-Zayas, 2004).

In New York City, the participation of Puerto Ricans in multiple ethno-racial worlds have enabled Nuyoricans to become both creators of and key contributors to influential cultural forms, including music from Salsa to hip-hop to reggaeton. Because of their population size, long history in the northeast, and bold nationalistic pride, Puerto Ricans have been important as a reference group. Reference groups simplify the great ethnic diversity characteristic of NYC. Because of their population size, economic prominence, or socio-cultural salience (or all of these) such groups are bases for comparison or models for categorizing people of different ethnicities. As a referent group, Puerto Ricans have greatly influenced native conceptions about Latinos in the northeast. Much like Mexicans have defined what it means to be Latino in the southwest. This helps explain why Roberto and others, including those who have only one Puerto Rican parent, invoke or emphasize Puerto Rican identity to defend their own claims to Latino identification, street-smarts, or New York grittiness. If the NYC Puerto Rican population continues to decrease (Marzán, Torres, & Luecke, 2008), other groups may gain prominence as indexing Latino identity in NYC. This could also have consequences for how NYC Puerto Ricans themselves identify.

While Puerto Rican identification was an important Latino point of reference for Roberto, for Abel Colombian identification predominated. In Jackson Heights, a successful ethnic enclave has established a strong Colombian middle class, with a per capita income is higher than that of Puerto Ricans, Ecuadorians, Mexicans, and Dominicans (NYC Department of City Planning, 2007). Jackson Heights has many

Colombian-owned businesses, which contribute to the political mobilization of Queens' Colombian community. Income and economic characteristics of Colombians are comparable to those found among Cubans. The median annual personal earnings for Cubans ages 16 and older were $26,478 in 2008 and $25,460 for Colombians. The median earnings for all U.S. Latinos were $21,488 (U.S. Census American Community Survey, 2008). Because of their aggregate economic status Abel and others positively evaluated Colombians. Alma, one of the two self-identified Colombian ethnographic participants in this study, deviated very little from her identification as Colombian, despite her many pan-Latino contacts and long-term romantic relationship with a Greek man. As she hints to, Colombians enjoy a privileged position in the Queens ethnic milieu relative to other Latinos:

> I feel proud to be Colombian. I don't feel sorry. I tell everyone that I'm Colombian because independently of thinking that Colombians work with drugs, Colombians are very educated, very educated. Manners – of the Colombians is better than that of other cultures, it seems to me. At the table, in everything. For example Dominicans, they eat with their mouth open, they talk when they're eating, they don't greet, and they don't say goodbye. We Colombians are very educated. And over there in Colombia, those manners come from Europe, from the Spaniards. Listen, I'm working with a Colombian gentleman in real estate. What an educated man, that man, it terrifies me, that man you can just see that he is Colombian. As soon as he started talking to me, like that so educated, so unhurried, so calm to talk; I said to myself this man is Colombian and he was Colombian.

Alma's account seems to deny Dominicans an ancestral connection to Spain, reserving an idealized European pedigree for Colombians. She then drew on a Latin American historical racial narrative that equates whiteness (read Colombian) with nobility and blackness (read Dominican) with the uncultured and crude. According to Alma, Colombian identity is communicated through manners of speech (independently of dialect or accent), in the way one carries oneself and in the way one treats others. Colombians are set apart from other groups not only by their economic success, but also by their social graces. During the course of my fieldwork, I often heard these perceptions from Colombians and non-Colombians alike. Thus, many Colombians in NYC see little need to invoke ethnicities other than Colombian; this identification is sufficiently advantageous outside of and within the Latino community. So while it was not uncommon to hear participants admiring and aspiring to identify with Colombians or Puerto Ricans (who tend to be lighter-skinned than Dominicans), Dominican or Mexican identification – associated with darker skin or indigenous heritage respectively – was less desirable. During my fieldwork the status of these two groups at the bottom of the perceived Latino pan-ethnic hierarchy became a recurring theme. Zentella (1990) reports that the low standing of Dominicans in this hierarchy has also had consequences for how the Dominican dialect is perceived and used. She found that while few Latinos used words associated with the Dominican dialect, Dominicans, in contrast, were the only subgroup that adopted from all other groups without exception. Zentella suggests that Colombians, Cubans and Puerto Ricans also contribute to Dominican linguistic insecurity through their widespread rejection of Dominican Spanish. In this vein, I would add that in my own study New York City Latinos similarly refrained from adopting the Mexican Spanish dialect. With the exception of expression like "*andale pues*" or "*orale*" to caricature or mock Mexicans, non-Mexican participants in this study did not switch or accommodate to this variety of Spanish. It is interesting to note that while some Latinos I encountered in the field, and especially South Americans, mocked nonstandard Puerto Rican Spanish (NSPRS)[10], perceptions of Puerto Ricans as a subgroup tended to be positive. Abel's best friend Marco, also Ecuadorian, proclaimed Puerto Ricans to be admirable for what he saw as their unwavering nationalistic pride. I cannot preclude that people withheld unfavorable opinions about Puerto Ricans because of my own Puerto Rican background.

What accounts for Mexicans unfavorable standing in NYC's Latino hierarchy? Race is certainly a factor, as is immigration status. Whereas Mexican immigrants to the southwestern U.S. have tended to

---

[10] A common example given by these critics is NSPRS's reportedly egregious affront to logic in "*pa'tra*", as in *Te llamo pa'tra* ('I will call you back'). "*Pa'tra*" or "*Para atras*" is a common Spanish calque from English used by mainland and island Puerto Ricans. Its standard translation in Spanish is 'backwards' or 'to the back' or as in the example sentence, 'I will call you backwards'.

originate and migrate from western and northwestern Mexican states like Jalisco, Zacatecas, Michoacan, Guanajuato (Durand & Massey, 2003), a new trend has developed regarding migration to New York City. The majority of Mexicans in New York come from south central Mexico, particularly Puebla and to a lesser extent Guerrero and Oaxaca (Durand & Massey 2003). Poblanos alone make up more than half of the Mexican population in New York (Dallas, 2001). According to the 2000 Mexican Census, Puebla was also among the top five Mexican states with the largest numbers of people identifying as "*Indigena*" or of indigenous ancestry (with Oaxaca being number one) (Schmal, 2004).

The increasingly restrictive anti-immigrant legislations of the 1980s attracted thousands of Mexican migrants away from the U.S. West. Regarded as more immigrant-friendly, New York saw a dramatic increase in its Mexican-origin population during this time period (Alonso-Zaldivar, 1999; Dallas, 2001). The Pew Hispanic Center estimates that 59% of undocumented immigrants in the U.S. are from Mexico (Passel & Cohn 2009) while just under half of the Mexican population in the U.S. has legal immigration status (Passel 2005). Undocumented immigrants are especially likely to hold low-skilled jobs that pay "off the books", including farming, groundskeeping and maintenance, construction, and food prep and service (Passel & Cohn, 2009). With the threat of discovery and deportation a persistent concern, undocumented immigrants are more easily subjected to exploitative work and living arrangements. These realities have contributed to the popular perception among Latinos in my field site that Mexican immigrants – who are more readily assumed to be in the country illegally - are willing to subject themselves to demeaning work conditions where their labor is pushed to extremes for low pay. In this perception, however, the Mexican man is seen as bereft of dignity and self-respect, betraying a weakness antithetical to traditional notions of Latino masculinity. When combined with the visible indigenous heritage of many NYC Mexicans, their perceived status at the bottom of the hierarchy can be easily understood. As Abel explained is the case in Ecuador, indigeneity is associated with low levels of education and backwardness – a view echoed throughout much of Latin American. Abel's wish to distance himself from this association – given his own indigenous heritage and status as an undocumented immigrant – motivated him to pass as "anything but

Ecuadorian" in an effort to expand his option for mobility against these factors which would otherwise limit them.

Abel's case further suggests that to get a sense of the relative standing of various Latino groups – and how those rankings might affect patterns of ethnic identification – one must also consider intra-ethnic divisions. According to Abel, Ecuadorians believe that a person from the coast (*costeños*) can trust other Latinos more than Ecuadorian compatriots from the Ecuadorian Sierras (*serranos*), and vice versa. As Abel, who is from the coastal city of Guayaquil, put it:

> What's happening is that in my country there's regionalism. Regionalism is that the people from the highlands don't get along with the people from the coast. There's- because those from the coast think they are a bit more attractive, more alive, more sharp...more cool. They think they are more attractive, yes. So, the people from the highlands are more conservative. A highland man is a hypocrite. They talk nice to your face and then behind your back; "that son-of-a bitch!" So there's regionalism in our country and that's what divides my country.

Regional conflicts that exist in Ecuador have been transplanted to New York City. The *costeño* refers to a *serrano* as *indio* and perceives him as backwards and conservative. *Serranos,* in turn, think of *costeños* as proud and pretentious. Thus, while intra-ethnic connections are important for Ecuadorian immigrants, there is some evidence that these form along the regional distinctions that order relations in Ecuador.

Conclusion

Interacting with America's own folk racial concepts, Latinos carry with them the burden of negative associations not only of *negro,* but also *indio.* These associations cut across boundaries of national origins so that a black Colombian or Panamanian immigrant may have better relations with a dark-skinned Dominican in New York than with the light-skinned residents of their own home countries. Similarly, an Ecuadorian from the Quechua-speaking, indigenous areas of the Sierra, may have more *simpatía* with a highland Peruvian or a *poblano* of Mexico, than with an Ecuadorian *costeño.* However, it would be both simplistic and baseless to assume that /Latinos of African heritage and indigenous heritage have in this a basis for creating bonds. While both groups are perceived to be at the bottom of the Latino ethnic hierarchy, the settlement patterns of black Latinos, predominantly from the Caribbean, and Latinos with indigenous heritage from Mexico and Ecuador have only recently begun to converge in New York City[11]. These previously divergent settlement patterns have allowed for fewer opportunities for the sort of *convivencia diaria* ('daily coexistence') that encourages pan-ethnic *collectividad*. A day after the April 2006 immigration rally in NYC I interviewed one Dominican man named Jon who had arrived to the U.S. with a tourist visa in the 1960s. He eventually overstayed the visa and lived without documentation in the U.S. for many years before petitioning for a green card through his wife. When I asked Jon for his opinions of the immigration rallies, his assured response was that no special rights or amnesty should be afforded to undocumented immigrants. "The Mexicans come here to abuse the system," he said, underscoring the association readily made between Mexicans and undocumented status. When I asked him to explain this stance given his own immigration experience, he explained that his case was different: his intention from the beginning was to work hard and get his papers as quickly as possible. His assumption was that Mexicans had little desire to become permanent residents and be a part of American society as he himself did. Despite a shared undocumented immigration history with those Latinos who demonstrated for amnesty, Jon saw little in common between himself and them.

Cross-generationally[12] we find another important bases for distinction among Latinos. The greater English-proficiency among second-and third-generation migrants opens up opportunities to build out-group relationships and greater opportunities for developing ethnic self-identifications tied to these relationships (e.g. American or Latino). These later generations grow up in a cosmopolitan New York. Through

---

[11] Large Mexican populations are now found in the historically Puerto Rican community of El Barrio in East Harlem as well as in the upper west side and the Bronx near Dominican enclaves. In Corona, Queens, home of a large Dominican population, the increase in the Ecuadorian and Mexican populations has meant greater contact between these groups.

[12] Considerable length-of-stay in the U.S. will be included as part of this generational distinction. So, an immigrant who arrived in the U.S. at a very early age and lived in the U.S. for most of their life is assumed to exhibit beliefs and behaviors consistent with a second-generation immigrant.

school and work, they branch out beyond the ethnic enclave. In some cases, if out-group relationships dominate the social network over long periods of time, the person can come to identify primarily with this out-group. For example in the case of Clarissa, the young, white, Puerto Rican woman raised in predominantly black neighborhoods with a largely black social network, who claimed a black identity for herself. Roberto, who we will shortly turn to, grew up among Puerto Ricans and had long-term relationships with Puerto Rican women. He had expertly adopted the Puerto Rican dialect, was familiar with Puerto Rican idioms and popular culture, and identified strongly with his Puerto Rican friends. Each of these two participants developed a repertoire of behaviors quite consistent with their adopted ethnic groups. In overcoming the structural barriers that limit more recent migrants, later generations tend to diverge economically, behaviorally and in identification, from their parents and grandparents.

Of course, there are exceptions to these two trends. For example, first-generation Mexican or Argentine finance and information sector professionals may experience similar patterns of integration as second and third generation migrants. Proficient in English, they may build diverse social networks that include members of other ethnic groups, including Americans of various ethno-racial backgrounds. They may live in Manhattan, rather than immigrant Queens. In turn, these immigrants would have little in common with undocumented migrant laborers and could develop more fluid ethnic self-concepts not tied to one national group. For thousands of Mexicans in NYC, restrictive immigration policies, high rates of undocumented immigration and dependence on kin networks offer few opportunities for developing non-Mexican or non-Latino affiliations. Submersion in Mexican-dominant daily life discourages English-language learning and flexible ethnic self-presentation. Census 2000 statistics support this (U.S. Census, 2000). Mexicans are more likely to be non-US citizens; 60% compared to 24% among other Latino communities. They are also less likely to be English proficient; 38.7% do not speak English well or at all compared to 21.6% among other Latinos.

These examples illustrate that even within specific Latino sub-groups is it difficult to link Latino individuals to neat, static ethnic categories. It seems the pan-ethnic Latino identification itself has been fortified by specific conditions of the immigrant incorporation process including anti-immigrant / anti-Latino policies, the automatic ascription of Latino identification to Spanish-speaking immigrants, discrimination, and neighborhood daily co-existence of people from throughout Latin America. These conditions and experiences are not common to all who may be labeled Latino. Moreover, as Oboler (1992: 32) pointed out, "aspects of personal identity may promote and/or hinder" the political articulation of Latino collective interests. These personal identities are formed and informed by a complex of factors, including socio-economic characteristics of individual immigrants, their mode of incorporation into American society, and perceptions of the relative standing among various Latino ethno-racial groups which imposes incentives and disincentives for using certain ethnic identifications.

CHAPTER 4

"I Can Roll Into Whatever": The Case of Roberto

INTRODUCTION

Roberto and I first met at a Starbucks in Astoria, where I conducted screening interviews for participants in the ethnographic phase. Just as he said he would, Roberto entered the café wearing a blue jump suit, white sneakers and a New York Yankees baseball hat. We greeted each other in English, as we would for most of our interactions. From the beginning Roberto struck me as an energetic and enthusiastic man. At this first meeting, I quickly recognized that he used this energy and enthusiasm to be persuasive.

During our time together, Roberto candidly shared his experiences with drug abuse, economic hardship, and family turmoil. Though I did not fully realize it until I listened to his recordings more than a year later, he was under intense financial pressure. Yet he was quite patient with my prodding and me and generally cool under pressure. Roberto also freely shared his knowledge of running *street* businesses. As we walked together in Manhattan and Queens, he explained to me how African street vendors make money on watches and wallets, why and how Chinese sellers peddle bootleg DVD's and the best way to compete with them, and the workings of a few other illegal operations. He also put me to work in his canopy business, assembling canopy set-ups and moving tables and chairs for street fairs.

His ethnically diverse upbringing coupled with personal upheavals and economic scarcity, had made it possible for him to develop ethnicity as a survival tool. If variation means adaptation, then

Roberto's example shows that in the demanding ethnic milieu that is NYC, ethnic and linguistic variation has clear adaptive advantages.

A Brief History of Roberto

At the age of nine, Roberto's mother sent him from Venezuela to live with his father in the US. In New York, he grew up in an ethnically mixed Queens neighborhood: with significant populations of European Americans, African Americans, and Latinos. Roberto recounted to me that he was often confused for Italian or Greek while growing up. As an adolescent, his closest childhood friends were Puerto Rican, Colombian, and Italian, yet he lived near a neighborhood with a large African American and West Indian population and his stepmother is black Haitian. With his father as his only real tie to Venezuela, Roberto learned to "walk the walk and talk the talk" of the other Latinos he came in regular contact with. For example, he recounts that his best friends' Puerto Rican mothers and grandmothers were like second mothers to him. These women cooked for him and welcomed him into their homes.

After high school, Roberto planned to enter the Marine Corps. He traveled back to Venezuela for four months to "clean up his system." However, within two months of his return to the US, Roberto's father died and he was thrown into a tailspin. Leaving his childhood community to wander the streets of New York City, he succumbed to substance abuse. For three years he lived in the homeless shelter system and was in-and-out of detox programs. During this period of his life he honed his urban survival skills, which undoubtedly included using ethnicity and language to avoid trouble and establish supportive bonds. One of the other things that Roberto became good at was making "fast money." During my time with him, I observed him use his ethnic and linguistic flexibility in attempts to secure financial stability.

Despite these periods of considerable instability, Roberto met and fell in love with Annie, with whom he now lived and helped to raise her 12-year-old daughter. Annie was Roberto's closest confidant and business partner. She identified strongly as Puerto Rican and expressed this identification in her occasionally use of Spanish, love for Latin dancing, and the Puerto Rican stickers and flags that adorned her car and home.

The graphic below (see Figure 1) depicts Roberto's ethnically diverse social network. Growing up in middle-class Queens Village, Roberto lived among a mix of people and languages. His close childhood friends were European-, Colombian- and Puerto Rican-American. Queens Village is close to Jamaica, an established middle-class West Indian neighborhood and Roberto reports being one of the few "white kids" in a predominantly black school. Roberto affirms that he was more drawn to the "Spanish crowd" and "the whites": the Spanish guys because they "got all the pretty girls" and the white guys because he felt he had more in common with them than with blacks.

Figure 1. Roberto's Personal Network

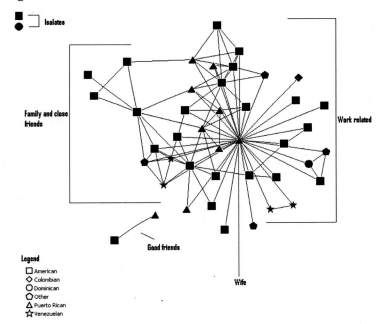

In Figure 1, the legend indicates the ethnic background of each of the 45 network members (alters) he listed. Roberto's network consists of four components. The largest component appears in the middle and includes work related, family and friendship ties. Next, at the bottom left of the graph, two nodes are connected to each other and no one else. These are women who are related to each other, and have been supportive to Roberto in his life. Finally, each of the two isolates is a separate component. These two are distant acquaintances (Roberto was unsure about the last name of one of them), who have no relation to each other or anyone else in the network.

Roberto's personal network is moderately dense with some areas more interconnected than others. His family and close friends share more connections than his work related contacts, for example. The people he has known in his moneymaking ventures have not all been from one employer or organization. We can see that most are spread out, several of whom are linked only to Annie. The largest component represents 41 of the 45 alters Roberto listed. His wife, Annie, can be seen in the middle, the most central person in his network. Except for the isolates and dyad on the bottom right, Annie has contacts with all areas of Roberto's network. In my week with Roberto (and in the other week he recorded on his own), he had contact with very few of the 45 people he listed. I personally met only his wife, step-daughter (represented by the square above and slightly to the right of Annie), and five or six of his work-related contacts who he spoke to in person and by phone.

The ethnic diversity of his upbringing and formative years is also represented in the figure above. Roberto described half of his network as American (square nodes). Three of these he further described as Nuyorican or of Puerto Rican descent. His American alters are mostly European American, but four were described as African American or mixed-race. Of the pentagonal nodes ("Other"), two he categorized as Russian, one as Jamaican, and another as Haitian (his step-mother appears as the pentagon above and connected to Annie). A number of his alters are Puerto Rican, more so than those who are Venezuelan. Finally, Roberto had weak ties to (based on levels of closeness to each alter evaluated by Roberto) to a Dominican man and a Colombian man. Thus, the two major network influences, both in terms of numbers and degree of closeness, were American and Puerto Rican. As we will see in his linguistic data, these influences are evident in his codeswitching and discourse.

Roberto's Ethnic and Regional Identifications

Any study analyzing how ethnic identifications are used in everyday life has to contend with potentially essentializing or reifying the categories that individuals use to identify themselves. In the following descriptions of Roberto's ethnic repertoire (as with Abel in Chapter 5),

I describe the identifications indexed (Jaffe, 2009; Ochs 1992; Silverstein 1976) by the linguistic styles and dialects he used in his daily interactions. I also draw on my interviews with Roberto, where he narrated the experiences and relationships in his life that influenced his perceptions of different ethnic categories and his bond to them. While this study emphasizes the malleability of ethnic categories, Roberto sometimes applied labels like "white," "Puerto Rican," and "Latino" in monolithic ways. For example, when invoking his connection to Puerto Rican ethnicity or performing according to popular conceptions about what Puerto Ricans "acted" like, Roberto drew on his knowledge of the New York Puerto Rican communities he was most familiar with. To accomplish this he used a non-standard Puerto Rican Spanish that indexed working class Nuyorican identity (Zentella 1997). He called this dialect "Puerto Rican" as in: "I don't speak New York Spanish, like I said, I can roll into whatever. Usually we talk more Puerto Rican than anything (Roberto, life history interview, April 25, 2005)." Roberto had developed certain attachments, especially via his self-identified Puerto Rican wife, to symbolic elements of Puerto Rican culture such as salsa music and dancing, traditional Puerto Rican food, and displaying the Puerto Rican flag. Frequent trips with his wife to Puerto Rico have also served to reinforce his connections to Puerto Rican culture and identity. In fact, he considered himself to be more knowledgeable about Puerto Rico than his native Venezuela:

> I know a lot about Puerto Rico. I know more about Puerto Rico than about my own country. You can drive me right now to Puerto Rico and I go boom! Give me the rental, I know where I'm going, I know what to do. Do that shit in Venezuela? *No joda, me encuentran en una montaña, allá al la'ito 'e Colombia. Perdi'o!* ('No kidding, they'll find me in a mountain, over there next to Colombia. Lost!')

I asked Roberto if he tried to pass as Puerto Rican when he visited the island and he exuberantly replied yes. When I asked him why, his immediate response was: "I don't know. Pathological liar maybe?" But then, he provided the example given in Chapter 3, in which he attempted to pass as Puerto Rican in order to purchase drugs. In that excerpt Roberto recounts speaking in a Spanish that he considered to be

"Puerto Rican" to convince drug dealers that he was not a white undercover cop. While Roberto thinks of his attempts to pass/cross as a character flaw, he unabashedly acknowledged his ethnic flexibility and the benefits that come from it.

As I will show below, Roberto had more relationships with Puerto Ricans than with Venezuelans. His U.S.- and island-born Puerto Rican contacts reinforced his general tendency to speak non-standard Puerto Rican Spanish. With his few Venezuelan contacts, on the other hand, he spoke what he described as Venezuelan Spanish. He further expressed his Venezuelan identity by using the "Venezuelan" label to describe himself: "I'm from Venezuela. / *Yo soy Venezolano*. ('I'm Venezuelan')". "Venezuelan" was one of two labels that I heard Roberto precede with "I am."

There are less than 20,000 Venezuelans in the NYC metropolitan area (U.S. Census American Community Survey, 2006-2008). The absence of a large Venezuelan community in NYC has had a distinct impact on ethnic identification among Venezuelans in this area. Because the Venezuelan community is not associated with a particular neighborhood, Venezuelan immigrants in the city draw more broadly on Spanish-speaking and/or Latino pan-ethnic connections for social, economic, and informational resources. At the same time, the absence of such a community means that there isn't a clear reference group for non-Venezuelans, particularly those not from South America, to form salient impressions, models, and stereotypes about Venezuelans. In Roberto's case, this fact meant that, while others frequently misjudged his nationality, he was able to use this ambiguity to his advantage.

Roberto attributed his ambiguous physical appearance – or his non-stereotypically Latino appearance – to his Spanish heritage. He strongly linked Spanish heritage with light skin – both he and his father were light-skinned and blue-eyed. Roberto's father was born in Spain and he further associated his father's background with strong values and education – "My father was born in Spain, he was very educated." and "My father is that type of Spaniard that, he brought me up with values! (Roberto, life history interview, April 25, 2005)." When I first met Roberto, I asked him how he identified himself on socio-demographic questionnaires, and he indicated Spanish. In the following excerpt Roberto explains why and confirms that a basis for his identifying someone as Spanish is their physical appearance:

Rosalyn: So when we first talked, when you first answered questions you said you were Spanish even though you were born in Venezuela.

Roberto: Yeah, I'm Spanish.

Rosalyn: Do you think it has to do with the closeness that you had with your dad?

Roberto: I don't believe that but that's where my roots are from, that's where my roots are from. You know my roots are all from Spain. I think and I believe that my mother is also from Spain. I really do, I don't know but I think you know. Like looking at my grandmother and you know her mother. Yeah, I believe that, yeah, her family has got be from Spain. So that's why I, I would say that I'm from Spain.
(Life history interview, April 25, 2005)

Because Roberto subscribed to the notion that Latinos are racialized as non-white, his phenotype challenged his Latino identification. Having grown up in a diverse community with European Americans, African Americans, and Latinos, he shifted between emphasizing his whiteness and other times working to de-emphasize it (as in the drug buying example). When he talked about European Americans he sometimes spoke in we/them terms, with European Americans as "them." Other times he blurred the boundaries between we/them. In the following two excerpts describing his kinship to white identity, Roberto details behavioral and stylistic qualities that both define him and define "white" for him:

And the whites were just, they were more like me in the sense of, you know, the whole crew likes to play handball, you know, we all like to ride our bikes, everybody worked on their bikes.

Like I could be a white boy. I would listen to classic rock and wear them jackets and the jeans, and you know "hi dude, how are you doing dude" and you know.
(Roberto, life history interview, April 25, 2005)

Notably, in the latter excerpt he doesn't quite appropriate white identification, but rather describes how he relates performatively to ethnicity. When he says that he "could be a white boy" he means that he could take on a "white boy" persona by changing the way he dressed and the way he talked. In English-dominant conversations, he usually used a New York English dialect historically – and popularly – associated with European American New Yorkers. English was also the language he spoke most regularly and most fluently.

Though he did not say it in so many words, Roberto clearly related perfomatively to Puerto Rican identification. And to some extent he performed a certain African American urban persona as well. Roberto held unambiguously racist opinions about African Americans, even using racial epithets such as *molleto* and *cocolo*. Yet he identified with African American urban culture ("I like my rap, I like my Hip Hop", Roberto, life history interview, April 25, 2005) and used African American Vernacular English (AAVE) and other linguistic styles indexing African American identity ("You know what time it is with this *nigger* right here, son!", conversation with a friend, June 11, 2005). In the days that I observed Roberto he deployed this style when talking to African Americans or in English-dominant conversations with other Latinos as a way to index a non-white urban identity (what he called "street" or "ghetto"). In others words he used certain ethnic markers to downplay the fact of his phenotype to those he deemed to fit properly within the non-white realm (African Americans and Latinos). As he compellingly explains:

Roberto: I stopped [hustling]. Annie doesn't want me to do the fast money shit. She gets mad at me.

Rosalyn: Why?

Roberto: Because she knows how I am. I like fast money. I mean, I like fast money (laughing) the quicker the money the better. The easier to get the better and she don't like this, you know what it is – and I got to respect that from her? –

Rosalyn: Yes?

Roberto: She doesn't like the spirit it brings.

Rosalyn: OK.

Roberto: Because I get ghetto real quick! I get ghetto real quick. I start wearing my pants down a little. I start, you know, I start a little hip on the walk and you know, I get ghetto! (laughing) I get street.

Rosalyn: But why is that?

Roberto: I don't know? When you've been brought up, I've been brought up... I've been brought up in the street. When you are in the street like I can't walk up to Harlem and roll up to a bunch, you know, *cocolos* hanging out in front of a building, playing dice.

Rosalyn: What do you mean *cocolos*?

Roberto: *Morenos*[13], and they're in front of a building playing dice, you're not just going to walk up to them and, "hey papa, que si que ('hey pop, what's up')", No. you got to be, you got have that spirit with you.

Rosalyn: Mhm.

Roberto: I'd be like, "Yo pa, check it out man I got these movies, yo what's up? Wha'chu need?"

Rosalyn: Yeah.

Roberto: You know, the whole, everything the lingo, everything. You got to have it all down. You can't be like, "Hey, how are you doing, would you like to buy some DVD's?" (in a voice mocking a nerdy persona).

Rosalyn: (laughing)

---

[13] Folk category commonly used in the Spanish-speaking Caribbean to describe a dark- or brown-skinned person.

Roberto: The nigga's gonna be, "yeah I buy DVD's, come here give me that that shit!". Take it right away! 'Cause what they're seeing is a white face. They don't see Spanish. if you look at me you don't see Spanish, you don't see Spanish! You can't tell! So you got to roll up there, you roll, you roll like, like you belong there. You got to make yourself a part of the environment and that's in everything you do.

Rosalyn: Mhm.

Roberto: That's just in everything you do. Man, wow, life is wicked, huh?
(Conversation during ethnographic observations, April 26, 2005).

As I will show in the analyses that follow, Roberto distinguished himself as someone who eagerly made himself a part of his environment. More specifically, he used his linguistic skills and cross-cultural fluency to forge and strengthen connections with strangers and friends.

Roberto's Linguistic Repertoire

In my analyses of Roberto's conversations I have considered both the formal linguistic descriptions of various dialects with Roberto's own descriptions. Roberto had clear ideas about what Puerto Ricans and Venezuelans are *supposed* to sound like - which didn't always correspond with the descriptions that linguists would use. His perception of what Puerto Ricans were supposed to sound like was informed by his relationship with other Puerto Ricans in Queens, where he grew up, and throughout the city in the 1980s and 1990s when Puerto Ricans were still the most prominent Latino sub-group in terms of population and contributions to urban popular culture. His wife was also an important influence. She identified as Puerto Rican though she was raised by her African American mother and was estranged from her Puerto Rican father. Finally, while he had traveled to the island on several occasions, his most consistent exposure to Puerto Rican Spanish was through Puerto Ricans in New York City.
In addition to these experiences, Roberto could, of course, draw on his experiences as a young boy, both in Venezuela and after

immigrating to the U.S. with his Venezuelan father. His exposure to multiple dialects while growing up in Queens further helped him to develop a way of talking that he described as "a flow." In his everyday speech – when talking in Spanish – this "flow" combined Puerto Rican Spanish (standard and non-standard varieties) with Venezuelan intonation and certain words that he had come to strongly associate with being Venezuelan. He described this speech style as a flow because it was automatic and did not involve consciously trying to "put on an accent." And it is this speech style that, according to Roberto, led people to assume he was Cuban:

Roberto: I guess I get a lot, I get a lot of (yawning) excuse me? I get a lot of that.

Rosalyn: A lot of what?

Roberto: If I'm Cuban?

Rosalyn: Oh yeah?

Roberto: When I talk Spanish. That's when I don't try to put the dialect in - you know, I just normally flow - they ask me if I'm Cuban.

Rosalyn: So when do you try, like what is…

Roberto: It depends what, what my surroundings…

Rosalyn: So give me an example of some surroundings where you might change your dialect.

Roberto: A bar on Roosevelt Avenue full of some freaking really mean Colombians.

Rosalyn: Ah yeah?

Roberto: I'll change the dialect. I'm either going to the Puerto Rican or just talk the mellow Colombian Spanish.

Rosalyn: Aha and ahm why?

Roberto: Some of them places are dangerous man, they fucking they don't like…Even like, Colombians for example, they don't like as far as they don't like you know, they just like their own kind. That's just the way they are. Not that I put myself in those predicaments anymore anyway but, but that's just an example of why I, where I would change it.

Rosalyn: And what's another example?

Roberto: Deep, deep Bronx, when it's nothing but Puerto Ricans. I go right into Puerto Rican mode. But that's easy. Puerto Rican mode is easy. I grew up doing… I grew up. I don't even got to try for that, that just comes automatic.

Rosalyn: Yeah, yeah. And what other modes do you have?

Roberto: The Cuban, the Venezuelan.

Rosalyn: Yeah, what is the Venezuelan? I don't even know how the…

Roberto: The Venezuelan, it's just a, it's just a flow, it's just. You ever seen a *novela* ('Spanish soap opera'), the Venezuelan *novelas*?

Rosalyn: No.

Roberto: You could tell the Venezuelan from the Mexicans, from the Colombians.

Rosalyn: Yeah.

Roberto: It's in the way they speak. I can't explain it. It just is. Like when I was talking to my boy yesterday. To Omar. That was a, that was Venezuelan.

Rosalyn: I noticed that, like you pronounced the s's. Like you...

Roberto: ((taking on an accent) *Chamo, que si esto que si lo otro* ('Listen man, this and that.') . I pronounce the s's, I pronounce the r's, I pronounce everything. Something I thank my dad for man.
(Conversation during ethnographic observations, April 26, 2005).

As I will shortly outline, formal descriptions of Venezuelan Spanish compare it to Caribbean Spanish forms, noting, for example, final –s deletion as a feature that Venezuelan shares with Caribbean Spanish dialects. Still, as Roberto explains in the preceding interview excerpt, he described Venezuelan – his particular version – as retaining s's and r's. Roberto's linguistic behavior highlights the limits of making strict comparison to formal dialectal descriptions in identifying the linguistic varieties that individuals use to index particular identities. Phonological deviations from a standard do not necessarily suggest that a given phonological variable has moved into another dialectal field. Rather such a shift away from a standard can reflect a speaker's perception of language varieties. These perceptions are formed by a constellation of factors, including ideologies about the value and propriety of language varieties and individuals' life experiences. In what follows, I provide descriptions developed by linguistics for the dialects that Roberto used most regularly. I accompany each description with examples from Roberto's naturally occurring speech.

Puerto Rican Spanish

Zentella (1997) distinguishes between Standard (SPRS) and Non-Standard (NSPRS) varieties of Puerto Rican Spanish. The most significant feature setting apart SPRS and peninsular Spanish is the aspiration or elision of syllable final /s/. This feature is shared by other Caribbean Spanish dialects. SPRS is further distinguished from other Spanish dialects by the pronunciation of word initial <r> and medial <rr> as a velar /x/ or uvular trill /R/, rather than the more common apico-alveolar trill /r/. Cited by speakers as the most distinctly *Puerto Rican* of all the sounds in Puerto Rican Spanish (Lipski, 2004), this feature renders words like *arroz* ('rice') and *rico* ('rich') with a raspy quality. Syntactic traits of SPRS include: lack of inversion of the subject in questions where the subject is a pronoun (e.g. *Que tu haces?* for *Que haces tu?*, 'What are you doing?'); conservation of subject pronouns, mainly *yo*, *tú*, and *usted*, where they would otherwise be implied in other Spanish dialects (Hochberg, 1986, Lipski, 2004), (e.g. *Yo tengo hambre* for *Tengo hambre*, 'I am hungry').

In her study of bilingual Puerto Rican children in New York City's *El Barrio*, Zentella (1997) described two pronunciations used by participants in her research and particularly associated with nonstandard or popular Puerto Rican Spanish: syllable final /s/ aspiration or elision even in formal speech and substitution of /l/ for syllable final /r/ (e.g. *recuelda* for *recuerda*, 'remember'). Zentella notes that these consistencies were found among those participants "who were born and raised in Puerto Rico in poor families, often those from rural areas who had little formal education (1994: 44)." Another common phonological feature of NSPRA is the weakening or elision of inter-vocalic /d/. This happens most frequently in words ending with – *ado* (e.g. *enojao* for *enojado*, 'angry'). A syntactic characteristic of NSPRS relevant for some of the research participants in this study is the use of phrasal calques (Otheguy et al., 1989) emerging from English syntactic influences. For example, *para atrás* (*patrás*), literally 'for back', as in *Te llamo patrá* from 'I will call you back', rather than *Te devuelvo la llamada*.

Roberto's Examples[14]:

((At a pre-Puerto Rican Day Parade festival in Brooklyn, Roberto passes out promotional materials to an anonymous woman (W))):

R: *Papo coje.* (1.3) *Vamo(-s) mami coje.* (*Ya*
     'Man take this. Come on dear take this. (Now
     te la) da do/h/.
     I) give two.'
W: *Que e/h/to?*

---

[14] In the following excerpts of Roberto's speech, as with other transcripts of naturally occurring conversations in this study, I have used Conversation Analysis transcription conventions (Sacks, Schlegoff, and Jefferson, 1974), see Appendix C.

'What is this?'
R: *No se? (.) Pero lo e/h/tan dando ahí gra?ti(-s).*
'I don't know. But they're giving it away free there.'
((Roberto laughs))
R: *Yo no se. Yo (   ). No me impo/l/ta.*
'I don't know. I (   ). I don't care.'

((During pre-street fair preparation in Manhattan, Roberto instructs fellow street fair workers on proper set up)):

R: Right there! Put the pan right there, in the
   bottom, right there. A:::::h! *Pa(-ra) que vea.*
                              'That's so you see.'

R: Alright Ange, let me go. ((Talking to his wife on the phone))

R: *AJA! PA(-RA) ESO CORREN!*
   'Aha! For that, run!'
   AJA! PA(-RA) QUE VEAN!
   'Aha! That's so you all see!'
   Pa(-ra) eso co/x/en.
   'For that, run.'

New York English (NYE)

Labov's (1982) classic study of the New York dialect provides the most comprehensive description of its phonological and syntactic attributes. An important expression of New York City's distinguished immigration history and character, NYE evolved through contact between the various languages spoken by those who moved to New York beginning with the earliest Dutch settlements. Provided that NYC's ethnic groups move further towards inter-ethnic contact and mixing, this would suggest that the dialect will continue to change, influenced by the relatively more recent and significant migrations from Latin American, Asia, and West Indies. Though not exclusively, today NYE is widely spoken by European Americans born and raised in New York City and neighboring areas.

The "New York City accent" is based on the following features analyzed by Labov. I will cover only those most relevant to the participants in this study:

Tensing and raising of the vowel sound /aw/ in words like *more*, *coffee*, *long*, and *talk*; tensing of the short <a> vowel in words like *banana* and *bad*, with /æ/ becoming /eə/; elision of syllable final and pre-consonant <r> in words like *butter* and *park*; dentalization of /d/ and /t/, and replacement of lingua-dental fricatives /θ/ and /ð/ with dentalized stops /d/ and /t/ (e.g. *dis* for *this*).

Roberto's Examples:

((Calls a friend he had not talked to in a long time to ask for help))
R: No, and I got these ice cream carts Bobby?
(Though) I got these ice cream carts that are ban/eə/nas!
I got the big Haggen Da/d/z ca(-r)ts.

R: It c/aw/st a dolla(-r) a piece.

((Pitching his services to a potential client))
R: I can organize stree:tfai(-r)s for you, f- for your
people if they want. >If they need somebody w- /d/at,
/d/at, knows how to organize it they need somebody that
< I can go out, I can get /d/e vendo(-r)s.

Venezuelan Spanish

Venezuelan Spanish is classified under the broader category of Caribbean Spanish. Therefore, while intonation patterns and lexicon differ from those of Cuban, Dominican, and Puerto Rican Spanish, some important phonological features are shared. According to Lipski (2004), these include: weakening of intervocalic /d/, and syllable and word final /s/ elision or aspiration. Traits unique to Venezuelan Spanish include strong pronunciation of /y/ and as an affricate in word / syntagma initial position, velarized word-final /n/, /rr/ pronounced as a slightly devoiced alveolar vibrant, and syllable final /r/ elision.

Roberto's Example:

((Talks to a Venezuelan friend outside of his apartment about
a Venezuelan acquaintance)):
R: *Y le engañaron. O sea, un pe(d-)o- no:: esa vaina*
'And they fooled him. In other words, a problem- no that
mess
lo tiene que pe?lea:r., (hue-)von. Porque aquí no ha
he has to fight, dude. Because here no one has
llama- a- a- aquí no llamo na?die.
call- h- h- here no one called.'

African American Vernacular English (AAVE)

African American Vernacular English was spoken to varying degrees
by six of the eleven participants in the ethnographic phase of this
research. Of the five who did not use AAVE, three are not native
English speakers. This usage speaks to New York Latinos'
identification with their African American peers, as discussed above.
Some researchers consider the use of AAVE by both African
Americans and Latinos as resistance to dominant, disparaging
discourses (Bailey, 2001; Morgan, 1994). In this study, a switch to
AAVE had social functions. Spoken mostly in informal registers,
AAVE codeswitches were used as contextualization cues, for ethnic
signaling, and more generally as a means of gaining acceptance by
others. AAVE was also used to provide emphasis to certain arguments
or expressions, to be humorous (not in a way mocking to AAVE), and
to imbue the speaker with a certain toughness or directness.

Among the AAVE features most used in this study were elision of
postvocalic and intervocalic /r/ (e.g. *car* pronounced as /ka/),
substitution of syllable final velar nasal <ng>, /ŋ/, with alveolar nasal
<n> in two syllable words (e.g. *notin'* for *nothing*), devoicing of /b/,
/d/, and /g/ (e.g. *secon'* for *second*), elision of syllable final /s/ and /'s/
(e.g. *50 cent* for *50 cents*), copula deletion (e.g. *You funny* for *You are
funny*), elision of subject-verb agreement marker <s> (e.g. *He make me
mad* for *He makes me mad*), double negation (*They don't want none* for
They don't want any), and replacement of *am not, isn't, aren't*, etc.
with *ain't*. As with New York English, there is also the tendency to
pronounce lingua-dental fricatives /θ/ and /ð/ with dentalized stops /d/
and /t/. This can depend on the sound's position in a word (Green,
2002). Habitual *be*, part of the tense-aspect system (Labov, 1972;

Morgan, 1994), and considered one of the most distinguishing features of AAVE, was also used by some participants. Habitual *be* expresses that an action is performed habitually or continually (e.g. *She be trippin'*, 'She often acts crazy'). Another component of the tense-aspect marking is the use of stressed *been* or *bin* (e.g. *I been done the work*) to denote an action that occurred in the distant past and either was completed in the past or continues into the present. So, in the example above, the translation would be 'I did the work a long time ago.' Finally, there were numerous words and expressions popularly associated with AAVE, used by participants in this study: *Yo* (an interjection), *bro* ('brother' or 'friend'), *word up* (used as a greeting on in place of *yeah*), *mad* ('a lot'), *'nuff* (from *enough*, also meaning 'a lot'), *son* ('friend') *tripping* ('going crazy', 'acting crazy', 'acting funny'). Constructions like *baby-mother* ('unmarried mother of a child') and *baby-daddy* ('unmarried father of a child') are more recent, but ubiquitous, additions to AAVE.

Roberto's Example:

((Talking to me about a friend (F) who he had recruited to help him with a street fair))
R: He didn't have to set up <u>cans</u>. He didn't <u>do</u> not(-h)in(-g).
He lazy. I'm putte- I'm put his ass to work today.

((Helping a friend to figure out how to get the recorder to work))
R: That shit is on, <u>baby</u>.
F: It wasn't on before /d/ough.
R: That's (be-)cause you ain't lookin(-g), sonny boy.

((Talking to friend on the phone about an upcoming street fair))
R: I got <u>mad</u> shit to drop off!

Data and Analysis

Codeswitching (CS) is the use of two or more linguistic varieties (i.e. distinct languages or two dialects of the same language) in an interaction. Here, I discuss dialect switching as a case of CS. A switch can occur between turns, within turns, and intra-sententially. Blom & Gumperz (1972) see switching as falling into at least one of three overlapping categories: *situational, metaphorical,* and *contextualization* switching. In *situational* switching, context (in which ethnicity can be a factor) determines which code will be used. For example, people look for a number of group membership indicators, including gender, age and status, and social setting to assess the appropriateness of a code choice or codeswitching itself. Becker (1997) suggests that speakers don't CS unless they know the linguistic background and social identities of interlocutors. This (and other types of switching) suggests conscious action, but it should be noted that some switches occur below the level of awareness. With *metaphorical* switching, the social setting remains outwardly unchanged, but the code-choice may signal a change in topic or social role. Finally, unmarked, *contextualization* switches center the act of switching itself as a conversational resource (Auer 1984; Bailey, 1999; Gumperz, 2001; Li, 1994). Thus, "individual switches serve instead as contextualization, or framing, cues to mark off quotations, changes in topic, etc. from surrounding speech (Bailey, 1999: 242)."

In terms of the identification or identity functions of CS, bilinguals can change the directionality of CS (from English to Spanish or from Spanish to English; regional dialect to a majority language). It is also common for bilinguals or multi-linguals to scatter words or phrases in a second language throughout a mostly monolingual conversation. For example, Spanish-speaking bilinguals may briefly switch to words and phrases such as *bueno, lo que sea, y todo, pos, andale pues,* to mark their Latino ethnicity (Jacobson, 1982; Toribio, 2002). A special case of CS is language or code crossing. This is characterized as the unexpected (and often viewed as "illegitimate" or "inauthentic") switch to an out-group code (Rampton, 2000; Rampton, 1995). One of the ways that code crossing differs from established conceptualizations of CS, is that crossing is said to require little competence (Rampton, 1995; see also Sweetland, 2002). Though not phrased as such in the literature, one feature of crossing that seems amenable to schema or cultural model analysis is described by Rampton (2000: 55) as follows:

> When a relatively unexpected language code gets used, it usually inserts images of a particular social type into the flow of interaction, and it both instantiates and sparks off heightened displays of the participants' orientations to one

another, to the representations, and to the relationship between them.

The identity functions of CS are among the most widely explored areas in bilingual studies (Bucholtz & Hall, 2005; Cutler, 1999; Greer, 2005; Bailey 2000a, 2000b; Gafaranga ,2001; Lo, 1999; Rampton, 1995; Sebba & Wooton, 1998; Williams, 2006; Zentella, 1997). The prevailing conceptual orientation is that identity is *constructed* or *co-constructed* discursively, rather than a pre-existing given of category or group membership (Bucholtz and Hall 2005). Within this framework, code-choice is but one of several linguistic strategies that encode a relationship between a social identity and aspects of the social context.

Emphasizing or hiding an accent is a possible way to either invoke a positively evaluated identification or de-emphasize a negatively evaluated one (Giles and Coupland 1991; Waters 1994). As Cutler (1999: 431) points out, scholars have "commented on the relative ease with which outsiders can acquire phonological and lexical features of another dialect vs. the difficulty of acquiring the grammar" (see for example Ash & Myhill 1986; Labov, 1972; Labov & Harris, 1986). Blom and Gumperz (1972) distinguish between dialect switching (co-occurrence of lexical, phonological, and morphological rules) and monolingual style-shifting, "which may take place at the phonological level only (Milroy, 1980: 34)." However, neither is a choice between discrete entities (Milroy, 1980).

Why Don't You Come in on this Man?

On my first day of observation with Roberto I accompanied him as he distributed promotional flyers for his business. At the time, Roberto and Annie were two years into their street fair equipment rental venture. Roberto had worked for many years for an established street fair production company before deciding to go independent. A rather enterprising man, Roberto had significant experience with various informal sector businesses. According to Roberto, one of his previous ventures was a lucrative, but illegal, donation collection setup in Manhattan. Roberto and his wife administered numerous street-side stands that asked for help-the-homeless donations from pedestrians. These donations were actually pocketed by the collectors, who in turn paid a large percentage to Roberto. Eventually, this and similar operations were shut down by then NYC District Attorney, Eliot Spitzer. Roberto's assets were confiscated and he was left penniless.

Roberto was strongly committed, at times desperate, to lift himself and his family from the financial hole. He jumped on any opportunity to make money, whether it was to sell colognes, bootleg DVD's, and Italian ices in the streets. Roberto also worked part-time as a lifeguard in an apartment building. The street fair rental business he promoted on our first day of observations was an attempt to legitimize his entrepreneurial aspirations. He was seriously focused on establishing connections with local businesses and building his clientele.

The transcript that follows was from one of many encounters with sales clerks and store managers as he distributed flyers store to store. The stores were situated in close proximity to each other in a busy commercial zone in Rego Park, Queens. Roberto was informed about a street fair that was to take place in that area within a few weeks. The flyers he distributed promoted a special deal on canopies, tables, chairs and set-up for street fair participants. Upon entering a cellular phone store to drop off a flyer, Roberto greeted James, the store's supervisor. In my observation notes I wrote that James, a stocky, fair-skinned man, was not immediately recognizable as Latino, which he happened to be. Also, his English did not have a discernable Spanish accent. Since Roberto is also not immediately identifiable as Latino, I believe both men entered into the interaction unsure about the other's ethnicity. The transcript reveals attempts on both their parts to test their assumptions and establish the appropriate linguistic and behavioral protocols. These were needed to create the rapport they both eagerly sought, each with their own businesses in mind.

1 R: H'you doing.
2 J: Alright.=
3 R: =You guys ah participating in the street faiz?
4   (0.7)
5 J: Yeah.
6 R: You are? (0.5) 'K. Just in case you need, ah, in
7   case you need canopies tables and chaiz,
8   (1.0)
9   j's gimee a call.
10 J: Yeah. I don't know when the next one is I
11   haven't got [any-]

```
12  R:              [May twenty-secon'.]
13  J:    Rea:.lly?
14  R:    That's the one with the Chamber and <Broadvie::wz
15        is in deh:: fawl>.
16        (1.0)
17  J:    Mm, well I do the Broadview one over at at my
18        other store.
19  R:    Ah, which store is [that-
20  J:                        [(By the), ah, Junction Boulevard.
21  R:    On Junction?, yeah?
22  J:    Yeah.
23  R:    Well, I got the canopies, tables and chairs. I
24        used to work for Broadview. I worked for Broadview
25        for 8 yeaz.
26  J:    [°Ok.°]
27  R:    [An' ] um I started a canopy company (0.5)
28        that's (0.8) direct contact with dem, so whenever you
29        need one or if you need tables, chaiz whatever
30        you need,[ j's give me a cawl ahead of time, let=
31  J:             [°Ok.°
32  R:    =me know what event, give me your spot nuhmbuh and
33        it will be there before you get der.
34        (1.0)
35  J:    Ok.=
36  R:    =And [it'll already be set up.
37  J:         [(    )=
38  R:    =>Yah.<
```

Most prominent in these first few lines of Roberto's exchange with James, is his use of pronunciation related to New York English. In lines 3, 7, 25, 29, and 32 he elides the syllable final /r/ in the words "fairs", "chairs", "years", and "number". Another feature of NYE used by Roberto is dentalization of /d/, which in most varieties of English is produced as an alveolar (with the tip of the tongue behind the teeth). He used dentalized /d/ in line 28 with "direct". Lines 15, 28, and 33 suggest that he tends to replace the lingua-dental fricative /ð/ with dentalized stop /d/, so that *the* → "deh" , *them* → "dem", and *there* → "der". A final NYE feature to point out in this segment is the quintessentially New York tensing of vowel sound /aw/ in the *fall* →

"fawl". Roberto introduced pronunciation from AAVE as well. In line 12 we see that he devoiced syllable final /d/, *second* → "secon'".

Pitching his canopy business had become a smooth and automatic process. He always began by asking potential clients if they planned to participate in the upcoming street fair. This opening functioned more as a way to legitimize his intial approach than a screening question, because regardless of whether they said "yes" or "no", Roberto handed a flyer and described his services quickly and concisely. Thus, the opening helped to distinguish him from *just any solicitor*, to a solicitor who might actually have something useful to offer. A common component of his pitches was name-dropping "Broadview." In the street fair business, this company was large and reputable and Roberto seized any opportunities to make explicit his association with them. In line 17, James reveals knowledge of Broadview and in lines 23-27 Roberto capitalizes on it by stating his association with Broadview.

As we will see, James was also partial to name-dropping and stressing his status and qualifications. In line 17, he refers to a store in Junction Boulevard as "my other store." It's not clear whether this was a statement of actual ownership, or an implication. I do know, however, that in other declarations of his background and qualifications he never mentions ownership of any store or stores. The reference to Junction Boulevard may also have been a very subtle clue to his background, as most of the businesses on Junction Boulevard in Corona, Queens are either owned, manned, or frequented by Latinos. Next, James is ready to bring ethnicity into the interaction.

39 J: Let me give you some information.
40   (5.0)
41 J: *Roberto?!*
42 R: Yeah.
43 J: I had a couple of other customers that that(.) do
44   fairs and stuff.
45 R: O?k.
46   (2.0)
47 J: °Try to give you some info.°
48   (2.0)
49   ((James searches for business card))
50 J: °(Ok)° ((James hands Roberto a business card))

James reads Roberto's name out loud (line 41), as it appears on the flier given to him. He says the name using Spanish pronunciation, with monophthongized vowels and a very slight velarization of word-initial /r/. Given the context of the speech preceding and following line 41, I belive this pronunciation of Roberto's name was intended to signal James's recognition of Roberto as a Latino and in turn signal his own ethnic orientation (he recognized or at least assumed Roberto was Latino because of his name). In this way, Latino ethnicity was made of special relevance to Roberto (Day, 1998). This also set the stage for the business card that he was about to give. In turn 42, Roberto's curt response does not reveal an inclination to communicate with James at that level. It was more of a "Yes, that's my name" response than "Oh, you know Spanish?!" I got the impression that he had accomplished his goal, dissimenated his information, and was ready to move on. For Roberto, these types of exchanges were routine, and ethnicity was of less consequence for him if there was not some immediately tangible benefit. James initiates a repair (lines 43-44) to line 41 by providing Roberto with more details to justify his getting and giving the business card.

51		(3.0)
52		((Roberto reads business card))
53	R:	*Cuchifrito* for Thought.
		'Puerto Rican soul food'
54		((Roberto laughs))
55	R:	I like that! [That's hot.]
56		((Roberto looking at business card))
57	J:	[(Yeah I),] I own an online magazine
58		called *Cuchifrito* for Thought, it's been around for 8
59		years.
60	R:	O?k.
61	J:	Ahm, (2.0) I'm working with a company called
62		*Asamblea Latina?*
		'Latino Assembly'
63		(.5)
64	J:	They did something really big in, ah, Flushing
65		Meadow Park last year.
66	R:	*No me diga/h/.=*
		'You don't say?'

67 J: =Yeah and >it's all *Latino*(-s)< and [(and from 21 countries?,]
68 R: [*O:h,coño, e(-s)/ta (bien).*]
                                    ('Oh, damn, that's good.')
69 J: >and they used a bunch [of canopies and stuff like that.]<=
70 R: [°Mm::::h, o?k.°]

The name on the business card catches Roberto's attention. Roberto, who reads *"Cuchifrito"* using Spanish pronunciation (monophtongized vowels and a vibrant /r/), is amused by the title and his interest is piqued. Notice that James did not explain the business card or mention his business as he handed the card to him. Instead, he allowed time for Roberto to get the full effect of the name on his own, and perhaps to gauge his interest. Having confirmed Roberto's interest, James enters immediately into his own pitch. He makes a connection between his ongoing projects and involvment with *Asamblea Latina* (lines 61-62) and Roberto's business (line 69). Thus offering the possibility for mutual support or collaboration. With his *Cuchifrito* magazine and link to a Latino organization James is succesful in communicating his affiliation with the Latino pan-ethnicity. Notice that more straightforward means of identification are not employed here. The subtle cues presented by both James and Roberto are up to this point based solely on presupposed cultural knowledge (the sort enclosed by schemas and models). At this point, Roberto recognizes the importance of confirming his own affiliation. This is accomplished by the codeswitch in line 66. Although it is too early at this point to be certain what dialect of Spanish Roberto will use for the rest of the conversation, the word final /s/ in *"digas"* is aspirated, so that *digas* → *"diga/h/"*. This is a characteristic feature in Puerto Rican Spanish.

Roberto's codeswitch in line 66 is an important move to align himself with James, who prior to that point had made several attempts to bring their ethnicity into the interaction. Still, James doesn't actually codeswitch himself. This supports the notion that Roberto's codeswitch was recognized as having an identification function rather than an invitation to continue the conversation in Spanish. Unlike Roberto, James did not use Spanish as a way to invoke a Latino identification. Instead, he discursively invoked Latino ethnicity at several points in their exchange (lines 41, 50, 62, and 67). He also subtly identifies himself as Caribbean, perhaps Puerto Rican, by the choice of *Cuchifito* for his magazine. The talk sequence in lines 66

through 68 explicitly establishes their common identification as
Latinos. First, Roberto switches (line 66), affirming the relevance of
Latino identification and his interest in what James had to say. Then,
with his emphasis on "all *Latino*" (line 67), James assumes and appeals
to Roberto's interest in working with other Latinos. Finally, Roberto
acknowledges this appeal and confirms his interest (line 68) with "*Oh,
coño, e'ta bien*" (syllable final /s/ is deleted as is common in Non-
Standard Puerto Rican Spanish (NSPRS)). At this point they have
both established a common frame of reference.

71 J: =They're actually really big out there.=
72 R: =Who ah::, who whose, who organizes that. Who
73   sent (.) who? does [it.]
74 J: [>Ah] I can give you all the
            contact information,<
75   just hit me up at the website.=
76 R: =At this website?=
77 J: =°Let me give you my email address.°=
78 R: =Yeah, give me your email man. I definitely,
79   what I'll do is (.5) I'll email you some'n' like
80   dis?
81 ((Roberto holds out one of his fliers))
82 J: Mhm.
83 R: Remember, Heavenly Canopy Rentals. That's mine
84 *papa.Y yo hago, mira yo hago* (1.3) *el el show
      >puertorriqueño*
      'man. And I do, look I do the the Puerto Rican show'
85   for the Bronx Borough President's office in the Bronx?<
86 J: Mhm?
87 R: I'm doing that this year. (.6) That's on June 26.

Speaking exclusively in English, most of James's utterances to this
point do not share the NYE features present in Roberto's speech. In
general his speech suggests a tendency towards Standard American
English. He does reveal some inclination for AAVE with the use of the
phrase "hit me up" ('contact me'). His switch to Spanish pronunciation
is limited to single words "*Cuchifrito*" and "*Latino*". On the other
hand, Roberto, who started out with a strong tendency towards NYE,
introduces more elements of standard and nonstandard Puerto Rican

Spanish and AAVE. For example, in line 79 and 80, *something like this* → "some'n' like dis"; with the substitution of syllable final velar nasal <ng>, in "something" with an alveolar nasal <n> and the production of the lingua-dental fricative <th> as a dental stop /d/. This last feature is also present in NYE. Roberto switches to NSPRS in line 84. I classify this utterance as nonstandard rather than standard PRS because of the use of "*papa*"- a common word in colloquial PRS with a function similar to slang *man* in English – and the Hispanicized English pronunciation of the word "*show*". One other thing to note in line 84 is the short pause between "*hago*" and "*el*". Here and with the false starts ("*el, el*") before "*show*" it seems that Roberto was looking for the appropriate Spanish word to describe the event. He finally settled on an English word but with Spanish pronunciation.

For the first time in their exchange, Roberto makes a specific reference to a Latino group, namely Puerto Ricans. It is significant that he switches to Spanish to state his participation in a Puerto Rican event. In combination with his use of Puerto Rican pronunciation, this seems to locate him closer to a Puerto Rican identification than any other up this point, and it could also signal his evaluation of James's identification. James, for his part, is consistent in his goal to promote himself and his website. In a move reminiscent of a typical sales tactic (lines 74-75), he directs Roberto to his website for information requested in lines 72-73, rather than give it to him upfront.

```
88  J:   Well [a::ctually]
89  R:        [Los salseros],[van, van estar/r/]
              'The salsa players, will, will be'-
90  J:        [I don't know if you guys are] doing anything on ah
91            (1.5) if you guys are doing anything on Saturday.
92            Actually my birthday party I'm having it in Park
93            Avenue on in the Helmsley Building (.5) at a little
94            lounge called Lea Lounge? (.5) I have a private one-
95            hour (.6) spot before the club actually opens up.
96  J:                        [(              )]
97  R:                        [>Righ', righ', righ'<.]
98  J:   Like little cocktail hour networking type of thing.
99            Ah:: a lot of people from La Mega ((popular Latino music
              station))
```

```
100      are gonna be there, a lot of people from Amo/l/ ((a romantic
101      Latino music station)), all the radio stations and stuff.=
102 R:   =Really?
103 J:   And then uhm (.) ah (.) my good friend, who I manage,
104      ah Flor Caceres she is a Latina comedian. She's actually
105      performing some comedy there, (.) during that time.
106 R:   Wo[w!
107 J:        [>When the club opens up<, it's gonna be a regular
108          club night, but (.6) if you guys wanna stop by just
109          send [me an email.
110 R:           [At what time, at what time is this?
111 J:   From 10 to 11, [that's the ( )] hour.
112 R:                  [At night?]
113 J:   Yeah.
114 R:   Oh, that's hot. I cou'do dat!
115 J:   Yep [it's right on] Park Avenue. It's a really classy [place.   ]
116 R:       ['Cause I got-]                                   [I know-]
```

Mentioning his participation in the Bronx Borough President's Puerto Rican celebration (lines 84 and 87), served to further signal a Puerto Rican connection with James. James in turn acknowledged this connection (line 90) by inviting Roberto and me to his birthday bash. According to James, not only was this private social networking event to take place at a classy Park Avenue club, but some of the biggest names in the New York Latino community were to attend. It is apparent in this transcript that James wished to create a grandiose impression on Roberto. His wish to come across as person actively involved in the Latino community is also clear. All of this makes sense, given that he was trying to secure Roberto's business, as will become obvious in a moment. As with his other switches, James reserved Spanish pronunciation for the names of people or organizations. In line 100 he pronounces the radio station name *Amor* in a way typical for many speakers of NSPRS; he substitutes word final /r/ with an /l/.

Turning now to Roberto, line 89 illustrates an attempt to appeal to James's knowledge and appreciation of Puerto Rican music. This exclamation of the fabulous nature of *salsa* events in general and the promise of the Bronx event specifically, is revealing in light of a conversation he had the day after with his Venezuelan friend Omar. In that later conversation he downplayed this very same event. It would suggest that he built up the event here (lines 84, 85, 89) to bolster the importance of his own business. In this section of the transcript Roberto once again uses AAVE phonological elements. "Oh, that's hot. I cou'do dat!" he exclaims in response to James's explanation. Roberto devoices word final /d/ in "could", bridging with /d/ in "*do*". He also dentalizes the alvelor fricative /th/ in "that".

While Roberto seems to be invoking Puerto Rican frames of reference, James consistently refers to a more pan-ethnic Latino orientation. We can return to the beginning of the transcript to find evidence of this (lines 62, 67, 99, 100, and 104). His mention of Puerto Rican comedian Flor Caceres (line 104) would have been a good place to make this connection more explicit, but instead he opts for the inclusive term Latina. He likely assumed that Roberto was not Puerto Rican. To make any one Latino ethnicity relevant in their conversation would counter James' tendency towards pan-Latino inclusivity. I visited James' website and found that James' philosophy of Latino unity is a consistent and powerful theme in his writings. It is also possible that James was uncertain about Roberto's background. A number of factors come into play when people make judgements about the ethnic backgrounds of others. Appearance is key factor. In New York there are strong mental models for what a Puerto Rican, Mexican, Dominican, etc. looks like. As a light-skinned, blue-eyed Latino, Roberto does not quite fit the mold of what a Puerto Rican is *supposed* to look like. Accent is another factor. Unless he consciously emphasizes one Spanish dialect or another in his speech, Roberto's accent is not easily identifiable. He admits to stumping people regularly. (As he says, leaving people thinking, "Damn, where the *fuck* is he from?") A person's appearance can lead a curious spectator in one direction and their accent in another direction. As we will see later in the transcript, James' guess about Roberto's ethnicity suggests a calculus for identifying ethnic background that draws on a combination of phenotypic, linguistic, and discursive factors. Assuming that people will self-identify in the way that most favorably aligns them with another (Banks, 1987; Barth, 1969; Haaland, 1969; Kaufert, 1977; Nagata, 1974; Padilla, 1984; Patterson, 1975), James opted for the more general, inclusive category.

117 R: I know exactly which one it is.=
118 J: = They play, they play a mix of everything. (.5) Umh, but

```
119      yeah we can definitely talk. And I [also build websites.]
120 R:                                   [Yo man? Listen man, if we can,
121 J:   I build websites.
122 R:   Yeah? You do websites!?
123 J:   Under 500 [bucks (    )]
124 R:             [Dude, I don't even] have, I don't even
125               have a website for Heavenly Canopies, man, so
126               we def'nitely need to sit down and tawk
127               [and try to kick some stuff around.]
128 J:            [Under 500 bucks], you, you won't
129               even pay for hosting.
130      (.5)
131 R:   Rea::lly?=
132 J:   =Everything's included.=
133 R:   =Everything's included?
134 J:   Every- We're talking about a five hundred dollar
135      package, everything, (.) your customers will be able
136      to put their order in right on the web.
137      (.7)
138 R:   °Oh, shit!°
139 J:   So, we're talking about some nice stuff here,
140      a'right?
```

Roberto and James begin to talk business in this section of the transcript. Almost simultaneously the two conversants attempt to promote their interests, overlapping in lines 119 and 120. Starting with the widely-used interjection "Yo", associated with AAVE, Roberto asserts his interest in working with James, but cuts-off mid-utterance, probably to let James go ahead with what he was saying. Taking advantage of this break (line 121), James repeats the information overlapped in line 119. While James assumes a more formal, sales-oriented register during his pitch, Roberto contrasts with his informal, at one point, vulgar (line 138) approach. His talk is peppered with colloquialisms: "Yo", "dude" (124), "man" (120, 124), "try to kick some stuff around" (127), and "shit" (138). Contributing to the informality of his speech, Roberto produces a nonstandard pronunciation of "definitely" (126), and NYE vowel tensing in the word "talk" (126). This contrast strengthens James's position as the

provider of important resources and Roberto as the receiver; a position
that Roberto attempts to change later in their conversation.

141 R: Yeah but listen man I just started, you know
142   my company is only two years old. It's only run
143   by me and my wife.
144 J: O?k. > <u>Cool.</u><
145 R: An' uhm, you know that's <u>it</u>, man, *pero*-
                                               'but'
146 J: When you have that website, you go [to anybody (for)]
147 R: [Yeah it's <u>cra?zy.]</u>
148 J: events and just hand them out, like **listen**.
149   (.5)
150 J: *La Mega* does <u>tons</u> of streetfairs, you [(know   )]
151 R: [Do they really?]
152 J: <u>Ye.ah?</u> They do all that stuff in the <u>Heights.</u>=
153 R: =Yo listen man, wh 'n chu, wh'n chu=
154 J: =Sponsors.=
155 R: =Y.'know. Wh 'n chu <u>come</u> in on this man?=
156 J: =(I, I   [   )
157 R: [Look at my- [I'll give you my -], listen, I'll give=
158 J: [(   )]
159 R: =you my prices (.) I got a <u>ninedeeni:ne</u> dolla' special. Less
160   than a hundred dollaz you get the canopy (.) a
161   table (.) and two chaiz.
162 J: Wawewewe [(wha' we do:: -)]
163 R: [Everybody's] charging over a hundred and
164   twenty five, a hundred and thirty, a hundred and forty.
165 J: If you do a website with us, we
166   (.)
167 R: >°Yeah°<.
168 J: usually (include) free advertising on *Cuchifrito*.
169   (.)
170 R: [>°Ok°<]
171 J: [That] sees 25,000 people a month.
172   (.6)
173 R: <u>Wa</u>::ow!=

Spanish, AAVE, and NYE are used by Roberto in this segment. First he switches to the Spanish discourse marker *"pero"* (line 145) to contrast the startup nature of his business with an unrealized utterance. It's likely that he intended to reassure James about interest in his website service despite the fact that his canopy business was small. Possible interpretations for the use of *"pero"* instead of "but" include: a) it is habitual for Roberto to do this; b) it is a contextualization cue to guide James's interpretation of Roberto's previous utterance; and c) a reminder to James about common linguistic and ethnic identity. Indeed, as past research suggests, Spanish-speaking bilinguals may briefly switch to words and phrases like *bueno, lo que sea, y todo, pos, andale pues,* to mark their Latino ethnicity (Jacobson, 1982; Toribio, 2002). My sense is that there was a bit of each of these factors contrbuting to his use of *"pero."*

After consistent efforts on James's part to *sell* himself and his services to Roberto, Roberto re-iniates his own pitch. He switches to an informal register and nonstandard English (most influenced by AAVE) to persuade James to contract his services (line 153, 155). Roberto's use of *street* sales talk rather than formal sales talk suggests that he's trying to appeal to James's familiarity and comfort with urban culture. In other words, he's trying to connect with James as a street mate (more intimate) rather than just a business contact. When this doesn't quite work, given James's false starts in line 156, Roberto returns to his previous, more canned, salesman-like approach. Once again, this approach is marked with various NYE elements, mainly elided /r/ in "dollar" (159), "dollars" (160), and "chairs" (161). Not to be deterred, James counters with his own offer in lines 165 and 168.

```
174 J:   =And a lot of people do adve- Like I said ah, I mean I have
175           stuff in Flo?rida. Like, [they have -
176 R:                                [>Yeah, yeah, yeah.<
177           (.)
178 J:   They have something called >La Fiestas Patronales<
                                      'The Patron Saint Parties'
179      [in Florida.]
180 R:   [Yeah.] I know, yeah.=
181 J:   =Where they do all the patron saints in one day, it's
182      like a big street fair, they see like eighty [thousand people-]
183 R:                                                 [La Calle Ocho?]
```

'Eight Street'
184   (.)
185 J: No. This is [ah-
186 R: [*La Calle Ocho* is something else?=
187 J: =It's a different town. Yeah.
188   (.)
189 R: Oh, wow?!
190 J: Different part of Florida. They do (this), they've
191   been doing it for <u>four</u> years and they basically
192   shut down the whole neighborhood or >whatever<.
193 J: [(   )]
194 R: [Yeah, yeah, [yeah.
195 J: [(They see about) 80,000 people in about four day(.)span.
196 R: *Mira <u>que</u> loquera, broder*!=
         'That's crazy, bro'
197 J: =So, an' I have all (the') emails, I have all the contacts.
198   I can contact any Latino streetfair organization,=
199 R: =*Yo lo que quiero hacer ahorita, broder* (.) *me quiero*
         'What I want to do now, bro, I want to
200   *situa/l/* (0.8) *con*,(.) *con >las feria/h/ aqui en Nueva Yor y los*
         situate myself with the fairs here in New York and the
201   *eventos aqui en Nueva Yor porque yo vivo en*
         events here in New York because I live in
202   *Nueva Yor ahora.<=*
         New York now.'
203   (0.6)
204 J: =Mhm.=
205 R: =*O sea que cuando me conviene::,* (0.8) *me conviene* °*coño*°.
         'I mean, when it serves me, damn, it serves me.'
206 J: °Yeah.° What's? up? [(*Tu eres*) *cubano, verdad.*
                             'You're cuban, right.'
207 R: [(   )]
208 R: No. *Venezolano.*
              'Venezuelan'
209 J: Yeah? Oh, ok.
210 R: *Venezolano.*
              'Venezuelan'
211   (0.6)
212 J: That's cool. (.) So definitely, just get in touch with

213   me like I said I have a lot of networking events
214   and stuff like that [and like I s-]
215 R: [Al?right.=
216 J: =A lot of what I do, has to do with –[(streetfairs.)
217 R: [(Bringing) outdoor events
218   J: °Yeah.°
219   R: Alright.

Roberto's codeswitching in this segment, particularly lines 199 – 202, serves to lend authenticity or a measure of sincerity to his statement. Like with his switch to street talk in the previous segment (line 155), this switch is another example of Roberto's skill in creating an interactional space where they can relate as connected equals. This contrasts with James's strategy, in which he consistently positions himself as the one with the upper hand. Ethnicity is important for this strategy to the extent that he can use it to illustrate his embeddedness in *important* Latino circles.

With his substitution of word final /r/ in "*situar*" → "*situa/l/*", and aspiration of word final /s/ in "*ferias*" → "*feria/h/*", Roberto uses NSPR for his switch. Though we cannot determine whether James interpreted Roberto's Spanish to be a Puerto Rican dialect, there's reason to believe he at least classified it as Caribbean. This segment shows that James speculated, gathered clues, and tested assumptions about Roberto's background. One clue, of course, was Roberto's pronunciation and intonational style. Roberto's appearance provided another clue, with other important clues materializing from statements made by Roberto: a) "[Yeah.] I know, yeah.=" (line 180), b) "*Calle Ocho?*" (line 183), and most subtly c) "*porque yo vivo en Nueva Yor ahora*" (lines 201-202). Each of these three statements gave the impression that he was familiar with Florida and may have even lived there before coming to New York ("I live in New York now"). This last statement might give anyone the impression that Roberto is not native to New York. Roberto *did* spend some time in a detox residential program in Florida, so the statement is not an outright lie. However, he seems to bend the truth. One possible interpretation is that Roberto did not actually mean to imply that he "lives in New York now but once live somewhere else." Perhaps this statement is purely an attempt to stress that what he really wants to do is get his business well-established *here* rather than look into opportunities in other states. It might have been a faint rejection of James's Florida boast. If this was the case, then his use of Spanish softened the rejection. Needless to say, taken together these and other clues throughout their conversation led James to assume Roberto was Cuban. His response in line 209 showed his slight surprise, particularly because his question about Roberto's background simultaneously functioned as a way to highlight James' ability to correctly categorize Roberto's identity. His incorrect guess meant that he had misread Roberto's discursive and phenotypic cues and so, in line 210, Roberto reiterates his ethnic background. There is a subsequent moment of silence as neither James nor Roberto move to further talk about the revelation of Roberto's background. This pause is suggestive of a number of things. On the one hand, James' query about Roberto's background was the first time that ethnicity was loudly and explicitly made relevant to the conversation. Previous to that moment, their ethnic backgrounds were subtly negotiated and generally assumed. The pause after James' incorrect guess and Roberto's clarification seems to signify mutual recognition of the interrupted flow of their subtle negotiations of multiple ethnic and social identities. The pause also highlights the disjuncture between Roberto's behavior and the ethnic assumptions that were made about him.

The cell phone store exchange just discussed highlights Roberto's fluid command of multiple languages, dialects, and registers. Compared to Roberto, James was much more consistent in his use of language. While Roberto jumped seamlessly from Spanish, to New York English, to AAVE, James employed standard, at times formal, American English, limiting most of his Spanish to proper nouns. Their respective linguistic strategies were compatible with each speaker's interactional goal. Roberto, who entered the situation as a solicitor, automatically assumed a subordinate role. Once James brought Latino ethnicity into the interaction as an important point of reference, Roberto's strategy was to invoke linguistically identifications that would best align him with James. James, on the other hand, made frequent references to extensive resources at his disposal, whether human, informational, or cultural. His identity was sufficiently implied in all of these references and language played a secondary role.

In the next and final example of his ethnic and linguistic flexibility, Roberto converses with a friend. Conversationally-situated power differences do not exist in this transcript, yet Roberto negotiates his multiple identities just the same.

Lo devolvieron al loco ('They sent the dude back').

On our second day of observations I met Roberto around noontime to accompany him and his wife Annie to a dental appointment. When I arrived outside of his apartment in Astoria, Annie was still inside getting ready and Roberto was waiting outside for a friend, Omar. Omar, who lived near Roberto, was one of the few Venezuelans Roberto knew personally (see Figure 1). In preparation for a big street fair, Roberto needed a van to transport the canopies, tables and chairs he rented out to a local hospital. He planned to borrow Omar's white van and waited to confirm this with his friend. The next transcript centers on an incident that happened to a mutual friend, Sergio. Apparently, had Sergio entered the U.S. from Venezuela on a visitor's visa. However, he made the critical error of revealing to U.S. immigration officials his intention to work while in the country. In a piece of their conversation not included here, Omar explained to Roberto that when Sergio was asked to provide a contact number in the US, he gave officials Omar's phone number. Officials then called and heard that the answering machine announced the name of Omar's business. This convinced authorities of Sergio's *illegal* intentions. Having entered and stayed in the U.S. under less than official circumstances themselves, Sergio's plight resonated with both Roberto and Omar.

1   R: Mañana quiero- mañana quiero llenarlo,
         ('Tomorrow I want – tomorrow I want to fill it,')
2   >tu va/h/ trabajar mañana?<
         ('are you going to work tomorrow?')
3   (0.6)
4   O: A que hora?
         ('At what time?')
5   R: [En la tarde.]=
         ('In the afternoon')
6   O: [(   )]
7   O: =Si, yo ([   )
         ('Yes, I')

8   R: [En la tarde a eso de la(-s)=bueno
                       ('In afternoon, like around, well')
9   >vamos a decir como la(-s)< cinco, la(-s) seis:
                       ('let's say like at five, at six')
10 O: A no, esta bien, [no-]=Oye.
            (Ah, no, that's fine. Listen')
11 R: [(és-)ta bien?]
                      ('that's alright?')
12 R: Dime.
            ('Tell me')
13 O: °Lo devolvieron al loco. °
            ('They sent the dude back')
14 R: >Como que lo< devolvieron?
            ('What do you mean that they sent him back?')
15 O: °En el aeropuerto°.
            ('In the airport')
16 R: De/h/ el aeropuerto? Mira esa vaina.=
            ('From the airport? Look at that mess')
17 O: =Sí, °no le dejaron entrar. °
            ('Yes, they didn't let him enter')
18   (0.6)
19 R: DEL AEROPUERTO DE <u>AQUÍ</u>?
            ('From the airport here?')
20 O: De acá de la- Florida.
            ('From here - Florida')
21 R: De Florida. (1.0) Pero <u>porqué</u>?
            ('From Florida. But why?')
22   (1.3)
23 O: Que el tipo le habia dicho que **pa(-ra)**
            ('That they guy had told him that why')
24   **que venia pa(-ra a-)cá::?, que venia trabajar?,**
            ('was he coming here, that he was coming to work')
25   (1.3) que no se cuan[to?-
            ('that I don't know what')
26 R: [Pe(-ro) que pendejo!, >haber dicho
            (But what a dummy, he should have said')
27   que venia de< <u>va:cac:iones:</u>.
            ('that he was coming for vacation')
28 O: Le han (>revocado<) la visa por cinco años.

		('They (revoked) his visa for five years')
29		(0.7)
30	R:	<u>Le qué</u>?!
		('They what?!')
31	O:	La visa que tenia se (>la=han=revocado<) por
		('The visa that he had they (have revoked it) for')
32		cinco años.
		('five years.')
33		(1.4)
34	R:	Como que- s- s- no puede hacer nada en cinco
		('What do you mean that- he can't do anything in five')
35		años?
		('years?')
36	O:	°Ya no ya. °
		('Not now')
37	R:	<u>Que CA:ga:?da!</u> °huevon°-
		('What a screw up, man')
38		(2.6)
39	O:	El me llamó. (.) Yo tambien, me llamó ayer. (0.7)
		('He called me. Me too, he called me yesterday')
40		En el trabajo, yo estaba trabajando allá.
		('At work, I was working over there')
41		(0.7)
42	R:	Coño, que vaina (huev-)on. Enton(-ces) tiene c:inco
		('Damn, what a mess, man. So then he's got five')
43		años >que no puede venir=pa(-ra) los< (Es-)ta(-dos)
		('years that he cannot come to the U.S.')
44		Unidos:. (1.7) >Pero=(-e)so lo puede< pelear? o no.
		('But can he fight it or no?')
45		No puede pelearlo.=
		('He can't fight it?')
46	O:	=Yo creo que sí, <u>claro</u> porque [q q aquí-
		('I think so, sure because here')
47	R:	[Que. bola(-s)?
		('What balls')

In contrast to his conversation with James, Roberto's exchange with Omar is marked by two unique paralinguistic elements: speed and intonation. In terms of speed, it seems that Roberto talks quickly more frequently when speaking in Spanish, at least in comparison to his conversation with James. There's also more latching (denoted by =) represented in this transcript. Most instructive, however, are Roberto's intonational practices. Since Venezuelan Spanish shares phonological characteristics with Puerto Rican Spanish, intonation is one way to tell the two dialects apart. As a speaker, Roberto is conscious of this. When compared to his conversations with James and other New York Puerto Ricans (including his wife), Roberto's performance of Venezuelan Spanish is marked by frequent rising intonation (either as part of a syllable or in longer utterances, see for example the intonation marked in lines 36, 43, and 46). Rising intonation is also notable in Omar's speech (lines 24-25). Throughout the conversation Roberto attempts to pattern his Spanish to that of Omar both intonationally and lexically. Omar, who is less fluent in English than Roberto, has retained Venezuelan dialect and speaks much more fluidly than Roberto. In fact, some of the pauses evident before Roberto's turns and mid-utterance may be due to second-language limitations[15]. Further proof of Roberto's constraints in Spanish-dominant conversations is his reliance on exclamatory phrases using lexicon common in Venezuela to complete his turns: "*Que CA:ga:da!* °*huevon*°" ('What a screw up, man' (37)), "*Coño, que vaina (huev-)on.*" (Damn, what a mess, man' (42)), "*Que. bola(-s)*" ('What balls' (47)). Notice also the verb conjugation error, "*haber,*", rather than "*hubiese*" or "*hubiera,*" in line 26, due to limited formal education in Spanish.

Therefore, Roberto, who had not been to Venezuela in many years and who did not have regular contact with other Venezuelans in the US, produced his own approximation to Venezuelan speech. I believe he did this in contrast to the Puerto Rican dialect he used more frequently. For example, where a Puerto Rican might aspirate syllable final /s/, he not only preserved but also lengthened the sound, even though this is not a feature of Venezuelan Spanish ("*seis:*", 9 and "*Unidos:*", 44; see also lines 53, 73, 138 below). This is not to say that Roberto did not drop or aspirate syllable final /s/, he did this consistent with either Venezuelan or Puerto Rican Spanish (lines 2, 8, 9, and 16). Roberto also produced strong apico-alveolar trills, particularly in word initial and word final /r/ (lines 63 and 144 below) and in cases where a Puerto

---

[15] While Roberto's first language was Spanish, he admitted that he had more command over English.

Rican might use a velar or uvular trill (for example *"arrechera* ('irritation' or 'infuriation')", lines 55, 62 below). I propose that Roberto uses these features (lengthened /s/ and strong trill), to both differentiate from PRS and to authenticate his Spanish. Both of these features lend a careful, well-pronounced quality to his delivery. It may be his way to compensate for Spanish language limitations that could call his claim to Venezuelan identification into question. These phonological elements also add emphasis to his statements, as with *"supe:r/r/"* in line 63 (see also line 89 in the previous section).

I mentioned earlier another rather noticeable characteristic of his speech when talking to a Venezuelan: frequent (even exaggerated) use of lexicon and exclamatory phrases associated with Venezuela or in cases syntactically and semantically distinct from PRS. So far in this segment of the transcript he uses *"vaina"* ('nuisance' or 'mess'), *"vale"* ('alright' or 'OK'), *"pe(-d)o"* ('problem'), *"coño"* ('damn' or 'fuck'), *"que bolas"* ('what balls'), and *"huevon"* ('dude' or 'man'); much more so, even, than Omar. These lexical insertions serve to further differentiate his Venezuelan Spanish from any other dialect.

```
48  R:  Coño que caga(-da) que le hizieron esa vai?na.
        ('Damn, they shit on him with that mess')
49      (0.6)
50  O:  Si va:le.=
        ('Yes, right')
51  R:  =Co/n:::/ño que bolas:.
        ('Damn, what balls')
52      (1.6)
53  O:  Lo devolvieron del aeropuerto, no lo dejaron pa?sar.
        ('They sent him back from the airport, they didn't let him
        pass')
54      (3.7)
55  R:  Coño que arrechera.
        ('Damn, how madenning')
56  O:  Si:, se regreso pa(-ra) allá, y (1.4) >yo le habia
        ('Yes, he went back, and I had')
57      pedido una botella de< aguardiente y viste=toda la
        ('asked him for a bottle of liquor and look, all my')
58      vaina me la devolvio.
        ('stuff they sent back')
```

59   (1.9)
60 R: .tsh
61   (1.0)
62 R: Que <u>arrechera</u>, pana. (2.5) Esa vaina debe estar
        ('How madenning, bud. That mess should be')
63   <u>supe</u>:r/r/ (0.9) coño el tipo ts una depresión debe
        ('super, damn that guy, should have a depression')
64   tener el tipo encima? ahorita, coño madre.
        ('on him right now, motherfuck.')
65 O: Sí (>yo no fuera a la calle=yo me iba a la casa?<).
        (Yes, (I would not have gone out to the street, I would have
        gone to my house')
66   (1.6)
67 O: (°   [°)
68 R: [Oye, vamo/h/=a ver, el tiene que
                     ('Listen, let's see, he has to')
69   pelear esa vai?na, bro(-d)er. Tiene gente <u>aquí</u>.
        ('fight that mess, bro. He has people here for him')
70 O: Porque el no puede hacer e?so.
        ('Because he can't do that')
71   (.)
72 R: No vale. Por cuanto tiempo se venía a toda(-s)
        ('That's not right. How long was he coming for')
73   maneras:?
        ('any ways?')
74 O: El se venia por uno(-s) tres o cuatro meses que le
        ('He was coming for three, four months that')
75   habian dado la visa cuatro mese(-s) permiso?
        ('they had given him a four month visa')
76   (3.7)
77 O: Pe:ro ya esta, lis?to.
        ('But it's all settled')
78   (1.1)
79 R: <u>En</u> Florida lo devolvieron. Que coños de madre!
        ('In Florida they turned him back. What motherfuckers')
80   (1.2)
81 O: Uno/h/ cubanos que lo, los tipos de la
        ('Some Cubans that, the guys from')
82   inmigración lo/h/ cubanos, lo lo pararon. (1.7) >Y

```
       ('immigration, the cubans, stopped him. And')
83     como yo cuando vine aquí< año(-s) atra(-s) vale,
       ('like me when I came here years back, right,')
84     >mira<,
       ('look')
85     ((Coughs))
86     era un cubano tambien. Y tu te va(-s) quedar? Y
       ('he was a Cuban too. And you are staying? And')
87     a ti=que te importa >chico?<. (1.0) Cua(-l)?
       ('what do you care man? What is')
88     e(-s e-)l problema.
       ('the problem?')
89  R: ((Laughing)) [A ti que te importa.]
       ('What do you care?')
90  O:               [(          )]
```

In this section, Roberto's use of Venezuelan exclamatory phrases as fillers becomes more pronounced. He does this at almost every turn between line 48 and 62. Additional to Venezuelan lexicon, Roberto produces other phonological elements of VS, eliding /d/ in *"broder,"* a Spanglishized word, and aspirates and deletes word final /s/ in "vamos" (line 68) and "todas" (line 72), respectively. Omar demonstrates a preference for deleting word final /s/ altogether (lines 74, 75, 83, and 86) than aspirating it as Roberto does. Multiple pauses in this same sequence suggest that the topic of Sergio's unfortunate return to Venezuela is close to becoming exhausted. Roberto attempts to revive the discussion by fleshing out his laments in lines 62 – 64. But eventually he finds further fodder for the discussion by suggesting that he and Omar find a way to help Sergio's situation (lines 68 – 69). *"Vamo' a ver...tiene gente aqui,"* is Roberto's way to confirm their mutual interest in their friend's dilemma, uniting them under a common cause, so to speak. This "we" statement figures well into the "they" discourse Omar offers in lines 81 – 88. In this case "they" are Cubans and it is not inconsequential that Omar chooses to invoke this distinction.

We/they distinctions were common among the Latinos in this study. Some familiar we/they distinctions recorded include: we-"Hispanics"/they-"Americans," we-*"Latinos"*/they-*"blanquitos,"* we-*"Latinos"*/they-*"judios ('Jews').",* and we-"citizens"/they-"illegals,".

The *we/they* distinctions made by Latinos about other Latinos were as compelling. Often, statements that began like Omar's *"Uno' cubanos"*, (*"Un Colombiano, ahí,"*, *"El Domincano, ese,"*, *"Una Boricua"*), functioned as neat vehicles for a great deal of cultural, stereotyped associations. The stereotyped association that Omar invoked about Cubans, or more specifically Miami Cubans, is a view commonly held among other Latinos encountered in this study: "Cubans rule Miami and they only look out for their own." My intention here is not to lend weight to these associations, but to make a point about the important role played by these models, stereotypes, associations for categorizing people, guiding interpretation, aligning affiliations, and encouraging *disassociation* from certain groups. As we will see in Chapter 5, disassociation from stereotypes is a key motivation for switching.

91 R: Coño que ma:lo:? (.) <u>pobresito</u> vale.
        ('Damn, that's bad. Poor guy, right.')
92 R: [Debe estar]
        ('He should be')
93 O: [Que **no te vayas**], no te va:yas (.) **no te va:yas,**
        (That, don't go, don't go, don't go')
94   dije yo. (Que no puedo hacer y que no venia
        ('I said. (That I can't and that he wasn't coming')
95   tan malo. El no   )
        ('too bad. He doesn't'))
96   Ahora (es-)ta ma(-s) luco.
        ('Now he's worse off')
97 R: Va estar <u>bien</u> mal a/y/í? (huev-)on. Ahí s- no se
        ('He's going to be real bad there man. Over there you can't')
98   puede hacer un <u>cara?jo.</u>
        ('do a damn thing')
99   (2.0)
100 R: (E-)sa vai?na. (1.0) <u>No</u> se, chao.
        ('That mess. I don't know, man')
101   (1.5)
102 R: Coño pero el tiene que ir a inmigracion allá
        ('Damn but he's got to go to immigration over there')
103   pel<u>ea:r?</u>lo.
        ('fight it')
104 O: A lo mejor voy ahora en Junio.

('I may be going in June')
105 R: En Junio va/h/ pa(-ra a-)llá?
('In June you're going over there?')
106 O: Sí. (   )
('Yes')
107 R: ((Coughs)) Yo no voy pa(-ra) ningun lado hasta que
('I'm not going anywhere until I')
108 arregle mi pa- mi mi: (1.1) mi vaina americana.
('fix my pa- my, my, my American mess')
109 >Yo no salgo (d-)el paí(-s) ni pendejo [que fuera=
('I don't leave the country even if I were stupid')
110 O: [((J   laughs))
111 R: =coño madre y si no me deja entrar yo los mato
('motherfuck and if they don't let me in I'll kill them')
112 ahí mi/h/.mo?,< me vuelvo loco!
('right there. I'll go crazy')
113 O: ((Continues to laughs))
114 R: >B 'like **_Wha'nigga'?_** **_You fuckin' crazy_**? Me van a
('They're goint to')
115 mandar a mi a un paí/h/ donde yo no cono/h/co un
('send me to a country where I don't know')
116 coño. Pa(-ra) quedarme?=No joda. M- me ven- me
('a damn thing. To stay? No shit. I- I'll co- I'll')
117 vengo nadando.
('come back swimming')
118 O: ((Laughs))
119 R: ((Starts to laugh himself)) Caigo en Puerto Rico.
('I'll end up in Puerto Rico')

This passage is an illustration of three of Roberto's identifications at work. First, considerable use of intonation to mark his speech as VS is evident (lines 91, 97, 98, 100, 103, and 112). His narrative in lines 107 – 119 juxtaposes the fact of his immigration status with the reality that he has few social or economic links to Venezuela. Having lived in the U.S. for most of his life, Roberto leads a life materially independent from his past in Venezuela. He feels more comfortable speaking in English and has few members of his social network who are Venezuelan. In fact, he has more ties to Puerto Ricans than to Venezuelans and his statement in line 119 provides proof of this connection. Yet, he shares uncertainties similar to immigrants who enter the country without documentation, limited English language skills, and close ties to kin and friendship networks in their native countries. Thus we see two identification discourses at work: Roberto as the "undocumented immigrant" and "Americanized Roberto" who has known little else but New York for most of his life. Finally, Roberto seamlessly switches language and register to emphasize the absurdity of a potential deportation (lines 114). It is fitting that he uses English to deliver these utterances. His statements clearly evoke an image of Roberto in this situation; a situation in which all connection to anything but "American" would be emphasized to avoid a deportation. It certainly would not be a scenario in which a bilingual would speak Spanish. Like Roberto, several participants in this study used AAVE and urban slang to provide emphasis, force, and/or humor to otherwise standard American English or formal speech. This jocular, emphatic presentation is consistent with one of the features of code crossing described by Rampton (2000).

120	O:	Oye. >Quedamos así entonces, nos vemos
		('Listen. It's settled then, we'll see each other')
121		mañana.<
		('tomorrow')
122	R:	Ahng?
123	O:	Yo voy (es-)tar mañana- (.) >a partir de la(-s) do(-s)
		('Tomorrow I'm going to be- after two')
124		de la tarde estoy aquí ya.<
		('in the afternoo I'm here')
125	R:	A partir de la(-s) do/h/?
		('After two?')
126	O:	Si, yo ( ) ha parquear la [guagua.
		('Yes, I'm ( ) to park the van')
127	R:	[Lo unico que tengo que
		('The only thing I have to')
128		hacer es llenar la camioneta. Tengo que meter die-
		('do is fill the van. I have to load ten-')
129		=tengo que meter die/h/ canopia(-s), doc- doce
		('I have to load ten canopies, twe- twelve')
130		canopias. (1.0) *Ok?* Tengo que meter como veinte
		('canopies. Ok? I have to load like twenty')

131		mesa(-s). Vente- veinte y- veinte y tre(-s) mesa(-)s
		('tables. Twenty- twenty- twenty-three tables')
132		por ahí, quiero meter.
		(around there, I want to load')
133	O:	Aha.
134	R:	Las- los *sandbags*, y las sillas, y se acabó.
		('The- the sandbags, and the chairs, and that' it')
135		((E gestures as if cleaning his hands of something))
136	O:	Nada, nada, casi nada.
		('Nothing, nothing, that's almost nothing')
137	R:	Eso no es nada. Compara(-d)o con lo que no/h/
		('That's nothing. Compared to what's')
138		viene Junio treinta? No, Junio veinte y seis:?
		(coming to us June thirtieth. No, June twenty-six')
139	O:	Hay que comprar [otra-
		('You have to buy another')
140	R:	[El garage completo huevo(-n).=
		('The entire garage man')
141	O:	=Hay que comprar otra guagua (en-)tonce-=
		('You have to buy another van, then')
142	R:	=No::!, que coño comprar otra guagua! Ese ya rento
		('No, fuck buy another van. For that I'll just rent').
143		un camión? Mira no la vaina e(-s) e/h/ta, (0.8)
		('a truck. No look, the things is this,')
144		r/r/ento un camión para *Praid Fes* (0.7) y la guagua
		('I'll rent a truck for Pride Fest and your van')
145		tuya va conmigo pa(-ra) el *Bronx*.
		('goes with me to the Bronx')
146	O:	Y que tu va (ha-)cer en el *Bronx*.
		('And what are you doing in the Bronx?')
147	R:	En el *Bronx* tengo una vaina::: un:- el el *Bronx*
		(In the Bronx I have this mess, a- the the Bronx')
148		Borough President.
149		(0.5)
150	O:	O::=
151	R:	=Que tiene una feria, una para(d-)ita chiquitita de
		('That's having a fair, a tiny parade, those')
152		esa:(-s) (.) chimbas. (0.7) Pero no joda(-s) huevon,
		('cheap ones. But no kidding, man')

153		<porque::/h/tra salsa live to(d-)a mie:rda:> no joda
		('because live salsa to the fullest. No kidding')
154		ahí bailando todo el día? (.) Gozando? un pe(d-)o y
		('over there dancing all day. Having a blast and a ')
155		medio?=
		('half')
156	O:	=A ti te gusta esa vaina.
		('You like that mess?')

Omar and Roberto's speech diverge in a few subtle ways diverge in this segment. It is possible that after his mention of how disruptive a deportation would be, the differences between himself and Omar were brought to the surface. In this section of the transcription he reduces his use of exaggerated VS intonation. While Omar drops /s/ in "*dos*" (line 123), in his repetition of Omar's statement Roberto aspirates word final /s/ in "*dos*" (line 125). In line 126 Omar uses "*guagua*" to refer to his white van and Roberto uses "*camioneta*" (line 128). In other words the obvious convergence to Omar's speech is no longer evident. It's not possible to say whether these changes were made consciously by Roberto. But it cannot be ruled out that a subconscious adjustment occurred in the face of a contradiction between his identification as a Venezuelan and the overstated use of VS on the one hand, and his American, New Yorker, and even Puerto Rican orientation on the other.

Finally, recall Roberto's enthusiastic declaration of his participation in the Bronx Borough president's Puerto Rican festival during his conversation with James. Here he describes the parade as "*chimba*" (152). I was unfamiliar with the word and did a search for it in a language forum (http://forum.wordreference.com). According to one of the participants of the forum: "in Venezuela it is a word broadly use to qualify persons or things in a derogatory manner or to say that something is false or of bad quality". Roberto also does not use "Puerto Rican" or "*puertorriqueño*" to describe the event like he did in his conversation with James. His diminishment of the event here likely means that he wished to make a favorable impression on James and presented the event as something more significant than what it really was. The two conversations considered together point to the usefulness of intertexuality, or the use one text to guide the interpretation of another, as applied to discourse analysis.

Discussion

Roberto is quite flexible in his use of ethnicity for achieving a number of interactive and material goals. He accomplished the three types of switching I outlined in Chapter 1: passing/crossing, accommodating, and featuring. In terms of passing or crossing, he especially aligned himself to Puerto Rican categorization. As seen in his network and discussed in his life history, Roberto had little contact with Venezuelans and Venezuelan culture; Puerto Rican influences were more present in his life. Major sources of Puerto Rican cultural knowledge came from both his current wife and ex-wife, who both identified as Puerto Rican. Additionally, influential neighborhood relationships during his adolescence were with Puerto Ricans. Finally, Roberto confirmed that he was much more familiar with the island of Puerto Rico than with his birth country.

These experiences have played important roles in shaping Roberto's ethnic self-understandings. Roberto occupies a gray zone, vacillating between the fact of his kin and birth ties to Venezuela and his experiential and interactional ties to Puerto Rican identification. His discourse suggests this. If he has no choice but to identify himself by a label, he will feature Venezuelan – as he eventually did at the end of his conversation with James. But if he has room to manage his ethnic self-presentation he draws readily upon his knowledge of Puerto Rican culture and behavior. This raises important questions about the use of ethnic labels in socio-demographic surveys and the assumptions that underlie their use to predict a number of outcomes, from health behaviors to patterns of political participation.

These elements of Roberto's ethnicity shed a new light on his conversations with Omar. Yes, Roberto was born in Venezuela. He uses this category as his primary identification. In his interactions with Omar, Venezuelan frames of reference figure prominently. Yet, his exaggerated use of Venezuelan Spanish features were accommodations or convergences to Omar's speech. They hint to insecurity about, or overcompensation for, his tenuous ties to Venezuela.

In the data analysis section I mentioned a number of schemas that directed areas of Roberto's interactions. The ethnic cooperation schema is one that was activated in both of his conversations. This schema fixes common ethnic identification as presupposing certain cooperative interests. As an abstract representation it positions social actors sharing a common ethnicity as also sharing common interests.

This schema has directive force and may help explain why Latino pan-ethnicity is persistent despite all the factors that complicate a common identification.

Evidence of this schema in Roberto's conversation is found, for example, in James's ready invocation of Latino connections: his relationship with various Latino organizations and his statement "Yeah, and it's all Latinos" in line 67. Roberto for his part, used codeswitching to highlight his willingness to play according to the rules set forth by the ethnic (Latino) cooperation schema. Similarly, in his conversation with Omar, Roberto said: "*Oye, vamo' a ver, el tiene que pelear esa vaina, broder. Tiene gente aquí* ('Listen, let's see, he has to fight that mess, bro. He has people here for him')". Appealing for their mutual friend, Roberto is basically saying "Let's do something." He is assuming there's a common cooperative interest. However, the ethnic cooperation schema was not as salient between Roberto and Omar, as it was between Roberto and James. This may be because with Omar he has a pre-established relationship upon which to base mutual support and cooperation.

Conclusion

The two transcripts discussed here are presented as evidence of ethnic identification switching, or the use of multiple ethnic identifications across contexts. Roberto's ethnic and linguistic repertoires are quite broad, making him an ideal participant for this research. In his conversation with James who had access to promising business contacts, he alternated between languages and dialects, invoking both pan-ethnic and Puerto Rican orientations. With a fellow Venezuelan, his use of VS became more pronounced, but aspects of his multiple identifications remained present throughout the interaction. Thus, Roberto's case demonstrates not only that people multiple ethnic identifications *across* situational contexts, but also *within* the same situational context (see also Bailey, 2000).

This study provides another example of the ways in which identity shifts occur in a span of minutes, during one interaction with the same interlocutor (see also Bailey 2000b). In the conversation between Roberto and James, there was enough ambiguity about the other's primary identification that both had to play an open field. To accomplish this, both men, but especially Roberto, tried identifications that suited each man's intentions and fit each man's continually tested assumptions about the other. Roberto's conversation with James is a good example of how ethnicity can be instrumental and yet remain implicit in an interaction. With the exception of James' direct question at the very end of the interaction, self-identification was never accomplished by naming categories out loud. This subtle navigation makes it possible for both participants to test the waters interactively, customizing their responses according to what is found to be appropriate. It also points to the ways that presupposed worlds drive an interaction, since so many things were left unspoken.

Finally, Roberto's case further suggests that ethnic and national labels can be misleading. Labels in social scientific research draw boundaries around populations assumed to share attributes and outcomes. But Roberto's daily practice reveals just how arbitrary these boundaries can be. U.S. Census conventions would categorize him as a white, Hispanic from South America. Yet his linguistic preferences, social network and cultural knowledge align him well with New York Puerto Ricans. Scientists have called attention to the inadequacy of race and ethnicity as explanatory variables, when what they actually capture is socio-economic variation (Collins 2001; Rivara & Finberg, 2001; Schwartz 2001). Promising alternatives or supplements to ethnic categories can be found in social network measures (e.g. distribution of ethnicities among network members) and in questions about language use.

CHAPTER 5

"I Want Them To Be Happy": The Case of Abel

INTRODUCTION

After seeing a flyer about my study posted in their ESL school, Abel and his friends called me to find out more. We agreed to meet at a Colombian restaurant, *"Cositas Ricas"* in Jackson Heights, Queens. On a weekday in June, I waited for them outside the always-packed restaurant on the all-important immigrant thoroughfare, Roosevelt Avenue. Abel and his friends greeted me, dressed in casual business clothes and carrying messenger-style bags. I was a little amused by the thought that I was meeting them to discuss some important business proposal. Rather than the interview of potential participants I was accustomed to doing, I readied myself to deliver a sales pitch.

As I later found is customary for this group, we sat down to eat before talking business. Abel and his friends generously treated me to Colombian beef stew and a papaya shake. We casually talked in Spanish about my project, which inspired some lively comments about immigrants in NYC. During our group conversation I was able to ask each of them about their background and daily routines - Abel, Marco, and Luis were Ecuadorians working as salesmen for DirectTV installation companies in Queens. Throughout our lunch, Abel took regular breaks to make and answer phone calls from clients. His close friend Marco urged him to relax and enjoy the meal, which he finally did. Knowing that I could not recruit all three of them I paid particular attention to how each described his daily routines. In the end, I asked Abel to participate. It turned out that Abel and Marco worked so closely together that my observations of Abel regularly included Marco who in turn provided a number of keen insights into immigrant and ethnicity issues, as well as to Abel's behavior.

Abel described himself as a married, church-going salesman. I was interested in experiencing how ethnicity came into play at church, having not attended religions services with other participants up to that point. Therefore, this was a key factor for asking him to participate. I was also intrigued by his relationship with his Mexican wife, who like him, entered the country without documentation and spoke little English. Abel's participation promised an inside view into a number of dynamics I had not yet explored in the research. In the end, however, most of my observations with Abel were at work; it was in the context of work that he made the fullest use of his ethnic and linguistic repertoire.

A Brief History of Abel

Much of Abel's time was spent working in the streets. Especially in the warm months of the year, he set up his DirectTV display on the busiest sidewalks of all NYC boroughs except for Staten Island. We set up our first interview in a small public park not far from his office in Corona. Sitting on a bench, Abel narrated an economic, personal, and spiritual passage that led him from Guayaquil in Ecuador to New Jersey to New York. He described his life as a series of ascents and precipitous descents, with his state at the time of our meeting the most stable. Born to a family of clothes and electronics vendors, since the age of eleven he learned how to make a living selling in the streets. "I worked, worked, and worked, always working," he said, and lived in a neighborhood where all his childhood friends eventually died violently or succumbed to drugs.

At the age of twenty-seven he immigrated to the U.S. While his two sisters would eventually decide to move to Spain, where entry was easier, Abel opted for the Mexican *frontera*. In 1995 he paid $5,000 to a *coyote* who helped him in his passage across the U.S. border. Travel took him through the Ecuadorian Sierras into Colombia, Venezuela, Panama, Mexico and eventually New Jersey. Upon his arrival he began working in construction with Portuguese contractors. Working alongside him were other Ecuadorians, many of them *serranos* from Ecuador's highlands. In construction Abel developed a set of beliefs that to this day influence his ethnic self-presentation. First, he described the Portuguese foreman he worked under as exploitative and callous.

"When I lived in New Jersey, I was ashamed to say I was Ecuadorian," he admitted. Mistreatment he received while working in construction led him to refrain from telling people he was Ecuadorian. His reasoning was that those looking for workers to exploit used his Ecuadorian identity to categorize and debase him. "They catalogue you," he said, "and then they put you in a group and they treat that group with kicks." Not only did he build resentment for the Portuguese bosses, who he perceived as racist, but also for the Ecuadorians around him who were complacent about their conditions. Additionally, since many of the Ecuadorians he worked with were not from the coast, *costeño*, like him, he also grew to distrust and disassociate from them. This is why he preferred the *"guayaquileño"* label to using "Ecuadorian."

Abel eventually became a taxi driver because he sought the sort of independence he had in previous jobs. During this time he was determined to learn English. One incident in particularly urged him to learn: a fellow Ecuadorian, who happened to be in better economic standing, refused to speak to him in Spanish. Nonplussed, he determined that language would never again be another source of ridicule. He also wanted to be accepted by Americans, to move beyond the Latino immigrant communities where all spoke only Spanish. While a taxi driver, Abel became involved in New Jersey's underground sex industry, catering to the immigrant community where he lived. As a *lider de mujeres* ('pimp'), he made frequent trips into Queens to find women, mostly Colombian, Mexican, and Dominican, to bring back to New Jersey. The money he made as a pimp helped him towards the purchase of his own taxi and livery license. With this new level of independence he was able to amass considerable savings. But as he relates, his involvement in this scene was not purely business. "My problem has always been women," Abel declares. After a night of heavy drinking, he drove under the influence and was arrested by the police. Not unlike Roberto in the previous chapter, Abel lost his taxi and his savings.

Queens was familiar to him and so he moved there to look for work; he moved with his girlfriend, now wife, Monica. Monica was a source of stability for him and it was upon her urging, and the encouragement of a neighbor, that they began to attend an evangelical church. The church catered exclusively to the Latino community in Corona. All services were conducted in Spanish, with the exception of one fledgling and unpopular English Sunday service. Abel found the church to be a source of redemption. He and Monica became born-again-Christians and married at the church. It also happened to be the source of his first significant work opportunity in Queens. A fellow church member recommended Abel to Marco, an Ecuadorian working in DirectTV sales. *Guayaquileño* himself, Marco felt instant chemistry with Abel and helped him get established as a satellite television salesman. For the most part, Abel liked the work and spent a significant amount of his seven-day workweek on it. Because of this, most of the observations and recordings were of Abel at work or with co-workers.

Abel's personal network reflects the important relationship areas suggested in his life history. His network comprises ten components, but nine of these are isolates. The main network depicted in the center of the graph includes his work contacts, fellow church members (including pastors) and his family. Similar to Roberto, Abel's wife, Monica, was the most central person in his network. The main network component is moderately dense, although more dense than Roberto's. Notice for example, more clustering than shown in Figure 1. Each of the sub-areas of his network is quite interconnected. Abel's network also spans international boundaries. Several of his family members live abroad in either Ecuador or Spain.

Abel spent most of his waking hours at work. But this work was a mostly independent endeavor. Marco was the only other person who regularly accompanied Abel during his day. They often worked together to sell satellite TV subscriptions and had developed a system of sharing profits. Although his church was an important facet of his life, he spent very little time in church activities while I was with him. Of all the participants with whom I worked, Abel was most apt to include me in his interactions with work colleagues and friends. Therefore, with the exception of his blood relatives, who do not live in the US, I met several of the people depicted in Figure 2.

It is evident from the list of nationalities that Abel interacted with a diverse range of people. Although many of his alters were Ecuadorian, if we omit the family component it is clear that his actual interactions in the U.S. were quite mixed ethnically. While ethnically diverse, Abel's personal network was entirely composed of Latinos. This fact was evident in my week of observations of him. The non-Latinos he encountered on a daily basis were potential clients in his sales forays. As will be demonstrated in his linguistic data below, most of his interactions were in Spanish.

Figure 2. Abel's Personal Network

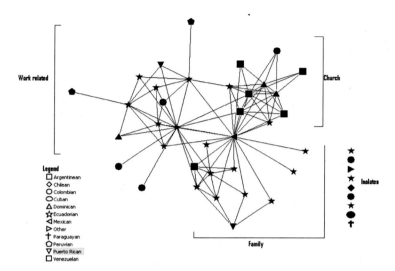

Abel's Ethnic and Regional Identifications

Contrary to prevailing patterns among Ecuadorians in the US, Abel did not maintain a transnational life between Ecuador and the U.S. (Jokisch & Pribilisky, 2002). While he had significant formative experiences in Ecuador, he maintained few relationships with family and friends back in Ecuador. Abel's Ecuadorian identity was bolstered by his many contacts with other Ecuadorians in Queens ("*Aquí somos todos ecuatorianos*" ('Here we are all Ecuadorian,' Abel, during work meeting with fellow salespersons, June 15, 2005). His best friend and sales partner, Marco, was Ecuadorian as were several of his co-wokers. Abel's closer Ecuadorian contacts provided a social environment in which to express ethnic pride and keep up to date with events back in Ecuador. These and his more fleeting contacts with Ecuadorians in Queens also served to reinforce the folk ethnic categorization system prevalent in Ecuador. This categorization system orders relationships and influence ethnic self-concepts among Ecuadorians in the U.S. context.

Abel subscribed to a racio-regional folk categorization scheme common in Ecuador. My fieldwork conversations with other

Ecuadorians in Queens suggested that it was persistent among Ecuadorian immigrants in the city. Personal anecdotes revealed that Ecuador was divided between los *costeños* ('the coast people') and los *serranos* ('the mountain people' or '*indios*'). According to the prevalent models in Ecuador, *costeños* are at once fun-loving, superficial, untrustworthy, open-minded, *machistas*. *Serranos* on the other hand are characterized as conservative, hard-working, ignorant, humble and (also) untrustworthy. The alleged differences are so deep that Abel once claimed that he, as a *costeño*, could get along better with Latinos from any other country than with *serranos* from his own.

Thus, Ecuadorian immigrants transplant these divisions on American soil suggesting that unity among all Ecuadorians in the U.S. is a tenuous claim. In keeping with this folk ethnic scheme, Abel more frequently identified himself as *guayaquileño*, rather than use the more inclusive *ecuatoriano* label. Because of what he perceived to be mistreatment of the predominantly *indio* and *mestizo* Ecuadorian population in NYC, Abel preferred to not tell people he was Ecuadorian and so *guayaquileño* was an important alternative. The coastal city of Guayaquil is Ecuador's largest. Pride in being *Guayaquileño* ("100% *guayaquileño!*", Abel, life history interview, June 13, 2005) thrived on the sentiment that to be from Guayaquil was to be street-smart and confident (not unlike the value that comes from identifying as a "New Yorker"). According to Abel, to meet a *Guayaquileño* is to be greeted by someone who will treat you like you've known each other for years. For Abel, to be from Guayaquil was also to disassociate from the negative associations made of *indios* or *serranos*.

While he avoided the label, Abel had also described himself to me as *indio*. The *indio* category is strongly connected to specific phenotypic characteristics, including brown skin color and short height. Abel made frequent reference to his convex nose shape as an undesirable *indio* trait he inherited. Actually, he held a few contradictory views about his indigenous heritage. On the one hand, he acknowledged that in Ecuador he was considered *indio*. He did not talk about his father, but he noted that his mother was *india* ("*Mi mamá es indiecita como ella.* ('My mother is Indian (diminutive) like her'), Abel, conversation during observations, June 18, 2005.) From his travels to Otovalo, he developed romanticized views about the "*indio* lifestyle." Yet, he identified so strongly as a *costeño* that he used derogatory labels like "*tira flecha*" ('arrow thrower') and "*cholo*" to describe Latinos with indigenous heritage and even himself ("*Yo soy cholo.*" ('I am cholo,' Abel, conversation with co-worker, June 25, 2005).

To counter how people could perceive him because of his phenotype, Abel occasionally said – or at least left people with the impression – that he was Colombian or some other Latino group that he had no biographical connection to. He opted for identifications he saw as having more prestige than Ecuadorian, and so Colombian was his preferred option. During his life history interview he explained: "*O sea a mi me daba vergüenza.* ('In other words, I was ashamed.') 'Where are you from?' 'Ah, from Colombia! From Venezuela! From Brazil!'" These categories were accessible because he had had much interpersonal contact with Latinos of all nationalities. He could cross to some of their Spanish dialects and had gained knowledge about idioms, popular culture, styles, norms, and status hierarchies of multiple Latino cultures. Abel had developed a Latino-specific cultural fluency that ingratiated him to others in Latino-dominant Jackson Heights/Corona. As such, he identified strongly with the Latino collectivity, even though he seldom used the Latino label to identify himself to others ("*Siempre yo soy Latino,* ('I'm always Latino,' Abel, life history interview, June 13, 2005).

Abel's Linguistic Repertoire[16]

Ecuadorian Spanish (ES)

Few studies have been conducted about Ecuadorian Spanish. Lipski (2004) cites a 1953 monograph by Humberto Mateus Toscano as the

---

[16] Abel was a familiar with phonology and lexicon from a number of other dialects of Spanish, specifically Colombian, Dominican, and Rioplatense Spanish. Because his speech in the recordings was characteristically Ecuadorian a great majority of the time, these other dialects will not be considered as part of his linguistic repertoire. However, as I will discuss later in this chapter, depending on with whom he was speaking, he introduced key words, phrases or pronunciations from other dialects into his speech. I should add that the Spanish from the Caribbean coastal regions of Colombia shares features of Ecuadorian Spanish. Both languages tend towards elision or aspiration of syllable final /s/ and velarization of word final /n/. Therefore, it would not be a complete stretch, linguistically, for Abel to identify himself as a Colombian from the Caribbean coast.

most comprehensive to date. According to Lipski, Quechua has made important contributions to the Spanish of Ecuador. While Quechua is more widely spoken in the highland regions, prolonged contact between the rural areas and the large cities has spread the influence of Quechua beyond the Sierras. Besides the indigenous connection, Afro-Ecuadorian populations both along the coastal region and in the highland Valle de Chota, have retained elements of ancestral African languages in their Spanish. The Spanish of Ecuador is divided into three primary regions: coastal, Andean highlands, and Cuenca / Amazonian. I will focus on the elements most relevant to Abel's speech, and outline the features of coastal ES only. These include: velarization of syntagma final /n/ and also in prevocalic words[17]; some tendency to neutralize preconsonant /l/ and /r/, frequent elision of syntagma final /r/; realization of /rr/ as an alveolar vibrant; weak intervocalic fricative /y/, at times elided in contact with /i/ and /e/; and aspirated or elided syllable and word final /s/. Voseo, the use of second person singular pronoun *vos* instead of *tú*, is common in the coastal area of Ecuador but stigmatized among the upper classes in Guayaquil (Toscano Mateus, 1953: 200). Therefore, while it is widespread in coastal communities, there is a tendency away from this practice in the city of Guayaquil. In fact, Abel did not use *voseo* except when addressing speakers of *Rioplatense* Spanish, Latinos from the Rio de la Plata region in Argentina and Uruguay.

    Abel's Examples:

((A co-worker asks if he received a call they were all expecting))
    A: *A mi y a Roberto >no(-s)=(ha-)**n**=llama(-d)o.< >A lo/h/*
        ('They called Roberto and I. To the
        do/h/ nomá(-s)= no(-s)=han=llama(-d)o/h/.<
        ('two of us only they have called.')

((Talks to Roberto over the phone about political problems at work))
    A: *A: claro (e-)so=si puche. Porq/h/- Porque así por así, meter*
        ('Ah sure, that's true pal. Because, like that, to put in
        ordene/h/ y a quien reclamamos. A quien le hacemo(-s) pito.
        orders and who do we complain to? Whose attention will we
        get?')

---

[17] Bold **n** in transcripts indicates velarized /n/.

((Standard information given to potential DTV clients))
A: *Activación y equipo totalmente gratis.*
('Activation and equipment totally free').

Hispanicized English (HE)

Abel learned about my study while attending a community ESL class. He was not fully fluent in English but among his fellow Ecuadorian salesmen he had the most command.   His English could best be described using Zentella's (1997) classification, Hispanicized English, a variety marked by the transfer of Spanish phonology and grammar. Features Zentella cites as common to HE are: tendency to reduce vowels to the five vowel sounds of Spanish; and tendency to reduce consonant clusters and replace English phonemes such as the interdental voiced and voiceless fricatives /θ/ and /ð/.   Grammatical transfers from Spanish can result in double negation.   And forms that transfer the form and meaning of a Spanish lexical item to English also occur (e.g. "She puts me nervous" from *Me pone nerviosa*) (Zentella, 1997: 47).
Abel's Examples:

((After teasing him jokingly, requests that the manager (M) of a DirectTV installation office address some concerns of Abel's sales team))
A: >I know you were /eh/smokin(-g).< >I know you were
       /eh/smokin(-g).<
M: Hello. How're you doing.
A: I /oo/nder investigation[18]. So be careful what you say.
       ((Laughs)).
M: Ah. Alright. That's good.=
A: =We need to ta/t/ to you. We need to ta/t/ to you.
       We wan(-t) a know wha(-t)'s goin(-g) on here.

((Apologizing to an English speaking-friend over the phone))
A: I promise. I promise. I'm feel really ba/h/ about /d/at.
       So sorry about that, I wan(-t) a do somet(-h)in(-g),

---

[18] This was the subtle, humorous way Abel customarily used to let people know that he was wearing an audio recorder.

to- to-. I wan(-t) say apology. I wan(-t) a say
apology so (   ). I wan(-t) eh- I wan(-t) do somet(-h)in(-g)
better…I'm feel really ba/h/ about /d/at.

Data and Analysis

Talking over the background sounds of a televised *futbol* match, Abel
announces, "Guys, guys, *quiero hacer un brindis* ('I want to make a
toast')." Abel, the English-speaker of the group, four other men and
one woman gathered at the Jaramillo Ecuadorian Restaurant in Jackson
Heights to welcome a new business prospect. The hopeful chatter
centered around an upcoming change in management and new
alliances, leading Abel to proclaim: "The sky's the limit." When the
futbol match was over, the music began. One particularly lively song
led Abel to exclaim proudly, "*Esa e' la musica de mi tierra* ('that's the
music of my land')." Finally, one hour into the gathering, long-awaited
guests arrived. The group of Ecuadorian sellers greeted a Colombian
manager and her colleague. Exchanging kisses, Abel introduced
himself to her, "*Quiubo, soy Abel* ('What's up, I'm Abel')."

This brief sketch of a one and half hour dinner among friends and
co-workers illustrates the ways in which Abel slipped easily into
multiple presupposed worlds. "Guys, guys" is familiar and playful and
helps Abel begin a warm, but often formal celebratory custom with a
casual tone. Few expressions capture the promise of the American
dream like "The sky's the limit[19]." Like all metaphoric phrases, there
is considerable cultural knowledge behind it. One thing is clear; Abel's
codeswitches are effective to the extent that the interlocutors share his
knowledge. With his public show of Ecuadorian pride, Abel revealed
an ethnic attachment not expressed in most of his recordings. Instead,
his data revealed a drive for accommodating or orienting himself to the
practices of other groups, as with his use of the Colombian greeting
"*quiubo.*"

---

[19] Without making too strong a connection between the phrase's metaphoric
meaning and the sentiment of this immigrant group, Abel's use of the word is
symbolic of the acculturation process. Because the expression is imbued with
cultural knowledge, knowing English is not sufficient to understanding it.
Likewise, some participants in this study have said, "To make it in America
you have to think like an American." It is not enough to know the language.

The data presented here illustrate three main patterns of ethnic self-presentation: a) tendency towards disassociating himself from Ecuadorian identification; b) tendency towards accommodating or converging to the speech of others; and c) tendency to invoke Ecuadorian identification only when among other Ecuadorians.

Todos Menos Ecuatorianos ('Everyone but Ecuadorians')

On a Jackson Heights sidewalk, with the 7 train passing above us every five minutes, Abel, Marco and I touched on the topic of "ethnic pride." Abel stood by calling out his usual DirectTV announcement, *"Venga, señor, instale DirectTV en casa! Pa' que vea los partidos de su país.* ('Come, sir, install DirectTV at home. So that you can watch your country's soccer matches')." Marco, meanwhile, sat with me and shared his perspective on the topic. People switch, he argued, because they are ashamed of who they are. He suggested that Ecuadorians in particular have no national pride. Marco added that Ecuadorians who switch don't want to be treated like "poor, ignorant *indios."* "What about you," I asked, "do you switch?" "No," he said. Marco described one occasion when he and a colleague went to a restaurant frequented by other Ecuadorians and *"mexicanos del campo* (Mexicans from the countryside)" – a veiled term for Mexicans of mostly indigenous ancestry. One of them asked him where he was from and he promptly told them he was Ecuadorian. "They didn't believe," he told me, "they insisted that I wasn't." Marco is euro-Ecuadorian. He provided this story as an example of how strongly he sticks to his identification. As he explained, he would never try to pass himself off as anything else and prefers to assert himself to show people "what he is" and "what he can do." The truth is that in Ecuador, like in most of Latin America, fair-skinned people like Marco have a sufficiently advantageous identification option. In a country where 90% of the population is either *mestizo* or *indio* (CIA World Factbook, 2010), whites are a privileged minority. Transplanted to New York ground, particularly New York's Latino immigrant society, Marco enjoys the same status and distinction. It could be argued that as a *white* Ecuadorian, "a rare breed," so much so that fellow Ecuadorians and Latinos don't believe he is, his identification is even more distinctive and uniquely advantageous[20].

Abel on the other hand, admits to feeling ashamed. Contrasting Marco's experience, to be *indio* <u>and</u> Ecuadorian is *exactly* what's expected. By performing non-Ecuadorian ethnic identifications Abel managed the impressions that he made on others. But taking on a non-Ecuadorian identification did not always entail performance. As Abel explained, it was not uncommon for people to incorrectly guess his background. When this happened he could simply go along with people's assumptions by staying quiet. During one of his trips to sell DirectTV in the Bronx, Abel encountered such a scene with a potential Puerto Rican client. The client (J) agrees to call Abel back at a later time because he was unsure if he was allowed to install DirectTV where he lives. The conversation is about ready to close but the client seems reluctant to end it:

1   A: *Me puede llamar.*
          ('You can call me')
2   J: Ok, *esta bien. Yo te llamo.*
          ('Ok, alright. I'll call you')
3   *Van a /Eh/taten Island tambien?*
          ('You go to Staten Island as well?')
4   A: Staten Island, Long Island, Brooklyn, Manhattan:,
5   (0.7)
6   E:m, Florida, Miami.
7   (1.2)
8   J: *Tu ere/h/ colombiano.*
          ('You're Colombian')
9   A: ((Abel silently nods his head yes))
10   (3.4)
11   J: Je je. ((C laughs)) *Yo soy boricua.*
          ('I'm Puerto Rican')
12   A: *(Es-)Ta bien papá.*
          ('Alright, pop')

---

[20] Marco spoke very little English and so did not have English as a tool for ethnic self-presentation. He was, however, extremely eager to learn and often insisted on speaking English with me.

13   J: *Tengo, tengo gente colombiana.*
          ('I have Colombian people')
14   A: *(En-)Tonce cualquier cosa (.) me e/h/ta- una*
          ('So then, anything you give me a')
15   *llamadita.*
          ('call')
16   J: *Si, yo ahora, (viste), estoy en Staten Island. Me le*
          ('Yes, right now I (look), am in Staten Island. I')
17   *escapé a mi hermana. Tú me entiende?*
          ('escaped from my sister. You know what I mean?')
18   A: *A: te (es-)capaste.*
          ('you escaped')
19   J: *Si porque, imaginate, le digo, vamo a Manhattan.*
          ('Yes because, imagine this, I say, let's go to Manhattan')
20   *Me dice que no.*
          ('She tells me no')

J spends the next three minutes venting about domestic troubles with his sister, with whom he lives. Responding mostly with, "*"Ta bien* ('Ok')," Abel listens patiently without giving much feedback. When it becomes clear that J depends on his sister and likely cannot make a decision about DirectTV without her, Abel's "Ok's" begin to take a tone of finality, urging the client to close the conversation. Turning to the excerpt, the first thing to notice is that J's turn in line 8 is an attempt to move the conversation from the transactional arena to the identity arena (Scotton & Ury, 1977). In light of the rest of their conversation, this move is meant to open up conversational possibilities. Lines 16 – 20 suggest that J has an isolated living arrangement, hence the use of "*me le escapé a mi hermana* ('I escaped from my sister')." In other parts of the conversation he lamented that he felt misunderstood by his sister and other family members. To further engage Abel in a conversation, J appeals to a possible ethnic connection by asking Abel if he was Colombian. As Abel silently passes for Colombian, J attempts to express his solidarity with Abel by highlighting his own Colombian connections. His possessive phrasing of this, "*tengo gente colombiana"* ('I have Colombian people'), suggests that his Colombian contacts are part of his personal network, legitimizing his claim to solidarity with other Colombians. Although Abel did not wish to spend too much time on J and miss other, perhaps more promising prospects, he recognized the need to keep him happy as a potential client. In line 9 he acknowledges to J that he is Colombian but his technique is revealing. Abel's nod in line 9 allowed him to "keep the client happy" without *over-committing* himself to Colombian identification. In this case, actions do not speak louder than words. I was present when Abel did this, and observed a certain reluctance in his gesture. The nod would best be described as the bodily equivalent of a whisper. His turns in lines 12 and 14 showed his reluctance for the conversation to turn to the topic of ethnic background. After their conversation ended Abel and I talked about what had just happened[21]:

Abel: And like that you find people with no one to listen to them.

Rosalyn: But you told him you are Colombian. Explain that.

Abel: It makes me happy to see him happy. If he says I'm Colombian, I'm Colombian. I like to see people happy ((Spoken in a sweet, but slightly sarcastic tone.))

Rosalyn: Why do you think that makes him happy?

Abel: Because he says that (   ) Colombian. OK. Because then I had the trust to talk.

Rosalyn: You don't say you are Ecuadorian?

Abel: I don't know, maybe because everyone encounters people, simply looks, and shares theirs things. But if I don't even know where you're from?
"Brazilian? Yes, I'm Brazilian". "Where are you from?" "From Paraguay? Yes, I'm Paraguayan."

Rosalyn: So you are not attached to telling people that you are from Ecuador.

---

[21] While all interviews with Abel were conducted in Spanish, only their English translations will be given here.

Abel: If people recognize my accent, or unless it's a client that lives here. That was from DirectTV. "Excuse me, where are you from? Ecuadorian. Yes! I'm Ecuadorian too, a pleasure!" Just so they buy from me.
(Conversation during ethnographic observations, June 18, 2005).

Abel chooses the ethnic option he believes will satisfy the potential buyer. In an extension of "The customer is always right," he takes the interlocutor's lead. Referring to Lakoff's (1973) work on politeness rules and Goffman's (1974) work on frame semantics, Sweetser (1987: 44-45) notes that "conversation often has its primary purposes at the level of social interaction; making someone happy, or negotiating the interaction – frame, may be a more important goal than informativeness." Inherent to Abel's reasoning (and reminiscent of the ethnic cooperation schema described in Chapter 4) is the assumption that people ask ethnic identification questions to build rapport and open up conversational opportunities. Because of ethnicity's potential as a way to connect with others, a guiding rule is that in fleeting in counters, "if I don't even know where the person is from," ethnicity can be used flexibly. Ethnic attachment figures little into this. In talking with Abel, I did not gather that he viewed such instances of passing as outright deception. In his own way Abel lives the notion that our identifications are just as dependent on the ascriptions of others as on our self-ascriptions. The anti-Ecuadorian rejections he had experienced contributed to Abel's ethnic flexibility if only as a way to negotiate the ethnic ascriptions made of him.

As the above example suggests, non-Ecuadorian identification is a strategy used only in fleeting encounters or in situations where people deal with each other on a surface level. It is clear that Abel's Colombian identification carries the risk of exposure. Therefore, Abel opted for another approach also designed to lessen the impact of his *indio* identity, opting for *guayaquileño* as his primary identification. Using this label had two key results: it allowed some distance from the *serrano/indio* association, and it was ambiguous enough to lead people *away* from "Ecuador." The short transcript that follows is an example of when and how Abel used this label to achieve the latter goal. In it, he has a conversation with a DirectTV sales office operator. These operators work locally in Queens providing support for sales people and technicians. Abel called to get a credit report on a potential client. While he waited for the results, Abel talked casually with the operator:

1   A: >*Tu ere(-s) colombiana? verdad.<Me diji(-s)te.*
         ('You're Colombian, right. You told me.')
2   (3.2) *Yo- yo soy de, Guayaquil.* (2.0) *Si. Soy*
         ('I'm from Guayaquil. Yes. I'm')
3   *guayaquileño.*(1.8) (*A-*)*donde queda, adonde*
         ('Guayaquilean. Where is it, where')
4   *queda e/h/tara pensando. A(-d)onde queda*
         ('is it, you must be thinking. Where is')
5   *Guayaquil.* (3.7) *Queda-* (0.8). (*Es-*)*ta (es-) ta*
         ('It's- it's, it's')
6   *cerquita de Colombia.* (5.6) A::::! *Por eso,*
         ('really close to Colombia. Ah...that's why')
7   *porque (es-)ta   cerca de Peru.* (1.5) *Yo soy*
         ('because it's close to Peru. I'm')
8   *calla(-d)o, de d- Santa Marina.*
         ('quiet, from Santa Marina')

Abel begins with a familiar conversation starter, asking about the background of newly met others. Consistent through Abel's recordings is his use of *guayaquileño* to identify himself, except in situations where he wishes to disassociate from Ecuadorian identification altogether. To make a positive impression on her he quite subtly takes her away from Ecuador. Without actually appropriating the Colombian label as he has done in other scenarios, he leads her in the direction of Colombia. The use of diminutive "*cerquita*" in line 6, serves to reduce the spatial distance and thus highlight the similarity between the two. Abel avoids using the "Ecuadorian" label all together. In fact, it appears that he implied that he was from Peru. Notice the last sentence, "*Yo soy calla(-d)o, de Santa Marina*, ('I'm quiet, from Santa Marina')." This is a word play on the Peruvian port city Callao and one of its urban zones, Santa Marina.
      Abel foretold such a scenario during the life history interview:

Rosalyn: You were explaining to me that at times you tell people that you are from Colombia or you're from-

Abel: Yes, so that they'll treat me- treat me with respect.

Rosalyn: You still-

Abel: No, not now-

Rosalyn: Not now, that was only in-

Abel: In New Jersey- because of the people that are over there, the people.

Rosalyn: Over there, yeah. But here is different?

Abel: Here is different, of course.

Rosalyn: How?

Abel: That you tell them you are from Guayaquil, and they know that you're from Guayaquil. And he says, "where is Guayaquil?" "Guayaquil is over there by, by Argentian. Between Argentina and Brazil", I tell them! "Really?" They go and find a map to look for Guayaquil.
(Life history interview, June 15, 2005).

The conversation between Abel and the Colombian phone operator suggests some intriguing things about the ways that Latino immigrants in NYC operate in cognitive transnational fields. Perhaps the relative positions of countries on a map correspond with people's own mental maps or folk concepts about various nations. These mental maps carry cultural information along with geographical information. This is why Abel's description of Guayaquil as "*cerquita*" to Colombia is possible as a way to highlight interpersonal similarities between them. He places the ostensible nation of Guayaquil on the map between two of South America's largest countries. It appears that for Abel, Guayaquil exists cognitively *outside* of Ecuadorian borders. In his conversation with the operator he placed it closer to Colombia, and so "closer to home" for the Colombian operator. Abel is using proximity as a proxy for similarity. With Colombia, Argentina, or Brazil as the reference point, he's able invoke the salient positive and impressive associations people have of these countries.

One final point about Abel's linguistic behavior merits analysis. According to the samples given earlier of Abel's use of Ecuadorian dialect, when talking to other Ecuadorians it is easy to pick out in his speech phonological and lexical features linked to ES. In his conversation with the Colombian operator he alters his speech slightly. He does not switch dialects but does soften certain ES traits. Mainly, he slows down the speed of his utterances, so that there is little blurring of boundaries within words. When talking to non-Ecuadorians there is also less velarization of /n/. The main reason for doing this, of course, was to be understood. He did this with clients, me, even his non-Ecuadorian wife.

Quiero que estén felices ('I want them to be happy')

In the preceding section Abel mentioned that he "likes to see people happy" and some times goes along with the ethnic option of least resistance. This is a central theme in his negotiation of multiple ethnic and linguistic identifications, even when it doesn't entail him feigning or emphasizing this or that identity. Like many New Yorkers, he has become keenly aware of clues into people's background: physical features, accents, dress, mannerisms, etc. This skill comes especially handy for salespeople as they work to improve their chances of making a sale by tailoring their approach according to customer attributes. For example, one of Abel's techniques when approached by a customer is to mention the channel he thinks will most appeal to them. Usually, this happens without the potential customer actually *stating* their background. A sidewalk salesman has only so much time to make an impression - quick decisions about people's background are standard practice. If Abel believes a potential customer is Puerto Rican, he will tell them about WAPA-TV, one of Puerto Rico's large national channels. Mexican? He will be sure to mention Azteca and perhaps all the international channels where one might have access to *fútbol* matches. For the Ecuadorian there's Ecuavisa. Abel may also opt for the more general approach, *"Tenemos canales de Argentina* ('We have channels from Argentina'),"* etc. This is good sales practice, but Abel is adept at accommodation. A charismatic man with a genuine interest (whether practical or affective) in the comfort of his interlocutors, to varying degrees he'll adapt himself to their speech. In this section I will illustrate how Abel used phonological, lexical, and language accommodation to invoke frames of reference familiar for his listeners, identifying with his interlocutors by reducing the distance between them and him.

As Abel's case will show, everyday examples of speech accommodation can be found in sales encounters, where salespersons converge to customers' speech much more than customers converge to the salesperson. Thus, the power element is among the most crucial determinants of the direction of the convergence.

Giles, et al. (1987) first developed Speech Accommodation Theory (SAT) in his study of interpersonal accent convergence during interviews. SAT addresses the motivations and constraints governing speech shifts during social interactions. The theory also accounts for the social consequences of these shifts. Giles and his colleagues (1987) describe speech accommodation as strategies that achieve social approval, distinctiveness, or communicative efficiency. Drawing on social psychological similarity-attraction research, speech accommodation theory states that a person can induce another to evaluate him or her more favorably by reducing certain differences between them. Giles, et al., (1973) note that in exchange theory terms (see Byrne, 1969; Homans, 1961) an accommodation may involve certain costs for the speaker. These costs include expanded effort and potential identity change. Therefore, such behavior may only be initiated if possible rewards are available. Research does indicate that the more effort a speaker puts into accommodating to a listener's speech, the more favorably they are viewed (Giles, et al., 1987; Giles, et al., 1973). Bucholtz and Hall (2005: 599) extend elements of SAT to their framework for the analysis of identity in linguistic interaction. They use the term *adequation* to emphasize, the fact that in order for groups or individuals to be positioned as alike, they need not – and in any case cannot – be identical, but must merely be understood as sufficiently similar for current interactional purposes. As in speech accommodation, adequation is a process whereby interactants emphasize similarities and de-emphasize differences to align themselves to others. But whereas Giles (1973) suggested that these sorts of accommodations can (but do not have to) lead to identity change (described above as a "cost"), Bucholtz & Hall (2005) highlight adequation as one of the tactics of intersubjective identity construction.

Phonological Accommodation:
In this first example, Abel adjusts his pronunciation to match that of an African American client (L). For much of their conversation, the client and a friend accompanying her showed a strong preference for AAVE:

1   L: But wha(-t) I gotta put up when the <u>ma:n</u> come to
2   /d/e <u>house</u>?
3   A: E::, <u>nothin(-g)</u>
          / nahtheen/
4   L: No(th-)i**n**(-g)?
          /nuh-i**n**/
5   A: /Nahtin/, /nahri**n**/.

In line 3 Abel's Hispanicized English is marked by pronunciation of the vowel sounds /uh/ → /ah/ and /i/ → /ee/. He does take care to pronounce the voiceless fricative /th/. Abel adds stress to "nothin," reassuring her that there is no money up front. In line 4, L repeats Abel's answer as a reassurance-seeking interrogative. She drops the voiceless fricative /th/ and produces a stressed, distinctly velarized and nasalized last syllable /in/. Rather than reproduce his pronunciation in line 3, in line 5 Abel attempts an approximation at L's pronunciation of "nothing." One key feature of his phonological convergence is the use of /i/ rather than the Spanish vowel sound /ee/. L's stressed, nasalized and velarization pronunciation of /in/ is trickier to reproduce. In his first attempt he devoices using /t/ rather than /d/. This did not quite result in his desired effect and self-corrects once more with a /r/ and a velarized /n/. Especially because he makes that second attempt to better approximate her pronunciation, I interpret his turn in line 5 as an accommodation.

Lexical Accommodation
Next is a conversation between Abel and an African American woman (S) who approached him for DirectTV information. She was unsure whether the satellite dishes would be allowed in her apartment complex and asked for Abel's opinion. Unsure himself, he offers the option of having a technician go to her home:

1   A: You- /dZ/ou wan- wan(-t)a try?, oh no. We can
2   go to the house and we try. (0.8) Is no- is no(-t)

```
3        go(-ing)na be a problem, wi- for you. No?
4        (.)
5    S:  I don't kno:w that's my problem. I'm a ask for it.
6        So, y(-ou)all cou- y(-ou)all cou(-ld) put like on top
7        of the roof?
8    A:  Mm, sometime(-s) on top of the roof. Sometime(-s) 9
         on the window. Si- in the side. In the right side.=
10   S:  =If I can it si- If I can't have it on the window,
11   A:  No?
12   S:  I cou(-ld) have it on the roof?
13   A:  Yeah. Gotta be on the roof. Is- Find out le(-t) me
14       know. I'm gonna give you my phone number, and
15       call me. /D/is my phone number, my cell phone, c-
16       call me. Gim- me- gimme holla when you,
17       you find out. (Be-)cause I don(-'t) wan(-t) a
18       problem wi(-th), you know, you guys have a
19       problem.
```

In line 16 Abel uses "gimme holla" for "give me a holla'" ('give me a call'). Though not exclusively, this expression is associated with African American speech and used in informal contexts. Twice in lines 15 and 16, Abel uses the standard "call me," therefore his use of "holla" is redundant as a request. However, as an accommodating gesture, it is indexically rich. By showing his familiarity with an African American expression at best, and American slang at least, he signals his multi-cultural savvy. During my time teaching ESL classes in Queens I observed that students first focus on the basics of English before they understand or use popular expressions. Their limited language skills constrain the quantity and quality of contacts they can have with English-speakers from a variety of backgrounds. Abel's knowledge and use of these and other popular American words and expression, distinguishes him from an immigrant with limited language abilities, and marks him as an immigrant with awareness of the world beyond the enclave. In this way, he attempts to reduce the linguistic and cultural distance that exists between himself and S.

In the preceding example, Abel demonstrated knowledge of popular American culture and language. The next example shows that his multi-cultural awareness extends beyond the US. Abel calls a Colombian DirectTV technician over the phone and leaves a short message. Once a client decides to purchase the DirectTV subscription Abel refers their case to an installation office where a technician will be found for the case. These technicians tend to work independently and on a case-by-case basis. Maintaining positive relationships with them is important because if they do not make the installation Abel does not get paid:

A: *¿Quiubo paisa?* (0.5) >°Ung°-< (0.7) *Llame patrá,*
     ('What's up countryman. Call back,')
     le saluda Abel. Para saber de=sobre la
     ('it's Abel calling. To know about the')
     instalación del señor Mal-=Mateo Carrion. Me llama.
     ('installation for Mr. Mateo Carrion. Call me.')
     Bye.

Just as he did when greeting the Colombian manager earlier in this chapter, he greets the technician with the familiar Colombian greeting, *quiubo.* Here he uses another familiar Colombian term, *"paisa."* Short for paisano, this characteristically Colombian form is used among "countrymen," in other words between Colombians.

Language Accommodation
In the following excerpt Abel calls a Puerto Rican client to confirm that an installation was made at his home. This example illustrates both the use of codeswitching and lexical items familiar to Puerto Rican Spanish speakers[22]:

1 A: Yeah. May I speak Bebo please? (.) Bebo. Abel.
       /Baybo/
2   From   Direct TV. (12.0) *Mr. Martínez, cuénteme,*
            ('tell me')
3   *que pasó.=le le hicieron la instalación. (4.0) Está*
   ('what happened did they do the installation. You're')
4   *poniendo ahora? (4.0)(Es-)ta todo bien* (right?) *De*
   ('putting it now? Everything's good)

---

[22] The expressions used in this excerpt are found in other Spanish Caribbean dialects.

5   *nada, papá.* You got somebody else to- *yo le*
         ('You're welcome, man.')   ('I')
6   *puedo ayúdar hacer la instalación,* let me know.
         ('can help do the installation,')
7   (4.0) Yeah. *Exactamente.* Alright. (.) Alright,
                              ('Exactly.')
8   *papá. Chévere.* Ok, bye.
         ('man. Cool.')

Abel called a household where English is spoken. He pronounces
Mr. Martínez's first name, Bebo, using English pronunciation but
changes to a more hispanicized pronunciation when the listener on the
other line did not understand who he referred to initially. Once Mr.
Martínez is on the phone, he addresses him with the formal English title
"Mr." using Spanish pronunciation (line 2). Abel uses Spanish to
confirm that the installation was made and that Mr. Martínez was
satisfied with the service. But he briefly switches to English to ask for
a referral (line 5). Abel uses Spanish as the "we-code", particularly
given his use of the informal, familiar, "*papá*" (lines 5 and 8) and
"*chévere*". Both of these play up the familiarity with which Abel
addresses Mr. Martinez because they are commonly used by Puerto
Ricans. However, it is not easy to classify his use of English as a
"they-code" (Sebba and Wotton 1998), or an attempt to formalize the
request. In line 6 he switches to English to close the request with "let
me know," an English closing frequently used in informal contexts.
Other examples of informal English usage included "Yeah" (7),
"Alright" (7) and "Ok" (8). Recognizing that Mr. Martínez is a
bilingual, Abel uses both languages. He does this despite his
preference for Spanish (see for example his switch back to Spanish in
line 5). The two languages in combination achieve a greater level of
familiarity than either would alone. Given his request for referrals, a
positive evaluation by Mr. Martínez is exactly what he needs.

A Special Case of Accommodation
The next case is not a straightforward act of accommodation in the
service of making an ethnic alignment. Rather, the behavior of Abel's
interlocutor (U) is of special interest. Their exchange took place while
Abel waited for Marco to meet up with him. Abel talks casually with a
Uruguayan acquaintance (U). U's attempts to have Abel acknowledge

his ethnicity results in a brief accommodation on Abel's part. It is not clear what benefit Abel gains from an accommodation and there are no evident power differences between the two, so the instrumental benefits are minimal. Actually, Abel seems slightly disinterested in the conversation and it is U that initiates and encourages the conversation to move further.

```
1   U:  No tengo gana ni de hablar.
        ('I don't even have the desire to talk')
2   A:  ((Laughs)). Porque no?
        ('Why not?')
3       (1.0)
4   U:  (No tengo gana, no.)
        ('I don't have the desire, no')
5   A:  Ah:::::.
6       (1.8)
7   U:  Hoy estoy si tomando café.
        ('Today I'm really drinking coffee')
8       (0.8)
9   A:  °Ah:: yeah. °
10      (2.4)
11  U:  (Es-)ta malo? o (es-)ta bueno este (sitio).
        ('Is it bad or is it good here, this place')
12  A:  E:- si se da m:. (0.5) Nosotros vamo(-s) a otro la(-d)o a
        ('Yes, it's ok. We go to another place to')
13      trabajar. Nosotros vamos a Bro::nx, a Brooklyn por
        ('work. We go to the Bronx, to Brooklyn over')
14      alla a trabajar. (1.3) Porque por aqui mucho- (2.3)
        ('there to work. Because around here there's a lot')
15      mucha compe- mucha- mu- mucha competencia.
        ('a lot of comp- a lot- a- a lot of competition')
16      Mucho-
        ('A lot-')
17      (11.7)
18  U:  Es que Uruguay es mi pais pero es muy lejo.
        ('It's that my country is Uruguay, but its very far')
19  A:  Si verdad.
        ('Yes, true')
```

20 U: *Yo vivia alla y conozco mucha gente.*
         ('I lived over there and I know a lot of people')
21 A: >*Vo(-s) so(-s) uruguayo.*<=
         ('You are Uruguayan?')
22 U: =(°   *lo invito*°)
                                 ('I invite')
23 A: (°lombi°)
24   (1.8)
25 A: *Vo(-s) so(-s) uruguayo*:?
         ('You are Uruguayan?')
26 U: ((Silent response))
27 A: *Vos sos urugua/sh/o*::?   ((with a surprised tone))
         ('You are Uruguayan?')

Despite the fact that U starts out by saying that he is not in a talking mood (line 1), he makes repeated attempts to engage Abel in a conversation. In line 1 he makes a subtle turn-yielding cue, which Abel responds to appropriately with an interrogative (line 2). Abel's question encourages U to elaborate, but he seems, at first blush, reluctant to speak, yielding once again to Abel. With a backchannel cue in line 5, Abel signals his wish to take no further turns. Contrary to his previous comments, in line 7, U demonstrates his interest in continuing the conversation. However, he once again provides a turn-yielding cue so open-ended in its options that Abel opts for a minimal response. Recognizing that previous attempts to engage Abel in a conversation were not effective, U changes his technique and asks a direct, turn-yielding question about the selling location he chose that day. While this successfully encourages a more detailed response from Abel, a lapse in their conversation occurs (line 17) when neither speaker opts to continue (in Abel's case) or take over the conversation (in U's case). Yet, U's turn in line 8 makes it clear that he is indeed interested in continuing a conversation. Perhaps because of timidity, he is insecure or unsure about how to best proceed and chooses a comment that seems obvious. But it is revealing that U chooses to raise the topic of his origins, particularly after the long pause that first transpires. It suggests that doing this was especially important to him and that he deemed the information he reveals about his background relevant to his interaction with Abel. In community where relatively few Uruguayans have settled, Uruguayan is a distinctive identification and U might have seen it as a positive status to feature. U's statement in line 18 is an invocation of his ethnic identification. Abel does not at first recognize it as such; perhaps during the conversation lapse in line 17 his mind had wandered to other thoughts and did not fully hear or register U's invocation. In line 19 he gives an automatic response. But U seems to communicate his wish to elaborate on this topic. His interest piqued, Abel shows his willingness to play U at his subtle negotiation in line 21. What is interesting is that he chooses to confirm U's ethnic invocation by switching to a hybrid between Rioplatense Spanish and his Ecuadorian Spanish. In his first "*vo(-s) so(-s) Uruguayo* ('you are Uruguayan')", he employs Rioplatense morphology but retains Ecuadorian phonology (word final /s/ deletion in both "*vos*" and "*sos*") and intonation. U passes over the question, latching with an inaudible comment (line 22) and Abel quietly echoes the comment (line 23). But Abel really is interested in confirming U's original statement about his Uruguayan identification. Once again he asks U if he's Uruguayan, this time employing Rioplatense intonation, and retaining Rioplatense morphology and Ecuadorian phonology. Finally, U confirms his original statement in line 18 with a silent response. To this, Abel reacts enthusiastically with a reply that reads like, "Are you really?!" In line 27 his "*vos sos Uruguayo*" takes on all characteristics of Rioplatense Spanish, including the distinctive intonation and lengthening of vowels associated with the dialect[23]. Adding authenticity to his pronunciation is the use of the fricative /ʃ/ (/sh/) instead of /y/ in "*uruguayo*".

In his understated transition from Ecuadorian to Rioplatense dialect, Abel demonstrates his sensitivity to inter-dialectal subtleties. Such subtleties are often learned through direct contact with a dialect, as was Abel's case given his relationships with Uruguayan housemates. In this way he communicates his basic familiarity with Uruguayan ethno-linguistic norms and validates U's attempt to make U's ethnic background relevant to their conversation. What is puzzling is U's passive response (or lack or response) to Abel's invitation to connect at this level. After Abel's statement in line 27 there is a considerable gap before U initiates the conversation again with an entirely different topic (see below). Perhaps U was sufficiently satisfied that Abel made a

---

[23] This intonational pattern originated and is most pronounced in Buenos Aires. Due to the prestige given *porteño* Spanish, the melodic qualities of this speech have spread beyond the city into other parts of Argentina and Uruguay (Lipski, 2004).

recognition of his identification as Uruguayan.   Like many such invocations, the goal may have been positive distinctiveness.   The intentions behind Abel's use of Rioplatense are also not clear. Was he accommodating to U's dialect, or invoking a distant connection to Uruguay, or both, or none?   Clues from the structure of their conversation suggest that Abel was attempting to create a positive space for their interaction to continue based on a commonality. This is an encouragement that U seemed to require in other parts of the conversation.   But like in other parts of their conversation, U's hesitation to elaborate ended *that* exchange.

U and Abel did not speak much for the remaining time that Abel waited for Marco to meet with him.   When Marco and other fellow Ecuadorian salesmen approach the spot where U and Abel wait, U initiates the following exchange:

1   U: *Ahí (tiene) uno, o dos mas.*
          ('There you have one, or two more')
2   A: *No lo(-s) viste.*
          ('You see them')
3   U: *(Se juntan   )=*
          ('They get together')
4   A: *Se juntan los ñaños ahí.*
          ('They get together, those Ecuadorians')
5   A: *Se juntan-=* ((directs comment to approaching co-workers))
          ('They get together')
6   M: =(   )= ((talking from a distance))
7   A: =*Se juntan los ñaños se jode todo.*
          ('When Ecuadorians get together, everything goes to hell')

In line 3, U jokingly refers to the ethnic-based cliquishness of the approaching salesmen. In the excerpt before this U demonstrated that ethnic-based distinctions were salient for U; hence his attempt at having Abel recognize his ethnic identification.   The current excerpt provides further evidence of this.   A model of inter-ethnic distinctiveness guides U. Recall that one of the characteristics of cultural models and other schemas is that they fill in what is left unsaid during interactions. Line 1 above, (*"Ahí (tiene) uno, o dos mas"*, 'there you have one of two more') is not a mere observation. It's a discursive trace of how he has interpreted the situation. While an ethnic cooperation schema assumes similarity-based cooperation, the type I refer to here orients a person towards points of difference. As such, U frames himself an outsider in the scene.

Abel adopts U's frame and refers to the group as "*ñaños*". This term is commonly used among Ecuadorians to mean "friend" or "brother". As Marco moves closer, Abel attempts to repeat this comment aloud so that the group will hear. Finally in line 7, Abel fleshes out his original comment by jokingly suggesting that when Ecuadorians get together "everything goes to hell." Abel's use of irony, humor, and familiar register is a sleek way to metaphorically distance himself from the (his) group in the presence of a non-Ecuadorian, even as he identifies with them by using the brotherly term *ñaños* to refer to them. Yet what he is really doing is identifying with them, as marked by his use of *ñaños*. In the preceding sections I illustrated how Abel disassociated from Ecuadorian identification. Next, I will provide two examples of when and how Abel typically affiliated with "his group."

Somos de Ecuador (We are from Ecuador)

Abel is ambivalent towards his Ecuadorian heritage. At times he expressed strong sentiments of ethnic pride, as in the comment about Ecuadorian music described in the beginning of the analysis section. Because of the void he perceived between *serranos* and *costeños* he was especially apt to identify as *guayaquileño*. In cases where he interacted with other *guayaquileños*, he positively invoked this identification to lessen the distance between himself and his listener. In the following excerpt, for example, he subtly refers to A as an in-group member in line 13, appealing to their common preferences and understandings as *guayaquileños*:

1   A: *Toni*! (0.8) *Di::melo bro/d/er.* (0.5) *Que hay*?
              ('Tell me, bro. What's up?')
2   (0.5)
3   ((Abel and Toni greet each other with a hug))
4   T: *Todo bien.*
              ('Everything's good')
5   A: *Cuenta me. Que hay*?
              ('Tell me. What's up?')

6   T: *A: ya, aquí. (.) Todo el dia:- (.) caliente, tu*
         ('Here. Every day- hot, you')
7   *ve=dejame sentarme=*
         ('know. Let me sit')
8   A: *=Si, no si- E:- este el clima de Guayaquil.*
         ('Yes, yes- this is the climate of Guayaquil')
9   T: *(Tú te va ir a Guayaquil.)*
         ('You're going to Guayaquil')
10 A: *Este el [clima de Guayaquil.*
         ('This is the climate of Guayaquil')
11 T: *[A: sí.*
                  ('Oh, yes')
12   (1.6)
13 A: *(Es-)te el clima que- que no/h/ gusta.*
         ('This is the climate we like')
14 T: *A: sí.*
         ('Oh, yes')

In other instances, the broader Ecuadorian identification was most appropriate for achieving his goal, particularly in sales encounters, of pleasing his interlocutors and forging potentially remunerative connections. This trumped Abel's general tendency to avoid identifying as Ecuadorian, and neutralized the sense of shame he sometimes felt about his ethnic background. In the next excerpt, recorded during one of his sales trips to the Bronx, he encounters an Ecuadorian woman. Unlike Abel, the woman (E) displays a reluctance to identify along regional lines, appealing to a pan-Ecuadorian ideal. Abel, on the other hand, reveals his ambivalent attitudes about Ecuador and her people.

1   E: *Cuánto valen esta/h/ bandera/h/?*
         ('How much are these flags')
2   A: *Son grati(-s)=señora*
         ('They're free, ma'am')
3   E: *O, sí?*
         ('Oh, yes?')
4   A: *Si. (Es-)tamo(-s) dando todo grati(-s).*
         (Yes. We're giving everything away for free')

5   E: *O, sí?*
         ('Oh, yes?')
6   A: <u>*Claro, pue(-s)*</u>!
         ('Of course!')
7   E: *A:::::!*
8   A: ((to someone on phone)) *Diga, paso? No le piden.*
         ('Tell me did it go through? They don't ask for it')
9   *Ya, haga el appointment con el para mañana. Tú le*
         ('Yes, make the appointment with him for tomorrow. You')
10   *puede llamar al señor? Ok, yo lo llamo ahorita, ok?*
         ('can call the man? Ok, I'll call him in a bit, ok?')
11   Ok, bye.
12 E: *O:, son gratis pero si es que cogen esto.*
         ('They're free, but this you take')
13 A: ((now talking to W)) DirecTV.
14 E: *O:,* DirecTV.
15 A: *Para que vea Ecuavisa de Ecuado/l/.*
         ('So that you can watch Ecuador's Ecuavisa')
16 E: *O:::::::.*
17 A: *Para- por que vea como votamo(-s) lo(-s)*
         ('So you can watch how we vote for the')
18   *presidente(-s).*
         ('presidents')
19 E: *A, si. Yo ya se.* ((laughs as she walks away))
         ('Oh, yes. I know.')

When E approaches Abel's display he is on the phone on hold. E is curious about the flags of several Latin American countries that Abel has on display. She specifically inspects the Ecuadorian flag, and Abel assumes that she is Ecuadorian. In line 6 he uses the exclamatory construction "*claro, pues*" a colloquial form of "*pues, claro*" ('well, of course'). As a colloquialism, it may be specific to Ecuador but similar constructions (e.g. "*orale, pues*", "*bueno, pues*", "*andale, pues*"), exist in other Latin American countries. While E stands by, the person on the other line returns to the call with Abel. Abel does not want to miss the opportunity to talk further with E, who continues to stand by, and he quickly attends to the call (lines 8 – 10). His repeated use of "Ok" in lines 10 and 11, expedite the conversation. Back with E, the older woman asks about the DirectTV display and he takes the opportunity to

mention a channel he thinks will interest her: Ecuavisa (line 15).
Throughout this interaction no direct mention has been made about
either of their ethnic identifications. Their shared identification
remains an undercurrent of the conversation. Abel attempts to make
this connection more explicit in line 15, using *"votamos* ('we vote')" in
a context similarly to *"nos gusta ('we like')"* in his conversation above
about the weather with a fellow Ecuadorian. The first person plural
form functions to identify both himself and E as Ecuadorian.
Nevertheless, at this point E begins to walk away, apparently not
interested in DirectTV, and delivers line 19 from some distance.

Less than five minutes later, E returns to the spot where Abel sells
subscriptions. She cannot find a store she believed was on that block
and approaches Abel once more to see if he knows where it might be
located. After approximately a one-minute exchange about the location
of the store and other buildings on that block, E initiates a topic change:

1 E: *Ustedes por si acaso, son paisanos mio/h/, verdad?*
       ('You by chance, are countrymen of mine, right?')
2 A: *De: Guayaquil.*
       ('From Guayaquil')
3 E: *(A pue(-s).) Viva Guayaquil!*
       ('Oh, well. Long live Guayaquil!')
4 A: *Eso e/h/.*
       ('That's it')
5 E: *Yo soy de Duran.* [Pero ahora (estoy aqui.)]
       ('I'm from Duran. But now I'm here')
6 A: [*De Duran? Sí*](*a (es-)[ta bien.*])
                          ('From Duran? Yes, alright')
7 E: [*Si,*]*si aja.*
                                              ('Yes')
8 A: [°*Claro*
                                              ('Of course')
9   *que si.* °]
                                              ('Yes')
10 E: *Somo/h/ de Ecuador.*
       ('We're from Ecuador')
11 A: *Si. (Es-)tamo(-s)-*
       ('Yes. We are-')

12 E: *A ya ya ya.*
        ('right, right, right')
13 A: *Eso lo que le explicaba a ella sobre el regionalismo*
        ('That's what I was explaining to her about the regionalism')
14   *que hay en nue/h/tro país.*
        ('that exists in our country')
15 E: *Aja.*
16 A: *Hay mucho regiona[lismo.*
        ('There's a lot of regionalism')
17 E: [*Ay! no, mire yo hace do/s/*
                            ('Oh, no, look, about two')
18   *año(-s) fui a la sie/rr/a. Mis padres son de la sie/rr/a,*
        ('years ago I went to the mountains. My parents are from the
        mountains,')
19   *mi madre de la costa. Pero amo tanto a lo/s/*
        ('my mother is from the coast. But I love so much')
20   *indiecitos de alla como lo/s/ campesino(-s) de aqui,*
        ('the Indians (dimunitive) from over there, like the rural
        people from here')
21   *porque de <u>ahi? soy yo</u>?*
        ('because that's where I'm from')
22   (1.0)
23   *Y mire, como me regocije, para mi fue una terapia*
        ('And look, how I rejoiced, for me it was a beautiful')
24   *hermosa de ver a esto/s/ indiecitos en la/h/*
        ('therapy to see those Indians (dimunitive) in the')
25   *montañas? <u>Pero que bello,</u> dije **Dios mio, que lindo***
        ('mountains. But how beautiful, I said my God, what')
26   ***paisaje veo. Mira a esos indiecito(-s). De ahi soy***
        ('a beautiful scenery I see.   Look at those Indians
        (dimunitive). That's where I am')
27   ***yo?! Porque mi padre era serrano. Por eso somo/s/***
        ('from. Because my father was from the mountains. That's
        why we are')
28   *mestizo(-s)?*
29 A: *Claro, somo(-s) mestizo(-s).*
        ('Of course, we're mestizo')
30 E: *Por eso somo(-s) mestizo(-s). No somo(-s) blanco,*
        ('That's why we're mestizo. We are not white')

31   *ni negro, ni (   ), ni amarillo, ni chino. Somo/s/*
        ('nor black, nor ( ), nor yellow, nor Chinese. We're
32   *mestizo(-s).*
33   ((laughs)).
34   *Y a <u>toda honra.</u>*
        ('And with all honor')
35 A: *Si, verdad?*
        ('Yes, right?')
36 E: *Mi hijo. Tengo un hijo que me dice- que vino*
        ('My son. I have a son that tells me- that came')
37   *chiquito de Ecuador de tre(-s) año(-s). Le digo, <u>**tu**</u>*
        ('small from Ecuador at the age of three. I say to him, you')
38   ***tiene/h/ que comer mucho mote, mucho deso,***
        ('have to eat your corn, lots of that')
39   ***porque lo/s/ indio/h/ allá ni cana/h/ tenian. Y-***
        ('because the Indians over there don't even have grey hair.
        And')
40   [(*le dije*   )]
        ('I told him')
41 A: [>*De=verda(-d)*?<
        ('Really?')
42 E: *Y- Si es verdad. Y enton(-ce) me dice, **Si yo naci***
        ('And- Yes it's true. And so he tells me, But I was born')
43   ***en Manhattan. [Yo le dije, Quien te pario!***
        ('in Manhattan. I said to him, and who gave birth to you?!')
44 A: [(((laughs))
45 E: ***Yo naci en Manhattan. Le digo y quien te pario.***
        ('I was born in Manhattan. I tell him and who gave birth to
        you?')
46   ((W laughs))
47 A: [*Y ahora que tiene ya- que edad tiene él ahora?*
        ('And now what does he have- what is his age now?')
48 E: *No, ya tiene cuarenta- es por molestarme.*
        ('No, he's already forty- it's to tease me')

Early in this exchange we can see the contrast between their two
approaches. In line 1, E asks if Abel and I (sitting close by) are her
"*paisanos*". This inquiry into ethnic background does not specify
region (e.g. "Where in Ecuador are you from"); in fact it does not even

specify Ecuador as the country in question. Instead, mutual recognition of ethnic background is implied, and only verbal confirmation of this in the most general sense is required to complete the request (e.g. "Yes" or "Yes, I'm from Ecuador")[24]. As is customary for him, Abel replies immediately with "De Guayaquil ('from Guayaquil')". E for her part enthusiastically acknowledges his city of origin (line 3). As her next turns suggest, this enthusiasm fits her general approach: inclusiveness rather than exclusiveness. In line 5 she states her own city Duran, (also a coastal city, neighboring Guayaquil), but adds *"pero estoy aquí ahora"* ('but I'm here now'). In conjunction with her statement in line 10 (*"Somos de Ecuador"* ('we're from Ecuador'), this demonstrates her wish to focus on what they had in common: a) "we're are both here now" and b) "we're both from Ecuador". It's revealing that Abel raises the topic of regionalism, which, as he suggests in lines 13 and 14, he had raised as an issue in our own conversations. This statement at this moment illustrates just how salient this dichotomy is for him. Diverging from Abel's view, E overlaps with him in line 17 and delivers a touching description of her own encounter with her indigenous heritage. Her proud narratives in lines 17-28 and lines 30-32 lead Abel to make statements of agreement. However, the content and delivery of his statement does not match the enthusiasm expressed by E. Finally, the rest of the conversation confirms E's romanticized views of *indios*. Abel's question in line 41, on the other hand, reveals a gap in his knowledge about the *indio* lifestyle E describes. In this exchange between Abel and E, Abel is confronted with that part of his background that causes him shame. Here, however, E encourages him to make a positive evaluation of indigenous heritage.

Final Thoughts and Conclusion

Abel's case highlights key points about ethnic identification. While Abel expressed some symbolic attachment (e.g. music, Ecuador's weather) to his Ecuadorian heritage, these were most salient in his interactions with other Ecuadorians. Although his identification as

---

[24] Consistent with his preference for not interrupting conversational flow and "keeping people happy" he also gives a response that does not exclude *me* from her inquiry. Rather than clarify that *he* was from Guayaquil and *I* was from Puerto Rico, he provided a response that allowed her to believe I was also from Ecuador.

Ecuadorian likely helped him land the job as a DirectTV salesman, most prominent was a tendency to disassociate from the Ecuadorian category. But to say that he disassociated from the Ecuadorian category should not be taken to mean that he rejected his heritage or possessed some dysfunctional psychological complex. He was firm in his insistence to control how others treated him as best he could. But he also portrayed earnest moments of ethnic pride. Abel's example affirms that ethnic identification (instrumental) often works independent of ethnic self-understanding (non-instrumental).

Social Identity Theory asserts that group membership leads to self-categorization in ways that favor the in-group at the expense of the out-group. Turner & Tajfel (1986) showed that just categorizing themselves as group members led people to display in-group favoritism. Thus, individuals seek to achieve positive self-esteem by positively differentiating their in-group from others. However, as Abel's case makes clear, this is not always the case. Often, Abel sought positive differentiation *from* his putative in-group. Basing his actions and interpretations on the negative stereotypes about *serranos* or *indios*, he preferred a regional category (*guayaquileño*). In some cases, he identified with the Colombian category. And he did so in a way that did not over-commit him to Colombian identification: by keeping silent or my invoking cognitive representations that did some of the talking for him.

Abel differed from Roberto in that he did not have ambiguous physical features that might have allowed him greater control over his ethnic self-presentation. Abel valued this sort of control, at the very least, because the potential to smooth sales transactions. He quite explicitly admitted the instrumental interests he had in ethnic identification. To compensate for this he frequently accommodated or *adequated* (Bucholtz & Hall, 2005), to non-Ecuadorians. Abel used whatever linguistic resources were available to him. But again, unlike Roberto, he lacked the proficiency in English that might have afforded him more flexibility. Furthermore, his phenotypic features further eliminated certain ethnic options (see Waters, 1990). Because of the negative stereotypes shared in Ecuador (and throughout Latin American) about *indios*, his options to use this identification as an instrumental tool are considerably limited.

His conversation with E in the last excerpt suggests that *indio* identification is an ambivalent area for him. It is not that Abel and E do not share the *serrano* / *costeño* cultural model so frequently expressed by Abel and other Ecuadorians I encountered. E's romanticized descriptions of the "*indiecitos en las montañas* ('Indians (diminutive) in the mountains') and her characterization of them as "closer to nature" are consistent with the model. This is suggestive of the point made by Quinn and Holland (1987: 12): "Socialization experiences may differ sharply in the degree to which they endow a given cultural model with directive force for an individual." While I cannot assume much about E's background, known points about Abel's life history are clear. Attributing, certain obstacles and mistreatment to his *indio* heritage, Abel tends to view *indio* in a negative light. Slotted into the model, this information guides Abel's interpretations and behavior differently from E.

CHAPTER 6

Challenging Ethnic Categories

INTRODUCTION

Drawing on the experiences of NYC Latinos, in this research I examined an important phenomenon: people switching their ethnic identification across multiple spheres of interaction. The study of ethnic flexibility is not merely an intellectual or methodological exercise. I believe that the growing diversity of our cities foretells a future where multi-ethnicity will be the order of the day. This will particularly be the case for ethnically diverse urban environments like NYC. This research documents what is becoming a prevailing trend in America: using multiple ethnic identifications. The 2000 U.S. Census suggests that multiple race and ethnicity reporting is common among the youngest members of the American population (Morning, 2003). Increases in reporting multiple race/ ethnic categories reflect a general trend over the past 30 years towards ethnic and racial diversity in the U.S, and foretells even more diversity in ethnic identification in the 2010 Census. My research substantiates and illustrates those statistics, showing how in people's daily interactions, as in socio-demographic questionnaires, multiple categories are necessary and used to navigate a complex and diverse ethnic landscape. Some individuals have quite broad ethnic identification repertoires, demonstrating that there is a certain empowerment that comes from knowledge about our ethnic flexibility. However, we must also be conscious that ethnic options are still constrained for many: marginalized racial groups, undocumented immigrants, and monolinguals.

Findings

Among New York Latinos, multiple ethnic identifications are common and for the most part, uncontroversial. All of the participants I interviewed or observed, including Roberto and Abel, reported using more than one label to identify themselves to others. Most common is the use of "Latino" along with a specific national label. These two ethnic options comprise the standard toolkit for ethnic identification among New York Latinos. Both the national and pan-ethnic labels are expressed situationally, but Latino identification functions as a base or a canvas onto which further detail is added as need be. For example, in Roberto's interaction with James, shared Latino ethnicity was assumed early on. Uncertain about each other's ethnic sub-group, both adopted a strategy that opened up interactional possibilities. Roberto kept identification options open by switching between multiple frames of reference, and using Spanish as an anchor to the more general Latino identification. James, who codeswitched very little, opted for the more inclusive Latino identification throughout, making no references to a specific ethnic or national group. Abel, for his part, identified strongly with other Latinos, having roomed and worked with men from several Latin American countries. Furthermore, his wife, Monica, is Mexican. Abel adopted elements of other Spanish dialects, namely Colombian and Rioplatense Spanish, and to some extent, Caribbean Spanish. He used these dialects with Colombians, Uruguayans, Argentineans, and Puerto Ricans, as a way to lessen any communicative or cultural distance. In general, both Roberto and Abel employed Latino identification when encountering other Latinos whose national origins were unknown. Compared to the nationality-based ethnic categories, inclusion in the Latino label is somewhat lax, and characteristically inclusive. Often, ascription of Latino identification by person A onto person B is based on surface assessments of person B's appearance or stereotyped interpretations of behavior. An individual's selection of Latino identification for himself is encouraged by frequent interaction with Latinos from throughout Latin America, as was the case with Abel and other participants in this study.

In contexts where Latino identification is in some way obvious or implicit, and specificity is required, national labels like "Venezuelan" and "Ecuadorian" are used. The use of these labels represents a commitment to one or multiple categories. Therefore, those wishing to preserve ethnic flexibility will tend to avoid using a specific label.

Roberto's case illustrates this. Banking on the ambiguity of his physical appearance, he rarely uses Venezuelan identification with non-Venezuelans unless asked directly. Venezuelan identification and cognate behaviors are employed in his interactions with other Venezuelans[25]. Similarly, Abel used *"ecuatoriano"* with other Ecuadorians, or when interacting with others on a long-term basis. In fleeting encounters, he admitted to using whichever identification was most advantageous, especially *"colombiano."*

Further ethnic specificity, as with Abel's *"guayaquileño,"* serves at least two purposes. One is to package information about socio-economic background, cultural preferences, disposition, and/or status, for presentation to compatriots. This information could serve to positively differentiate oneself from others or as a basis for further interactions and mutual support. Another function of a specific ethnic or regional label is to disassociate from a more inclusive, negatively evaluated category. It is the "yes, but" move in ethnic self-presentation: "Yes, I'm Ecuadorian, but from Guayaquil." This was clearly evinced by Abel. Wishing to distance himself from negative associations made of Ecuadorians and *indios*, he used *guayaquileño* as a way to draw attention from negative generalizations, taking more control over how others viewed and categorized him.

In Chapter 2, I included an excerpt from field notes I took during my research in Astoria, Queens. The notes described an urban environment in which ethnicity was both ubiquitous (as with the numerous stores selling targeted ethnic goods) but also, on the surface, a non-issue. Similarly, for the participants in this study, in some contexts ethnicity guided interactions and in others it was irrelevant. Contexts in which ethnicity was made relevant by participants and their interlocutors included sales encounters, social gatherings dominated by one or another ethnic group, and in scenarios where a person wished to make themselves ethnically distinct. In some cases, ethnicity was mostly unimportant to an interaction but was introduced early on as a way to understand how to proceed with an exchange or to help a conversation proceed smoothly. From my observations in New York City I gather that ethnicity has saturated so many dimensions of daily

---

[25] In at least one case not analyzed here, Roberto used a more Venezuelan presentation (dialectally) when talking to a South American (non-Venezuelan) man. This led to the only instance I recorded in which someone correctly identified him as Venezuelan.

life that it is a taken for granted backdrop. Based on evidence from Roberto and Abel's cases, and other participants, my research suggests that ethnicity is most relevant when crucial resources and opportunities are at stake. Only after I completed the analysis for both participants did I fully realize the parallels in Roberto and Abel's experiences. The life histories of both men revealed significant periods of economic hardship, childhood traumas, legal troubles, and emotional instabilities. Basing my selection *only* on the frequency of switching, I did not intend for such experiences to be the only view into Latino realities. Yet, these honest stories may reveal something unique about EI switching. Perhaps the periods of hardship and scarcity experienced by these men encouraged their ethnic and linguistic flexibility as a survival tool. These experiences underscore the difference between ethnic flexibility and situational ethnicity as analytical foci. Whereas past literature on situational ethnicity has highlighted the importance of the social situation for understanding how ethnicity is mobilized, my own approach additionally considers the ways in which people develop ethnic flexibility in response to personal historical circumstances.

An important distinction in the matter of context and ethnic identification is whether the context entails a long-term or short-term encounter. Short-term encounters, ones in which actors are unlikely to come in contact again, allow more possibilities for ethnic self-presentation. Indeed, risky ventures like *passing* are most effective in contexts where exposure or challenges are improbable. Recall Abel's claim to being Colombian to a Puerto Rican potential client. Abel had never met the Puerto Rican man before and their relationship was limited to a short sales exchange. Roberto, who felt *at home* with Puerto Rican identification, could to some extent defend a claim to Puerto Rican identification; mainly, through his use of Puerto Rican dialect and knowledge about the island and Puerto Rican culture. Thus, Roberto reported letting people assume he was Puerto Rican when he traveled to Puerto Rico with his wife. To help people's interpretations along (people he encountered in passing), he highlighted Puerto Rican dialect in his speech. This points to another helpful feature of short-term encounters: people can create more ethnic possibilities for themselves by letting others' assumptions take the lead. At the intersections of context, physical appearance, and behavior, a number of assumptions can be made. Roberto, who was often mistaken for Cuban or Italian because of his appearance and aspects of his speech did not often contradict these assumptions. Instead, like Abel, he subtly went along with people's assumptions. Both Roberto and Abel have unsteady nationalistic attachments to their places of origins. Still, they use these affiliations to mobilize a number of economic and practical resources (e.g. jobs, sales, transportation).

Ethnic identification in long-term encounters or relationships tended to conform to the normative influences of relationship histories, habit, and group dynamics. Roberto was consistent in his language use and expressions of his ethnicity when with his wife. Ethnicity was not an explicit factor driving their interactions. That being said, their initial relationship was enhanced by Roberto's knowledge of Puerto Rican culture and language, and his attraction to Puerto Rican women. Abel worked daily with a group of Ecuadorian salesmen and women. Thus, he was free to use Ecuadorian dialect and often engaged in banter steeped in references to Ecuadorian politics, people, and places. In Abel's case, it was during time spent with other Ecuadorians that he expressed a positive evaluation of and connection to Ecuadorian identification.

With my focus on Roberto and Abel this research highlighted the use of ethnicity in workplace or commercial encounters with economic resources at stake. These include forging business contacts and selling and buying products/services. To this end, a broad schema of ethnic cooperation guided Roberto's and Abel's long-term and short-term interactions. This schema served to set interactive (and instrumental) goals that hinged on the presupposition that common ethnic identification is one condition of cooperation.

Following with the distinction outlined above between short- and long-term exchanges, in long-term relationships, (shared) ethnicity was a way to strengthen and maintain already existing bonds. These bonds were key components of participants' social support networks. For Abel, his relationship with Marco was decisive for his financial stability. When they were originally introduced by a mutual acquaintance, the introduction was framed as one Ecuadorian (Marco) helping another (Abel). Not only were they both from Ecuador, but they were also *guayaquileños*, a fact that was significant for both Abel and Marco. They each described their relationship as comfortable and familiar. Both felt that their chemistry was due in large part to their shared background. In Roberto's case, Venezuelan identification provided a basis from which his relationship with Omar emerged, making mutual support possible.

My research adds to the literature on ethnic networks, which has found that fruitful business arrangements emerge from ethnically homogenous interactions (Bonacich, 1973; Ooka & Wellman, 2003; Patterson, 1975; Sanders & Nee, 1987). My own contribution is nuanced in two respects. First, while true that shared ethnicity is a strong basis for business cooperation, the literature tends to focus on the advantages of *one* shared ethnicity. Both Roberto and Abel demonstrated ways in which multiple ethnic identifications (albeit within the Latino pan-ethnicity) are adapted to forge varied ethnic ties. How multi-ethnic people build economic or political networks corresponding to each of their identifications is an under-studied area. This research provides some insights about how such a differentiated mobilization of resources works. It is clear, for example, that bilingualism and bi-dialectism are crucial tools for such mobilizing. Second, the literature on economic ethnic networks has focused on the established and lasting connections that sustain ethnic enclaves. A web of weaker, but nonetheless effective, inter-ethnic ties is formed by the types of multi-ethnic negotiations Roberto and Abel made everyday. Immigrant New York, with all of its well-established ethnic enclaves, also thrives from the fleeting cross-ethnic encounters. Neighborhoods like Astoria and Jackson Heights / Corona in Queens are good examples of immigrant communities that have been transformed by the daily, small, social and economic exchanges of its diverse people.

The digital audio recordings in the ethnographic phase captured that EI switching is accomplished through a range of linguistic feats. The data presented here consistently show that linguistic flexibility opens up possibilities for ethnic self-presentation. To varying degrees, both Roberto and Abel had access to two languages and multiple dialects. As a result, codeswitching (including dialect switching), style shifting, and lexical insertions were employed as ways to varyingly align themselves to interlocutors.

Besides these linguistic acts, Roberto's and Abel's discursive work also lent support to their switching. As mentioned above, in some cases, Roberto and Abel used straightforward ethnic labels to identify themselves to others. Often, switching was achieved through references that signaled their (in-group) knowledge of Puerto Rican, Colombian or African American culture, behavior, expectations, etc. Making references to in-group knowledge was a subtle means of negotiating multiple ethnicities. It was a way to *imply* affiliation without necessarily committing to an identification.

Implications

In eighteen months of research, I worked closely with eleven Latino men and women and spoke candidly with more than two hundred other Latinos who represented a range of backgrounds and experiences. Their experiences suggest that there is no one-to-one relationship between biographical ethnicity and the use of ethnic markers. Often, flexible identification spans multiple levels of inclusiveness (e.g. Latino, Ecuadorian, *serrano*, Quechua). Intriguingly, these repertoires also cross seemingly distinct boundaries (e.g. American, Ecuadorian, Colombian). Ethnic markers, particularly language-related ones, are manipulated in a number of creative ways by members and non-members alike, pushing the limits of what constitutes ethnic group membership and challenging notions of ethnic authenticity. People tended to switch ethnic identifications by changing to or emphasizing a certain language or dialect (including accents), or simply by keeping quiet and letting others' assumptions take the lead. The reasons for switching ranged from the relatively minor (getting free drinks), to the quotidian (connecting with friends or landing better dates), to the vital (avoiding problems with immigration, making a sale, or in a job interview). When unpacked, these subtle and routine acts of flexibility reveal a number of compelling features about ethnicity. Ethnicity cannot plainly be said to be *who* a person is, but rather a way of *seeing* (Brubaker, 2004) and *doing*.

Additionally, by analyzing which ethnicities are invoked and for what purposes, as this research has done, divisions within the Latino pan-ethnic group (or even within just one national group) are revealed. For example, it was not uncommon to observe or hear about people who feigned Puerto Rican or Colombian ethnicity because these are groups with a measure of visibility and respectability in New York City's ethnic landscape. However, in my research, not one participant crossed to a Mexican identification in my presence. Some argue that the differences between various Latino subgroups are too significant for Latinos to be grouped together for analysis or policy treatment. In fact, this makes Latinos an ideal group for examining the salience and negotiation of multiple ethnic identities, including the pan-ethnic Latino identity. Ethnographic evidence from this study shows that the resonance of Latino pan-ethnicity differs from context to context and is mediated by influences of generation, immigrant status, and class. With several issues related to Latinos playing prominently in the national stage (e.g. immigration legislation and bilingualism), my research documents intimately how these themes play out in people's everyday lives.

By describing the ethnically flexible person and how they respond to dynamic and hyper-diverse urban contexts, my hope is to highlight ethnicity deployed in creative and unexpected ways. Such creativity and flexibility calls into question the validity of ethnic categories used in socio-demographic surveys like the Census. Focusing on Latinos, this research project challenges some of the assumptions that underlie the use of ethno-racial classifications in social and demographic research. Namely, the validity of ethno-racial categories in such research rests on the assumption that the habitual, biographical labels people use in questionnaires faithfully reflect personal social histories and social environments. I hope to have shown that patterns of self-identification are based on a complex interplay among interactional, cognitive, and situational factors as well as personal predispositions and skills.

Understanding what exactly is captured by Census ethno-racial categories is important given the reliance on these categories for prioritizing needs and distributing resources. I interviewed Latinos for this study, particularly of second and third generations, who perceived the "Hispanic" label to be relevant only within the context of the socio-demographic survey. Within this context, the Hispanic response is "automatic" and limited in its ability to capture meaningful, everyday realities. Even the more specific nationality-based labels are misleading, as the evidence from Abel and Roberto revealed. Abel's case illustrates how conflicting self-reported ethnic identity states can be. Having developed negative associations of his indigenous heritage, he altered his behavior to disassociate from this identity during interactions. To be sure, there are strong emotional and psychosocial attachments to identifying with a group. Yet in everyday lived experience, people such as Abel behave according to what is most advantageous for them. The sum of these actions translates to predictable patterns of behavior that may not correlate with emotional or symbolic attachments.

Alternatives based on social interaction measures (such as

languages and dialects spoken and / or social network attributes) are promising. Ethnically diverse social networks help cultivate the sort of ethnic flexibility Abel and Roberto displayed. Through our participation in social networks we learn the models of thought and behavior that enables us to be recognized as part of a group. The ascription or acceptance of others as belonging to a group plays a mutually reinforcing role with ethnic self-presentation. Accordingly social networks may serve as proxies for ethnic identification because they often reflect the major ethnic influences on people's daily life and interactions. A person's social network that is heavily represented by one ethnicity will exert unique pressures on that person to identify (through crossing, accommodation or featuring) according to the dominant ethnicity in the social network. Furthermore, people with ethnically heterogeneous social networks have more opportunity (and need) to learn and use multiple ethnic identifications. As normative influences on behavior, networks may be more reliable predictors of social, economic, and health outcomes than the context-bound labels used in socio-demographic questionnaires. The in-depth study of ethnic flexibility may shed some light on how (and why) people decide what to enter in socio-demographic questionnaires and what such choices indicate about ethnicity in the 21st Century.

Life History Interview

I. Childhood:

1. Where were you born?
2. Where were your parents born?
3. What did your parents do for a living when you were a child?
4. Do you have siblings?
5. How would you describe your relationship with your parents?
6. How would you describe your relationship with your siblings?
7. Did you grow up with extended family near to you? Where did your relatives live when you were growing up?
8. Describe the neighborhood where you grew up.
9. Describe the first time you had an awareness of your ethnicity or race?
10. What was your earliest experience with race?
11. What was your earliest experience with ethnicity?
12. What did your parents teach you about race or ethnicity?
13. Describe one or two family traditions you enjoyed as a child?
14. What were your favorite pastimes as a child?
15. Did you attend church as a child?
16. Describe your school?
17. Was your school racially or ethnically diverse?
18. Were your school friends from the same or different ethnic background as you?

19. What did you learn in school about people from different national, racial or ethnic backgrounds?
20. Did you ever experience any racial or ethnic discrimination as a child?
21. What were some of your most memorable moments as a child?

II. Adolescence and Early Adulthood:

1. When did you have your first job?
2. Describe your first jobs?
3. Was your workplace ethnically or racially diverse?
4. Did you spend time with your co-workers outside of work?
5. Did your work provide the opportunity to meet people from a different racial or ethnic background than you?
6. What were your early career or occupational goals?
7. Did you go to college? If yes, where did you go? What did you study?
8. Did you join any clubs or organizations in college or elsewhere?
9. Did you attend religious services as a teenager or young adult?
10. What was your favorite music when you were a teenager?
11. Who did you look up to as a teenager or young adult?
12. What was your favorite pastime?
13. What were some of your most memorable moments as a teenager or young adult?
14. When did you start dating?
15. Did you date anyone from a different racial or ethnic background as you?
16. How did your parents or family feel about this?
17. What were some experiences you had with race or ethnicity at this time in your life?
18. Did you have friends who were from a different national, racial, or ethnic background as you?
19. Were you interested in learning more about your family's background as a young adult? If so, what kinds of things did you do to learn more about your family's heritage?

20. Try to recall some of the earliest times when someone asked you where you were from or what your ethnicity was. What did you tell them?
21. Explain why you gave this response.
22. Did you experience any racial or ethnic discrimination as a young adult?

III. Present:

1. For immigrants: Describe your immigration experience. Why did you migrate? How did you (and/or your family) decide where to migrate to?
2. How were you treated when you arrived in this country?
3. What were some of your most negative immigration experiences?
4. What were some of your most positive immigration experiences?
5. Did you know English? If not, how long did it take you to learn?
6. Do you have family back home?
7. How often do you keep in contact with them?
8. How often do you return home to visit?
9. What do you currently do for a living?
10. How long have you had this job?
11. Describe your workplace.
12. Do you have co-workers who are from the same ethnic background as you? Different?
13. Are you married? Have you ever been married? Are you in a long-term relationship?
14. How / where did you meet your spouse / ex- / partner?
15. What is your partner's ethnic background?
16. How is your relationship to your partner's family?
17. How often do you spend time with your partner's family?
18. Do you have children?
19. What do you teach your children about race or ethnicity?
20. How would you describe your children's race or ethnicity?
21. Describe one or two family traditions you enjoy now?
22. Describe your neighborhood?

23. Describe the meals you serve most regularly?
24. Where / how did you learn to prepare these meals?
25. When people ask you where you are from or what your ethnicity is, what do you tell them?
26. Do you have friends who are from a different national, racial, or ethnic background than you?
27. Have you traveled?
28. Where did you go?
29. Describe your experiences meeting people abroad.
30. Do you belong to any community organizations? Describe this organization?
31. Do you attend religious services?
32. Do you attend ethnically oriented events?
33. Do you speak Spanish in your household? English?
34. Have you had any experiences with racial or ethnic discrimination?
35. Do you teach your children your native language?
36. What do you like the most about your ethnic or cultural heritage?
37. What do you like least about your ethnic or cultural heritage?
38. Are there people from certain ethnic or racial backgrounds that you have no or little contact with? Why do you think this is so?
39. Have you ever been involved in demonstrations or protests? Describe some of these experiences.

Social Network Questionnaire

I. Ego Questions (questions about respondent):

    1.   How would you describe your ethnicity?
    2.   How would you describe your race?

II. Name Generator:

Please list the name of 45 people that you know. Knowing means that you know the person by face and name, that you could contact them if you had to and that you have had some contact in the last two years. Please list the name of those you are closest to first then contine with the names of those you are less close to.

III. Alter Questions (questions about network members):

    1.   What is this person's gender?
           a.   Female
           b.   Male
    2.   What is this person's nationality?
           a.   American
           b.   Argentinean
           c.   Bolivian
           d.   Brazilian
           e.   Chilean
           f.   Colombian
           g.   Costa Rican
           h.   Cuban

i.	Dominican
j.	Ecuadorian
k.	Guatemalan
l.	Honduran
m.	Mexican
n.	Nicaraguan
o.	Panamanian
p.	Paraguayan
q.	Peruvian
r.	Puerto Rican
s.	Salvadorian
t.	Uruguayan
u.	Venezuelan
v.	Other

3. How would you describe this person's nationality?
4. What is this person's race?
    a. Black or African American
    b. Asian or Pacific Islander
    c. Native American or Alaskan Native
    d. Mixed-Race
    e. Other
5. How would you describe this person's race?
6. Please rate on a scale from one to five your closeness with this person?
    a. 5 = Extremely Close
    b. 4 = Very Close
    c. 3 = Close
    d. 2 = Minimally Close
    e. 1 = Not At All Close

IV. Alter Pair Question (relationship between network members):

1. What is the likelihood that person A and person B would talk to each other if you were not around?

APPENDIX C
Transcription Conventions

(.)	brief pause (below half a second)
(0.5)	longer pauses in seconds
<u>xxx</u>	strongly accentuated syllable or word / spoken with more emphasis than surrounding talk
.	falling or final intonation
,	continuing intonation
?	rising intonation
°xxx°	spoken more quietly than surrouning talk
=	connects utterances with no intervening delay / latching
::	lengthened sound
> <	spoken more quickly
< >	spoken more slowly
x-	talk cut off in mid- production
[	overlapping talk
(xxx)	unclear talk
( )	unintelligeable talk
(( ))	transcriber's descriptions
bien	text in itallic is in Spanish
'good'	English translation of Spanish text
xxx	register change: quoting self or other from another conversation

References

Alba, R. (1990). *Ethnic Identity: The Transformation of White America*. New Haven: Yale University Press.

Alonzo-Zaldivar, R. (1999). Big Apple takes on a Flavor of Mexico. *Los Angles Times*, February 19.

Appadurai, A. (1996). *Modernity at Large: Cultural dimensions of globalization*. Minneapolis: University of Minnesota Press.

Aronsson, K., Jonsson, L. & Linell, P. (1987). The Courtroom Hearing as a Middle Ground: Speech Accommodation by Lawyers and Defendants. *Journal of Language and Social Psychology*, 6(2): 99-115.

Ash, S. & Myhill, J. (1986). Linguistic correlates of inter-ethnic contact. In D. Sankoff (ed.) *Diversity and diachrony* (pp. 33-44). Philadelphia: John Benjamins.

Auer, P. (1984). *Bilingual Conversation*. Amsterdam: John Benjamins.

Auer, P. (1998). Introduction: Bilingual Conversation revisited. In P. Auer (ed.) *Codeswitching in Conversation: Language, interaction and identity* (pp. 1-24). London: Routledge.

Bailey, B. (2001). Dominican-American Ethnic/Racial Identities and United States Social Categories. *International Migration Review*, 35(3): 677-708.

Bailey, B. (2000a). The Language of Multiple Identities among Dominican Americans. *Journal of Linguistic Anthropology*, 10(2): 190-223.

Bailey, B. (2000b). Language and negotiation of ethnic/racial identity among Dominican Americans. *Language in Society*, 29: 555-582.

Bailey, B. (1999). Switching. *Journal of Linguistic Anthropology*, Special Issue 9 (1-2):241-243.

Banks, M. (1996). *Ethnicity: Anthropological Constructions*. London: Routledge.

Banks, S. P. (1987). Achieving 'Unmarkedness' in Organisational Discourse: A Praxis Perspective on Ethnolinguistic Identity. *Special Language-Fachsprache*, 9(1-2): 60-62.

Barth, F. (1969). Introduction. In F. Barth (ed.) *Ethnic Groups and Boundaries*. Boston: Little, Brown.

Becker, K. R. (1997). Spanish/English Bilingual Codeswitching: A Syncretic Model. *Bilingual Review*, 22(1): 3-31.

Bell, A. (1997). Language style as audience design. In N. Coupland and A. Jaworski, (eds.) *Sociolinguistics: A reader* (pp. 240-250). New York: St. Martin's Press.

Betancourt, J.R., Green, A.R. Carillo, J.E. & Ananeh-Firempong II, O. (2003). Defining cultural competence: a practical framework for addressing racial/ethnic disparities in health and health care. *Public Health Report*, 118(4): 293–302.

Blom, J. P. & Gumperz, J.J. (1972). Social meaning in linguistics structures: codeswitching in Norway. In, J. J. Gumperz & D. Hymes (eds.) *Directions in Sociolinguistics: The Ethnography of Communication* (pp. 407-434). New York: Holt, Rinehart & Winston.

Bonacich, E. (1973). Theory of Middlemen Minorities. *American Sociological Review*, 38: 583-594.

Bourgois, P. (2002). *In Search of Respect: Selling Crack in El Barrio*. Cambridge: Cambridge University Press.

Brubaker, R. (2004). *Ethnicity without groups*. Cambridge, MA: Harvard University Press.

Brubaker, R., Loveman, M., & Stamatov, P. (2004). Ethnicity as Cognition. *Theory and Society*, 33(1): 31-64.

Bucholtz, M. (1999). You da man: Narrating the racial other in the linguistic production of white masculinity. *Journal of Sociolinguistics*, 3(4): 443-460.

Bucholtz, M. & Hall, K. (2005). Identity and Interaction: A Sociocultural Linguistic Approach. *Discourse Studies*, 7(4-5): 584-614.

Business Wire. (2001). Claritas Study Ranks Racial/Ethnic Diversity in Counties Nationwide; Analysis Shows California Leads Nation In Diversity Among Counties Of 100,000-Plus Population.

http://findarticles.com/p/articles/mi_m0EIN/is_2001_July_23/ai_7
6689304. Last retrieved January 10, 2010.

Byrne, D. (1969). Attitudes and attraction. *Advances in Experimental Social Psychology*, 4: 35-89.

Campinha-Bacote, J. (2002). The Process of Cultural Competence in the Delivery of Healthcare Services: A Model of Care. *Journal of Transcultural Nursing*, 13 (3): 181-184.

CIA World Factbook. (2010). Ecuador. https://www.cia.gov/library/publications/the-world-factbook/geos/ ec.html. Last retrieved February 1, 2010.

Cohen, R. (1978). Ethnicity: Problem and Focus in Anthropology. *Annual Review of Anthropology*, 7: 379-403.

Cohen, R. (1974). Introduction: The Lesson of Ethnicity. In A. Cohen (ed.) *Urban Ethnicity* (pp. iv-xxiv). London: Tavistock Publications.

Coles, F.A. (1992). Isleno Spanish /s/ Variation and Speech Accommodation. Paper presented at the Annual Meeting of the Linguistic Society of America, 66th, Philadelphia, PA, January 9-12.

Collins, F. (2001). Transcript of "2001 Genomics Short Course Dr. Francis Collins: 'The Human Genome Project And Beyond. http://www.nhgri.nih.gov/DIR/VIP/ShortCourse01/SC_01collinsTranscript.html. Last retrieved June 15, 2009.

Córdoba, D. & Cervantes, R.C. (2010). Intergroup and Within-Group Perceived Discrimination Among U.S.-Born and Foreign-Born Latino Youth. *Hispanic Journal of Behavioral Sciences*, 32(2): 259-274.

Cornell, S. & Hartmann, D. (1998). *Ethnicity and Race: Making Identities in a Changing World.* Thousand Oaks, CA: Pine Forge Press.

Cutler, C. (1999). Yorkville Crossing: White teens, hip hop and African American English. *Journal of Sociolinguistics*, 3(4): 428-442.

Dallas, P. (2001). The Big Apple's Mexican Face. *Hispanic Magazine*, July/August.

Day, D. (1998). Being Ascribed and Resisting, Membership of an Ethnic Group. In C. Antaki & S. Widdicombe (eds.) *Identities in Talk* (pp. 151-170). London: Sage.

DeWalt, K.M. & DeWalt, B.R. (1998). Participant Observation. In H.R. Bernard (ed.) *Handbook of Methods in Cultural Anthropology* (pp. 259-299). Walnut Creek: Altamira Press.

DiMaggio, P. (1997). Culture and Cognition. *Annual Review of Sociology*, 23: 263-287.

Duany, J. (1998). Reconstructing Racial Identity: Ethnicity, Color, and Class among Dominicans in the United States and Puerto Rico. *Latin American Perspectives*, 25(3): 147-172.

Durand J. & Massey D.S. (2003). *Clandestinos: Migración México Estados Unidos en los albores del siglo XXI*. México D.F.: Editorial Miguel Angel Porrua.

Eastman, C.M. (1981). Language planning, identity planning and worldview. *International Journal of the Sociology of Language*, 32: 45-53.

Eschbach, K. & Gomez, C. (1998). Choosing Hispanic Identity: Ethnic Identity Switching among Respondents to High School and Beyond. *Social Science Quarterly*, 79: 74-90.

Evans-Pritchard, E. E. (1937). *Witchcraft, Oracles and Magic among the Azande*. London: Faber and Faber.

Fishman, J. (1977). Language and ethnicity. In H. Giles (ed.) *Language, Ethnicity and Intergroup Relations* (pp.15-57). London: Academic Press.

Fishman, J. (1999). Sociolinguistics. In J. Fishman (ed.). *Handbook of Language and Ethnic Identity* (pp. 152-163). Oxford: Oxford University Press.

Frank, R., Akresh, I.R., & Lu, B. (2010). Latino Immigrants and the U.S. Racial Order: How and Where Do They Fit In? *American Sociological Review*, 75(3): 378-401.

Gafaranga, J. (2001). Linguistic identities in talk-in-interaction: order in bilingual conversation. *Journal of Pragmatics*, 33: 1901–1925.

Geertz, C. (1973). Thick Description: Toward an Interpretive Theory of Culture. In *The Interpretation of Cultures: Selected Essays* (pp. 3-30). New York: Basic Books.

Gil-White, F.J. (2001). Are Ethnic Groups Biological "Species" to the Human Brain? *Current Anthropology*, 42: 515–553.

Giles, H. (1973). Accent mobility: A model and some data. *Anthropological Linguistics*, 15:87-105.

Giles, H., Mulac, A., Bradac, J.J. & Johnson, P. (1987). Speech Accommodation Theory: The First Decade and Beyond. In M.L.

McLaughlin (ed.) *Communication Yearbook* 10. Newbury Park, CA: Sage Publications.

Giles, H., Taylor, D. M. & Bourhis, R. (1973). Towards a theory or interpersonal accommodation through language: some Canadian data. *Language in Society*, 2: 177-192.

Giles, H. & Coupland, N. (1991). *Language: Contexts and Consequences*. Milton Keynes: Open University Press.

Giles, H. & Johnson, P. (1981). The Role of Language in Ethnic Group Relations. In J.C. Turner and H. Giles (eds.) *Intergroup Behavior* (pp. 199-243). Chicago: The University of Chicago Press.

Gluckman, M. (1958 [1940]). The Analysis of a Social Situation in Modern Zululand. *African Studies*, 14 (1940): 1-30; 147-74. Reprinted as Rhodes-Livingston Paper No.28. Manchester: Manchester University Press.

Goffman, E. (1974). *Frame Analysis: An essay on the organization of experience*. Cambridge, MA: Harvard University Press

Goodenough, W.H. (1956). Componential Analysis and the Study of Meaning. *Language*, 32(1):195-216.

Green, L.J. (2002). *African American English: A Linguistic Introduction.* Cambridge: Cambridge University Press

Gumperz, J. (2001). Interactional Sociolinguistics: A Personal Perspective. In D. Schiffrin, D. Tannen, & H. Hamilton (eds.) *The Handbook of Discourse Analysis* (pp. 215-228). Malden, MA: Blackwell.

Gumperz, J. (1982). *Discourse Strategies.* Cambridge: Cambridge University Press.

Gumperz, J. (1972). Introduction. In J.J. Gumperz & D. Hymes (eds.) *Directions in Sociolinguistics: The Ethnography of Communication.* New York: Holt, Rinehart & Winston, Inc.

Gumperz, J. (1964). Linguistic and social interaction in two communities. In J. Gumperz and D. Hymes (eds.) *The ethnography of communication. American Anthropologist* 66(6): 137 – 53.

Haaland, G. (1969). Economic determinants in ethnic processes. In F. Barth (ed.). Ethnic *Groups and Boundaries* (pp. 58-73). Boston: Little, Brown.

Hochberg, J. (1986). Functional compensation for /-s/ deletion in Puerto Rican Spanish. *Language* 62:609-621.

Homans, G.C. (1961). *Social behavior.* New York: Harcourt, Brace and World.

Horowitz, D.L. (1985). *Ethnic Groups in Conflict.* Berkeley: University of California Press.

Horowitz, D.L. (1975). Ethnic Identity. In N. Glazer & D.P. Moynihan (eds.) Ethnicity: Theory and Experience (pp. 111-140). Cambridge, MA: Harvard University Press.

Jacobson, R. (1982). The social implications of intra-sentential codeswitching. In J. Amastae & L. Elías-Olivares (eds.) *Spanish in the United States: Sociolinguistic aspects.* Cambridge: Cambridge University Press.

Jaffe, A. (2009). Introduction: The Sociolinguistics of Stance. In A. Jaffe (ed.) *Stance: Sociolinguistic perspectives* (pp. 3-28). Oxford: Oxford University Press.

Kaufert, J.M. (1977). Situational Identity and Ethnicity among Ghanaian University Students. *Journal of Modern African Studies,* 15: 126-135.

Kelly, M.E. & Nagel, J. (2002). Ethnic Reidentification: Lithuanian Americans and Native Americans. *Journal of Ethnic and Migration Studies,* 28: 275-289.

Labov, W. (2001). *Principles of Linguistic Change (Vol. II).* Oxford: Blackwell Press.

Labov, W. (1982). *The social stratification of English in New York City.* Center for Applied Linguistics, Washington, D.C.

Labov, W. (1972). *Language in the Inner City: Studies in the Black English Vernacular.* Philadelphia: University of Pennsylvania Press.

Labov, W. & Harris, W. (1986). De facto segregation of black and white vernaculars. In D. Sankoff (ed.) *Diversity and Diachrony* (pp. 1-24). Philadelphia: John Benjamins.

Labov, W., Cohen, P., Robbins, C. & Lewis, J. (1968). *A Study of the Non-Standard English of Negro and Puerto Rican Speakers in New York City.* Philadelphia: U.S. Regional Survey.

Lakoff, R. (1973). The logic of politeness; or, minding your P's and Q's. Papers from the 9th Regional Meeting of the Chicago Linguistic Society (pp. 292-305). Chicago: Chicago Linguistic Society.

LePage, R.B. & Tabouret-Keller, A. (1985). *Acts of Identity: Creole-based approaches tolanguage and ethnicity.* Cambridge: Cambridge University Press.

Levine, H.B. (1999). Reconstructing Ethnicity. *The Journal of the Royal Anthropological Institute,* 5(2): 165-180.

Levinson, S.C. (2002). Contextualizing 'contextualization cues'. In S. Eerdmans, C. Prevignano, & P. Thibault (eds.) *Language and interaction: discussions with John J. Gumperz* (pp. 31-39). Amsterdam: John Benjamins.

Lipski, J.M. (2004). *El Español de América.* 3ʳᵈ Edition. Madrid: Catedra.

Li, W. (2002). "What do you want me to say?" On the Conversation Analysis approach to bilingual interaction. *Language in Society,* 3 1: 159-180.

Lo, A. (1999). Codeswitching, speech community membership, and the construction of ethnic identity. *Journal of Sociolinguistics,* 3/4: 461-479.

Logan, J. (2001). The new Latinos: who they are, where they are. Lewis Mumford Center for Comparative Urban and Regional Research, http://mumford1.dyndns.org/cen2000/ HispanicPop/HspReport/HspReportPage1.html. Last retrieved February 1, 2011.

Lynch, E.W. (1992). Developing cross-cultural competence. In E.W. Lynch & M.J. Hanson (eds.) *Developing cross-cultural competence: A guide for working with young children and their families* (pp. 35-62). Baltimore, MD: Paul H. Brookes Publishing.

Marzán, G., Torres, A. & Luecke, A. (2008). Puerto Rican Outmigration from New York City: 1995-2001. Centro de Estudios Puertorriqueños Policy Report, 2(2): 1-24. http://www.centropr.org/documents/working_papers/Outmigration 091108.pdf. Last retrieved February 1, 2011.

McCarty, C. (2003). *Egonet: Software for the Collection of Egocentric Network Data.* Baltimore, MD: MDLogix.

Milroy, L. (1980). *Language and Social Networks.* Oxford: Basil/Blackwell.

Mitchell, J. C. (1974) Perceptions of Ethnicity and Ethnic Behavior: An Empirical Exploration. In Abner Cohen (ed.) *Urban Ethnicity* (pp. 1-36). London: Tavistock Publications.

Morgan, M. (1994). The African American speech community: Reality and sociolinguists. In M. Morgan (ed.) *Language and the social construction of identity in Creole situations* (pp. 121– 48). Los Angeles: Center for Afro-American Studies, UCLA.

Morning, A. (2003). Race by the Book: Depiction of Human Difference in U.S. High School Curricula. Working Paper #25, Center for Arts and Cultural Policy Studies. Princeton University.

Nagata, J. (1974). What is Malay? Situational Selection of Ethnic Identity in a Plural Society. *American Ethnologist*, 1: 331-350.

Nagel, J. (1994). Constructing Ethnicity: Creating and Recreating Ethnic Identity and Culture. *Social Problems*, 41: 152-170.

New York Department of City Planning. (2010). Community District Needs, Queens Fiscal Year 2011. http://www.nyc.gov/html/dcp/ pdf/pub/qnneeds_2011.pdf. Last retrieved February 1, 2011.

New York Department of City Planning. (2007). Socioeconomic Characteristics by Race/Hispanic Origin and Ancestry Group. *NYC 2007: Results of the 2007 American Community Survey*. http://www.nyc.gov/html/dcp/pdf/census/acs_socio_07_nyc.pdf. Last retrieved February 1, 2011.

Nishina, A., Bellmore, A., Witkow, M., & Nylund-Gibson, K. (2010). Longitudinal Consistency of Adolescent Ethnic Identification Across Varying School Ethnic Contexts. *Developmental Psychology*, 46(6): 1389-1401.

Ochs, E. (1992). Indexing gender. In A. Duranti & C. Goodwin (eds.) Rethinking context: Language as an interactive phenomenon (pp. 335–358). Cambridge & New York: Cambridge University Press.

Okamura, J.Y. (1981). Situational Ethnicity. *Ethnic and Racial Studies* 4: 452-465.

Ong, A. (1999). *Flexible Citizenship: The Cultural Logics of Transnationality*. Durham, N.C.: Duke University Press.

Ooka, E. & Wellman, B. (2006). Does Social Capital Pay Off More Within or Between Ethnic Groups? Analyzing Job Searches in Five Toronto Ethnic Groups. In E. Fong (ed.) *Inside the Mosaic* (pp. 199-226). Toronto: University of Toronto Press.

Otheguy R., Fernandez. M. & Garcia O. (1989). Transferring, switching, and modeling in West New York Spanish: an intergenerational study. *International Journal for Sociology of Language,* 79:41-52.

Paden, J.N. (1967). Situational Ethnicity in Urban Africa with Special Reference to the Hausa. Paper presented at African Studies Association meeting in New York, November.

Padilla, F.M. (1984). On the Nature of Latino Ethnicity. *Social Science Quarterly*, 65: 651-664.

Passel, J.S. (2005). Estimates of the Size and Characteristics of the Undocumented Population. Pew Hispanic Center Research Report, March 21. http://pewhispanic.org/reports/report.php? ReportID=44. Last retrieved February 1, 2011.

Passel, J.S. & Cohn, D. (2009). A Portrait of Unauthorized Immigrants in the United States. Pew Hispanic Center Report, April 14. http://pewhispanic.org/files/reports/107.pdf. Last retrieved February 1, 2011.

Patterson, O. (1975). Context and Choice in Ethnic Allegiance: A Theoretical Framework and Caribbean Case Study. In N. Glazer & D.P. Moynihan (eds.) *Ethnicity: Theory and Experience* (pp. 305-349). Cambridge, MA: Harvard University Press.

Paul, B. (1953). Interview Techniques and Field Relationships. In A.L. Kroeber (ed.) *Anthropology Today* (pp. 430-451). Chicago: University of Chicago Press.

Pool, J. (1979). Language planning and identity planning. *International Journal of the Sociology of Language*, 20: 5-21.

Portes, A. & Böröcz, J. (1989). Contemporary Immigration: Theoretical *International Migration Review*, 23(3): 606-630.

Portes, A. & Truelove, C. (1987). Making Sense of Diversity: Recent Research on Hispanic Minorities in the United States. *Annual Review of Sociology*, 13: 359-385.

Quinlan, E. (2008). Conspicuous Invisibility: Shadowing as a Data Collection Strategy. *Qualitative Inquiry*, 14(8): 1480-1499.

Quinn, N. & Holland, D. (1987). Culture and Cognition. In D. Holland & N. Quinn (eds.) *Cultural Models in Language and Thought* (pp. 3-42). Cambridge: Cambridge University Press.

Ramos-Zayas, A.Y. (2004). Implicit Social Knowledge, Cultural Capital, and Authenticity" among Puerto Ricans in Chicago. *Latin American Perspectives*, 31(5): 34-56.

Rampton, B. (2000). Crossing. *Journal of Linguistic Anthropology*, 9(1-2): 54-56.

Rampton, B. (1995). *Crossing: Language and Ethnicity among Adolescents*. London: Longman.

Ricourt, M. and Danta, R. (2003). *Hispanas de Queens: Latino Panethnicity in a New York City Neighborhood*. Ithaca: Cornell University Press.

Rivara, F.P. & Finberg, L. (2001). Use of the Terms Race and Ethnicity. *Archives of Pediatrics and Adolescent Medicine*, 155:

119.
Roberts, S. (2006). A 300th American. Don't Ask Who. *The New York Times*, October 18.

Rosario, R.D. (1983). Ser Puertorriqueño. *Claridad Suplemento en Rojo* (5-11): 16-17.

Rumbaut, R. (2009). Pigments of Our Imagination: On the Racialization and Racial Identities of "Hispanics" and "Latinos". In J.A. Cobas, J. Duany. & J.R. Feagin (eds.) *How the U.S. Racializes Latinos: White Hegemony and Its Consequences* (pp. 15-36). Boulder, CO: Paradigm Publishers.

Rumbaut, R. (2006). The Making of a People. In M. Tienda & F. Mitchell (eds.) Hispanics and the Future of America. Washington, D.C.: National Academies Press.

Rumbaut, R. (2005) Sites of Belonging: Acculturation, Discrimination, and Ethnic Identity Among Children of Immigrants. In T.S. Weiner (ed.) *Discovering Successful Pathways in Children's Development: Mixed methods in the Study of Childhood and Family Life* (pp. 111-164). Chicago: University of Chicago Press.

Sacks, H., Schegloff, E. & Jefferson, G. (1974). A simplest systematics for the organization of turn-taking for conversation. *Language,* 50: 696-735.

Sanders, J. M. & Nee, V. (1987). Limits of Ethnic Solidarity in the Ethnic Enclave. *American Sociological Review*, 52: 745-773.

Schwartz, R.S. (2001). Racial Profiling in Medical Research. *The New England Journal of Medicine*, 344(18):1392-1393.

Schmal, J.P. (2004). Indigenous Identity in the Mexican Census. The Hispanic Experience: Indigenous Heritage. Houston Institute for Culture. http://www.houstonculture.org/hispanic/census.html. Last retrieved February 1, 2011.

Scotton, C. M. & Ury, W. (1977). Bilingual Strategies: The Social Functions of Codeswitching. *International Journal of the Sociology of Language* 13: 5-20.

Sebba, M. & Wooton, T. (1998). We, They and Identity. In *Codeswitching in Conversation: Language, interaction and identity* (pp. 262-289). London: Routledge.

Seda Bonilla, E. (1975). Qué Somos: puertorriqueños, neorriqueños or niuyorriqueños? *The Rican: Journal of Contemporary Puerto Rican Thought*, 2(2-3): 81-107.

Silverstein, M. (1976). Shifters, linguistic categories, and cultural description. In K. Basso & H. Selby (eds.) *Meaning in anthropology* (pp. 11–56). Albuquerque: University of New Mexico Press.

Spickard, P.R. & Fong, R. (1995). Pacific Islander American and Multiethnicity: A Vision of America's Future. *Social Forces*, 73(4): 1365-1388.

Stephan, C.W. & Stephan, W.G. (1989). After intermarriage: Ethnic identity among mixed heritage Japanese-Americans and Hispanics. *Journal of Marriage and the Family*, 51: 507-519.

Stepick, A. & Stepick, C.D. (2002). Power and Identity: Miami Cubans. In M. Suárez-Orozco & M.M. Páez (eds.) *Latinos: Remaking America* (pp. 75-96). Berkeley: University of California Press.

Suárez-Orozco, M. & Páez, M.M. (2002). Introduction: The Research Agenda. In M. Suárez-Orozco & M.M. Páez (eds.) *Latinos: Remaking America* (pp. 1-38). Berkeley: University of California Press.

Sweetland, J. (2002). Unexpected but authentic use of an ethnically-marked dialect. *Journal of Sociolinguistics*, 6(4): 514-536.

Sweetser, E.E. (1987). The definition of *lie*. An examination of the folk models underlying a semantic prototype. In D.Holland and N. Quinn (eds.) *Cultural Models in Language and Thought* (pp. 43-68). Cambridge: Cambridge University Press.

Tajfel, H. & Tajfel, J.C. (1986). The social identity theory of inter-group behavior. In S. Worchel & L.W. Austin (eds.) *Psychology of Intergroup Relations* (pp. 7-24). Chigago: Nelson-Hall

Toribio, A.J. (2002). Spanish-English codeswitching among U.S. Latinos. *International Journal for the Sociology of Language*, 158: 89-119.

Torres-Saillant, S. (2002). Epilogue: Problematic Paradigms: Racial Diversity and Corporate Identity in the Latino Community. In M. Suárez-Orozco & M.M. Páez (eds.) *Latinos: Remaking America* (pp. 435-456). Berkeley: University of California Press.

Torres-Saillant, S. (1998). The Tribulations of Blackness: Stages in Dominican Racial Identity. *Latin American Perspectives*, 25(3): 126-146.

Toscano Mateus, H. (1953). *El Español de Ecuador*. Madrid: Revista de Filología Española, Anejo LXI.

U.S. Census Bureau. (2005-2009). American Community Surveys 5-Year Estimates. http://factfinder.census.gov. Last retrieved February 2, 2011.

U.S. Census Bureau (2000) United States Census 2000. http://www.census.gov/main/www/cen2000.html. Last retrieved February 2, 2011.

Waters, M. C. (1994). Ethnic and Racial Identities of Second-Generation Black Immigrants in New York City. *International Migration Review*, 28: 795-820.

Waters, M.C. (1990). *Ethnic Options. Choosing Identities in America.* Berkeley: University of California Press.

Williams, A.M. (2006). Bilingualism and the Construction of Ethnic Identity among Chinese Americans in the San Francisco Bay Area. Ph.D. Dissertation, Department of Linguistics, University of Michigan.

Williams, S. & Mejia, S. (2001). Voices of New York. Astoria: A Little Greece in New York. http://www.nyu.edu/classes/blake.map2001/greece.html. Last retrieved February 2, 2011.

Wolfram, W. (1974). *Sociolinguistic Aspects of Assimilation: Puerto Rican English in New York City.* Washington, DC: Center for Applied Linguistics.

Wolfram, W. & Schilling-Estes, N. (1998). *American English: Dialects and Variation.* Oxford: Blackwell.

Zentella, A.C. (1997). *Growing Up Bilingual.* Oxford: Oxford University Press.

Zentella, A.C. (1990a). Returned migration, language, and identity: Puerto Rican bilinguals in dos worlds / two mundos. *International Journal for the Sociology of Language* 84: 81-100.

Zentella, A.C. (1990b). Lexical Leveling in Four New York City Spanish Dialects: Linguistic and Social Factors. *Hispania*, 73(4): 1094-1105.

Index